The Shell Countryside Book

THE SHELL

COUNTRYSIDE BOOK

Richard Muir & Eric Duffey

J. M. Dent & Sons Ltd

LONDON MELBOURNE

Although sponsoring this book Shell UK
would like to point out that the authors
are expressing their own views.

First published 1984
© Richard Muir and Eric Duffey 1984

Printed in Italy by
International Publishing Enterprises s.r.l., Rome, for
J. M. Dent & Sons Ltd
Aldine House, 33 Welbeck Street, London W1M 8LX

British Library Cataloguing in Publication Data

Muir, Richard, *1943*–
 The Shell countryside book.
 1. Country life—Great Britain 2. Natural
history—Great Britain
 I. Title II. Duffey, Eric
 941'.009'734 DA667

ISBN 0-460-04626-8

Contents

List of Maps and Diagrams *Page 6*
Introduction *Page 7*

—1—
FIELDS, WALLS AND HEDGEROWS
Page 15
—2—
DOWN IN THE GREENWOOD
Page 49
—3—
COUNTRY ROADS
Page 77
—4—
THE VILLAGE CHURCH
Page 103
—5—
THE COUNTRY COTTAGE
Page 133
—6—
EXPLORING VILLAGES
Page 157
—7—
COUNTRY PARKS AND COTTAGE GARDENS
Page 177
—8—
THE CHANGING WORLD OF THE FARM
Page 211
—9—
MOUNTAINS
Page 237
—10—
WETLANDS
Page 249
–11–
THE COAST
Page 273

Conservation Issues *Page 295*
Appendices *Page 299*
Bibliography *Page 305*
Acknowledgements *Page 306*
Index *Page 307*

List of Maps and Diagrams

Maps

Great Britain: Geology   *10*
Great Britain: Physical Relief   *11*
Great Britain: Climate   *14*
Gamlingay 1601   *19*
Kingston Wood   *21*
Roman Roads in Britain   *82*
Known Medieval Routes   *85*
Coach Roads of Britain 1771   *90*
Some Yorkshire villages as they appear in Jeffrey's
   map of 1772   *168*
The Distribution of Royal Forests 1066–1200   *179*
Medieval Deer Parks in Eastern England   *181*
Regional Farmhouse Styles in Ireland   *222*
Planning for Leisure   *300*
National Nature Reserves   *301*
RSPB Reserves   *302*

Diagrams

Stages in the construction of a drystone wall   *30*
A cruck-built open-hall house   *141*
Timber-framed cottage built with clam, staff and
   daub method   *145*
A classic long-house   *149*
Reconstruction of an early long-house   *149*
A laithe-house   *151*
Plan of a baffle entry house with entry against the
   fireplace jambs   *151*
Plan of a double-pile house with four rooms on each
   floor   *152*
Typical single fronted cottage plan   *154*
Plan of a Wealden house with cross passage and
   open hearth   *156*
Reconstruction of Prior's Manor House, North
   Elmham c1300   *214*
Lurgashall Mill, Museum of East Anglian Life   *228*
Stevington Post Mill, Bedfordshire   *230*
Diagrammatic representation of habitats on a dune
   system   *277*

All photographs © Richard Muir with the exception of
the large copper butterfly on page 264 (Eric and David
Hosking) and Orford Ness on page 284 (University of
Cambridge Committee of Aerial Photography)

Introduction

The countryside of Britain is probably more deeply loved than any other in the world. Over the centuries it has inspired hosts of artists, writers and naturalists. Now, in our highly urbanized society, it provides relief, recreation and fascination for millions of strollers, ramblers, bird-watchers and other amateur enthusiasts whose interests range from archaeology to botany and from cottage architecture to butterflies. Almost every member of this vast country-loving community is a supporter of conservation, yet the countrysides of Britain are still being dismantled at a frightening and unprecedented rate, while native plants and wildlife are retreating into fewer and fewer, smaller and smaller habitats. To preserve our rural landscapes we must learn to love them even more strongly – and to do that we must gain a deeper appreciation of the events and natural laws which have moulded the landscapes, formed the habitats and sustained the plant and animal communities.

While the handiwork of man the destroyer of good countryside is all around us, much of the richness, interest and detail is also man-made. One may tend to

regard the rural scene as Nature's world, yet almost every countryside in Britian owes a large part of its character and biological contents to human intervention and husbandry. Even seemingly wild and untouched places like the Scottish Highlands, Lakeland Fells or the Moors of Devon and Cornwall were completely transformed by our peasant forbears. The landscapes that we love have been shaped by man over a period spanning more than seventy centuries, during which time communities explored and evaluated the contents of each local environment, designated different patches of ground as hay meadows, commons, ploughlands, woodlands and pastures according to their qualities, and then reappraised and reshaped the countryside as different needs and farming patterns evolved. In this way, if we take a typical patch of the Scottish Highlands as an example we might find that the natural wildwood of pine forest survived little changed there until the Dark Ages or even later. Then it would probably be cleared to form an open, ill-tended range where the black cattle roamed and where clansmen grew oats beside their ramshackle settlements in the small pockets of better ground. Centuries of overstocking led to the erosion and deterioration of the sour, shallow soils and in the eighteenth century the notorious Highland clearances removed the clansmen and the bare, depopulated mountains became vast sheep grazings. A century or so later our patch of ground might easily have become a deer forest or grouse moor and more recently, a dark and rather lifeless plantation of conifers.

Much of the human exploitation of the British environments was more benevolent and as man explored and developed the assets of the contrasting pieces of terrain, so a host of new ecological niches was created. The natural contents of the landscape became more diverse, as walls and hedgerows, abandoned ground and deserted settlements, old industrial workings, pastures, fell grazings, water meadows and managed coppices offered new opportunities to plant and animal colonists.

Diversity is the hallmark of the British scene. While man has exploited and accentuated this diversity by adjusting his activities to the inherent characteristics and potentialities of the landscape, developing distinctive regional lines in cottages, churches, field patterns and livestock, much of the amazing variability is rooted deeper in the patchwork complexity of the geological and climatic endowment. In the far north-west of Britain are the islands of the Outer Hebrides, with tough rocks that may be as much as 1000 million years old and which can be washed by 100 inches of rainfall each year, while in the deep south-east around the Thames estuary are soft, youthful rocks less than ten million years old which enjoy an almost semi-arid climate and receive less than twenty inches of rainfall each year. Anyone travelling between these two regions will pass across rocks of almost every type and of virtually every period marked on the geological timescale and will traverse landscapes as different and personable as those of the Lakeland Fells, the Pennine Dales, the limestone scarps of Northamptonshire and the chalk downlands of the Chilterns.

The rocks of Britain vary not only in age, but also in their origin, structure, hardness and mineral composition. There are volcanic rocks like the basalts of Co. Antrim, and granites which solidified in great domes deep beneath the surface of the earth and are now exposed to form moors like Dartmoor and Bodmin and many summits in the Cairngorms. There is also a wide spectrum of sedimentary rocks, formed from hard-packed deposits consisting of the weathered remains of older rocks, accumulations of the chalky skeletons of marine organisms or beds of organic debris. They include the coarse Millstone Grits seen in the Pennines, the russet, desert-formed Old Red Sandstone which gives much of Devon its rosy glow and the olive Greensand which rings the Weald, as well as calcareous rocks like the tough, silvery Carboniferous Limestone of most Yorkshire dales and the Mendips and the softer chalks of the Yorkshire Wolds and southern downlands. There are also 'metamorphic' rocks, created by the geological transformations wrought by intensities of heat and pressure, like the tough schists and gneisses of the Scottish Highlands. Each rock type weathers to create its own distinctive scenery, and each eventually crumbles to form a soil which will favour some plant communities and repel others.

No country of a comparable size can sport such a geological coat of many colours. The intricate diversity of our rocks has made Britain an ideal training ground for geologists, but it also renders futile any attempt to summarize the rocky roots of our landscape in a few paragraphs. Even so, it is possible to make a broad but crucial distinction between the different worlds which exist on either side of a line drawn roughly between the River Tees in the north-east of England and the River Exe in Devon. To the east of this Tees-Exe line lies Lowland Britain, a gentle, mellow land of vales, scarps and plains. This land is largely a composition of fruitful countrysides which have traditionally been thickly-peopled and rich in farming resources. To the west of the line is Upland Britain, a land dominated by rugged hills, moist plateaux and steep and narrow valleys, and one whose tough old rocks bear the brunt of the **rain-laden cyclones which spin in from the Atlantic.**

Great Britain: Geology

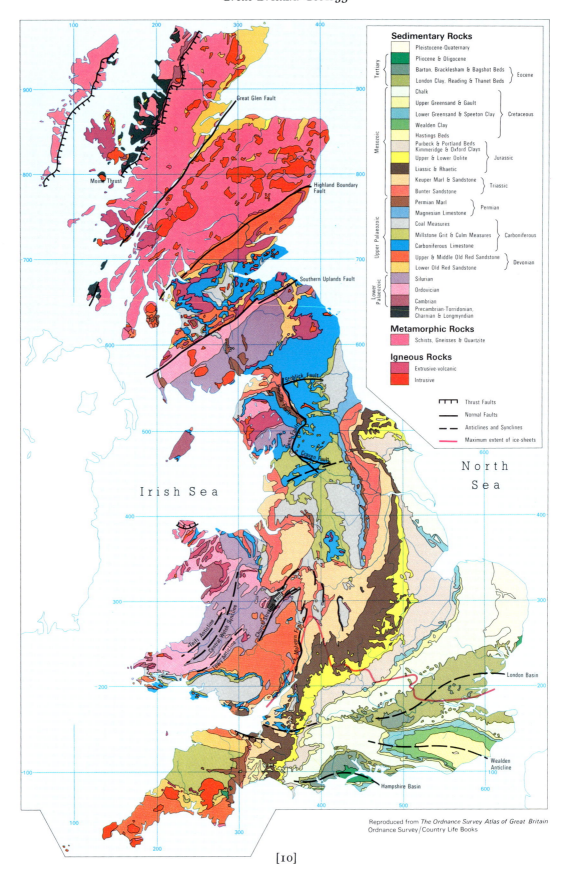

Reproduced from *The Ordnance Survey Atlas of Great Britain*
Ordnance Survey/Country Life Books

Great Britain: Physical Relief

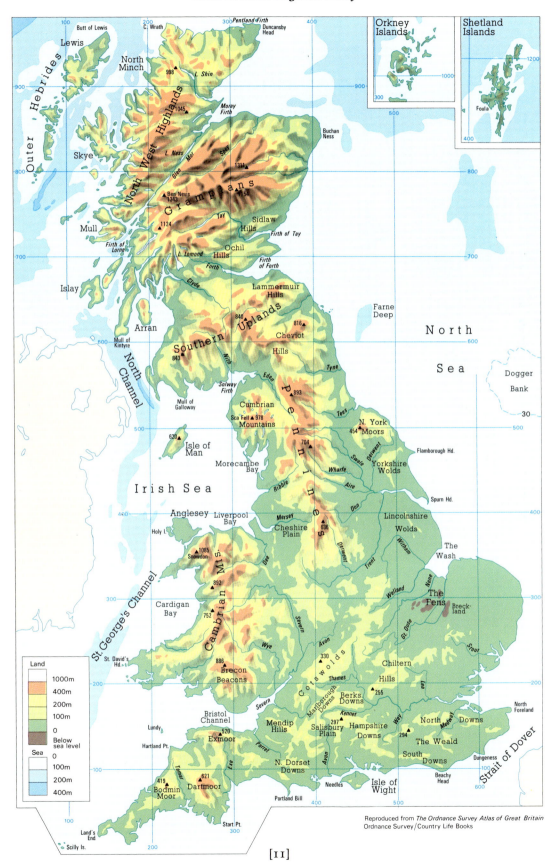

Reproduced from *The Ordnance Survey Atlas of Great Britain*
Ordnance Survey/Country Life Books

Though rich in lake, fell, moor and crag, Upland Britain has generally been a relatively impoverished land, home to small and resilient communities of stockmen, miners and quarrymen. Of course, there are plenty of pockets of exception to this Upland/Lowland rule; Upland Britain as coarsely defined here includes the Cheshire Plain, great industrial towns like Glasgow, Belfast and the conurbations of Manchester, Liverpool and South Wales as well as fruitful places like the Vale of Strathmore, while Lowland Britain includes areas of rough country like the Charnwood Forest and the North York Moors. Even so, the distinction between the Upland and Lowland zones of Britain remains a valid and important one.

The story of man's occupation of the British landscape may have begun some 400,000 years ago. We know very little of the first British settlers, and during the millennia which followed, bands of hunters entered and abandoned what was then a British peninsula of the European continent as the climate alternated between inviting temperate conditions and arctic glacial extremes. Around 12,000 years ago the ice sheets melted and the glaciers withdrew. On more than one occasion glacial conditions briefly returned to the northern mountains, but then the climate quite rapidly became warm and humid. Trees swiftly advanced across the debris-strewn landscape, displacing the established cold-resistant alpine plants. Pioneering species like the pine and birch were in turn displaced from the lowlands as deciduous trees like the hazel, alder, lime, oak, elm and ash inherited the countryside. Perhaps around 8000 BC the low, swampy land-bridge which has linked Britain to the continent was overwhelmed by the sea, with important consequences determining which species could and could not now reach these islands.

During this Middle Stone Age or 'Mesolithic' period most of Britain was populated by groups of semi-nomadic folk who fished the shores, lakes and rivers, hunted wild horses, deer and small game and gathered the rich woodland resources of edible roots, fruits, nuts and shoots. At first the Mesolithic folk may have made no attempt to reshape their environment, but then man distanced himself from the natural world by deliberately burning areas of the wildwood to create lush pastures and open hunting ranges, and it is probable that beasts like the red deer were domesticated before the period had run its course. Man had begun his long career as a maker rather than a mere inhabitant of the landscape.

Around 5000 BC the most important revolution in the creation of the countryside was launched with the introduction of farming from the continent. The new agricultural lifestyle was probably first adopted in areas endowed with good, free-draining limy or alluvial soils, but it rapidly expanded outwards to affect hosts of much less promising environments. Vast expanses of primeval forest were felled to create the new croplands, pastures and meadows and the demand for axes was such that special axe factories where raw materials were quarried and roughly shaped were established in the flint-rich chalklands of Norfolk and Sussex, amongst the volcanic rocks of the Scafell and Langdale Fells of Cumbria and in several other locations in Cornwall, Wales and Northern Ireland. As agriculture prospered, so the population expanded, increasing the pressures on the land and before the first age of farming or 'Neolithic' period ended, phases of severe soil exhaustion and abandonment of land were experienced. Meanwhile, the creation of pastures and commons and other areas of disturbed ground and worn-out cropland provided new habitats for scores of plants and animals. As the forest blanket was rolled further and further back and the economic possibilities of the different environments were developed, the basic outlines of the British countryside were slowly established.

In the thematic chapters which follow we carry the story of the creation of the countryside through to the present day, exploring the natural and man-made components of the British rural scene, explaining the evolution of fields and lanes, cottages and churches and describing the different plant and animal communities which populate the broad woodland, wetland, moorland, field and shoreline environments and the smaller ecological niches within them.

Great Britain: Climate

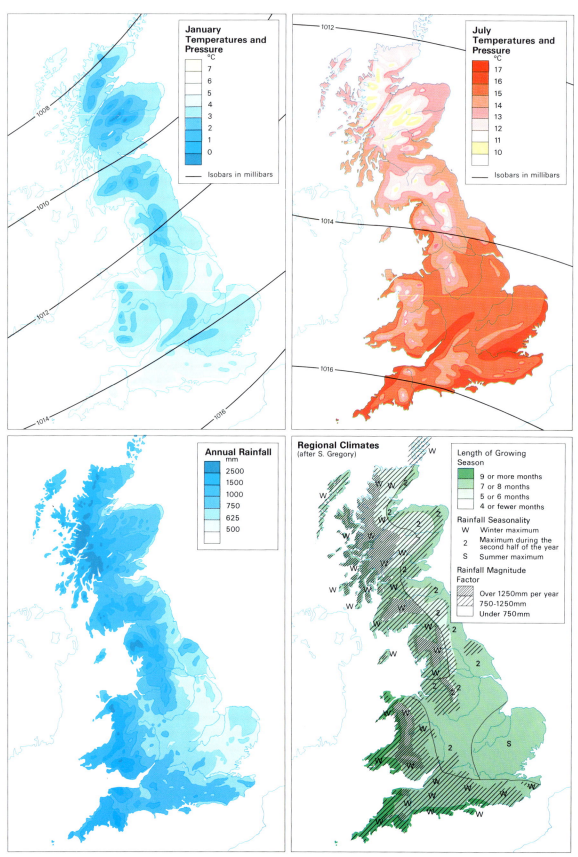

January Temperatures and Pressure

°C
- 7
- 6
- 5
- 4
- 3
- 2
- 1
- 0

——— Isobars in millibars

July Temperatures and Pressure

°C
- 17
- 16
- 15
- 14
- 13
- 12
- 11
- 10

——— Isobars in millibars

Annual Rainfall

mm
- 2500
- 1500
- 1000
- 750
- 625
- 500

Regional Climates
(after S. Gregory)

Length of Growing Season
- 9 or more months
- 7 or 8 months
- 5 or 6 months
- 4 or fewer months

Rainfall Seasonality
- W   Winter maximum
- 2   Maximum during the second half of the year
- S   Summer maximum

Rainfall Magnitude Factor
- Over 1250mm per year
- 750-1250mm
- Under 750mm

Reproduced from *The Ordnance Survey Atlas of Great Britain*
Ordnance Survey/Country Life Books

— 1 —

FIELDS, WALLS AND HEDGEROWS

*Stone walls enclosing the old infield at Wasdale Head
in Cumbria. Wast Water lake appears in the distance and the
scene is viewed from the slopes of Great Gable.*

Each landscape has its own colours, texture, contents and personality. Greenland has its icy mountains and elsewhere there are the famous coral strands, painted deserts and primeval rain forests. But for natives and foreigners alike, the essential landscape of Britain and Ireland is a rumpled patchwork quilt of green and golden fields, each colour patch hemmed by a fluffy viridian hedgerow thread, while sap-green bobbles of elm, oak and ash dot and dapple the gentle vistas. These archetypal British landscapes took thousands of years to form and flourished in their glorious maturity in Victorian and Edwardian times. The pioneer photographers could capture the world of creaking carts; pitted, dusty lanes; the crowded, poppy-spattered grain fields, and the sturdy and well-tended hedgerows which outlined the intricate agricultural mosaic. Over vast areas of England this patchwork landscape has disappeared, although in parts of Clwyd, Dyfed, Shropshire, the West Country, Kent and some other places large fragments of this intoxicating heritage still survive.

Away from the modern minimalist prairie landscapes which threaten to rip the loveliness out of the countryside there are few field patterns which are solely the products of a single epoch of field-making. Most blend or half conceal the products of several different episodes of creation and, with a little care, anyone can learn to recognize the tell-tale traces and perhaps date the different components in the fieldscape jigsaw. Fields of one kind or another must be as old as farming, which arrived in Britain about 5000 BC. Over the millennia that followed, the fieldscapes will have been modified and transformed on several occasions as worn out farmlands were temporarily abandoned to weeds and scrub, areas were reclaimed and old arrangements gave way to new. Ploughlands became pastures and grazings were ploughed, while ranches could expand across the peasant plots, and ploughmen ancient and modern have scoured away almost all the traces of the really ancient Neolithic field patterns. In a corner of Co. Mayo, however, a set of Stone Age fields which were bounded by stone walls became engulfed by peat, and recent peat cutting has now exposed parts of the fossilized farming landscape.

Prehistoric farming patterns must have had much in common with those which still linger in unspoilt places. There were sweeping upland commons which were probably shared by neighbouring communities; grainfields on the valley slopes and the better-drained plains; pasture enclosures, and hay meadows in the damp valley bottoms that were cut a couple of times in summer to yield a store of winter fodder, while around the ancient dwellings were more intricate patterns of little paddocks, stock pens and garden plots. Typically, the ancient fields were small and rather square. This was probably imposed by the methods of ploughing available. In some places the fields may have been dug with a spade tool like the *caschrom*, still used by crofters in the nineteenth century. More usually they were ploughed with a curved and pointed bough known as an 'ard', which was drawn by a pair of small oxen. The ard could groove and furrow the ground, but had no 'coulter' to slice the sod and no 'mould board' to turn it. Consequently, fields seem to have been 'cross ploughed' in two directions to create a tilth. Excavations like those at Gwithian in Cornwall have revealed ancient subsoils which are criss-crossed by ard marks. On sloping ground, soil exposed by ploughing would drift downslope to accumulate as a bank at the bottom of each field. After some time such banks became quite prominent, and in places where modern ploughing has not destroyed the evidence they can still be clearly recognized. When the old fields were in use they probably carried hedgerows which could be deliberately planted or have grown from natural seedlings which germinated in the unploughed ground where the ard team turned.

Prehistoric fields can sometimes be found as fossils in the living farming landscape. In the chalk downlands of Wessex there used to be many places where the hillslopes displayed networks of these so-called 'Celtic' fields, which variously dated to the Ages of Bronze and Iron. The scramble for subsidies and green pounds, caused by the artificial EEC grain prices and the recent fashion to plough up old pastures which are rich in grassland species and sow a grass monoculture, have resulted in the obliteration of much of our legacy of

*From Malham Cove in Yorkshire one can recognize fossil field patterns. Black stone
walls and white ribbons of snow outline the living fields, but in the upper right section
of the photograph the shadowy traces of an older network can be seen.*

ancient farming. But in the harsher upland environments the relics may endure. As climate changed
towards the end of the Bronze Age many upland areas
were deserted, while carpets of sour peat spread across
the sodden plateaux. Dartmoor is littered with Bronze
Age relics and it has recently been recognized that the
low, overgrown stone walls or 'reaves' which traverse
miles of rough moorland were built in the Bronze Age
to define the fields and farming territories. On the
close-grazed flanks of Rough Tor in Cornwall one can
see not only the time-worn relics of Bronze Age
dwellings but also the remains of stone walls which
bounded the adjacent paddocks and stock pens. In
many other parts of Cornwall the basic pattern of living
fields perpetuates an Iron Age partitioning of the
landscape. Most of the walls must have been repaired
and rebuilt on several occasions and many have been
removed, but the essential frameworks of Roman, Iron
Age or older enclosures often survive; the field patterns

flanking the coast road running westwards from St Ives
are particularly fascinating. There are other relics in
the north, as on Big Moor in Derbyshire, where the
boundaries of Bronze Age fields form ridges in the
peatland vegetation around Bar Brook reservoir. More
obvious are the ancient field patterns in the rough
pasture above Grassington in the Yorkshire Pennines,
where one can also recognize the shallow grooves
which are ancient field tracks and droveways.

Such fieldscapes once blanketed the greater part of
Britain and pageants of ancient fields which stretch for
mile upon mile can be recognized in air photographs.
Now from ground level they can only be glimpsed in
dry chalklands or rugged, uninviting places which
have discouraged the generations of ploughmen which
followed.

Although the Romans transformed the settlement
and transport map and created vast new markets for
country products, in most places the traditional field

patterns endured. Later, many old ploughlands and pastures surrendered to weeds and woodland as disease, skirmishing, economic decay and uncertainty stalked the Dark Age landscape. Small bands of Saxon settlers seem to have adopted the traditional fieldscape patterns that they found in England, and gradually the stage became set for recovery, but not yet for revolution.

The revolution which transformed most of the British lowland landscape probably began around the ninth century AD and in some places its full impact may not have been felt until as late as the thirteenth century. It involved the adoption of 'open field' farming, a form of agriculture which survived until the nineteenth century in many parishes and the legacies of open field farming can still be recognized in most parishes which have escaped the heaviest assaults of modern farming.

The origins of this complicated but productive way of working the land are still shrouded in mystery, but at least we know how the system worked and the sort of landscapes that it forged. In late-Saxon and medieval times farming involved almost the entire community. Each village or township had its own hallowed package of life-giving lands and, although some estates may have specialized in certain types of production, in most localities the emphasis was on a balanced subsistence. The community needed hay meadows to yield the fodder which sustained the livestock through the winter, hedged pastures where the beasts could graze until they were turned on to the fallowing grain land, and it needed ploughlands to produce grain, peas and beans for bread, gruel, seed and fodder. People also needed more grazings for their stock, timber supplies and fuel – and these essential demands were met by the 'waste' or common. Peasants also had crofts or house plots where vegetables or grain could grow or where pigs, geese or chickens could be kept and near to their dwellings there were often little closes, paddocks or garths where a dairy cow, ox or goat could graze. People tend to think of open field farming in terms of the strip fields where the crops were grown, but the pastures, meadows and commons were seldom less vital, and good grassland could be the most valuable asset of all.

Throughout the lowlands, most village ploughlands were divided into two or usually more vast open fields. These are termed 'open' because they were not enmeshed in hedgerow networks (although many of the 'furlong' boundaries carried hedgerows). Each open field was divided into large blocks or furlongs. The furlongs consisted of a substantial package of parallel 'strips' or 'selions' and each strip comprised a small group of 'plough ridges' and the furrows which separated the ridges. The average strip was just a few yards in width but around 200 yards in length and had an area of about an acre, although in eastern Yorkshire and some other places 'long strips' and 'long furlongs', some over a mile in length, have been discovered. A peasant household tenanted a series of strips and, for reasons which are still not clearly understood, these strips were scattered throughout the village furlongs. In some places at least the share-out of land seems to have been arranged so that throughout the furlongs a peasant tenant always had the same neighbours.

Often the most obvious legacy of this long-lived method of farming is formed not by the strips themselves, but by their constituent plough ridges or 'lands'. Most readers will have seen parks or old pastures which display a corduroy texture and there one is seeing the grassed-over remains of ridge and furrow ploughland. A particular method of ploughing was deliberately used to build up the ridges and the creation of these artificial corrugations assisted the drainage of the land. In some dry places like the East Anglian chalklands drainage will not have been a problem and the ploughlands may have had strips but not ridges.

Pure description without examples can become tedious, so let us focus on a specific place and see how the fields in a particular parish – Gamlingay in Cambridgeshire – appeared in the days of peasant farming. Because Merton College, Oxford, had a large holding in the parish a map of the village lands was drawn in 1601 – this map has survived and is reproduced here. It depicts a very typical arrangement. The ploughland is seen to be divided into three vast open fields: East Field, Middle Field and South Field. These fields are divided up into furlongs, while the fine banding within each furlong represents the strips. Weaving through the fields is a curving ribbon of meadowland which follows the moist valley bottom and brookside: West Meadow, Grymes Meade, Short Meade and Pightle Green are its components ('pightle' means a little piece or wedge of land).

The village of Gamlingay with its cross-like layout lies amongst a patchwork of hedged pastures and closes. Some are the ribbons of land attached to the village dwellings, while other long pastures running back from the track which heads eastwards towards Cambridge seem once to have been strips, but were then enclosed in hedgerows and severed from the open fields. Stranded like a beached whale in the open field land to the north of the village is an expanse of useful woodland. It is divided into three properties: Mertonage Wood, Avenalles Wood and Sugley Wood. But if we follow the woodland boundary around to the west we

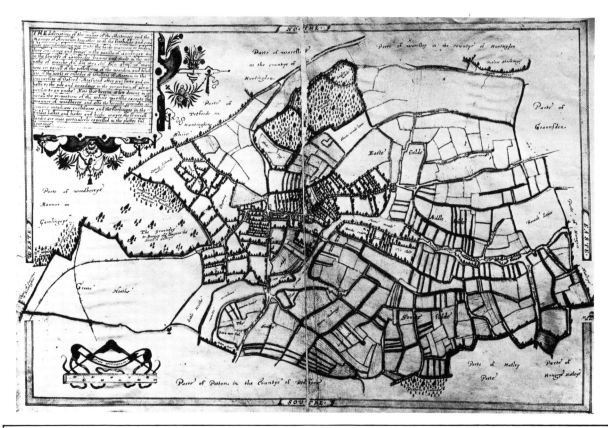

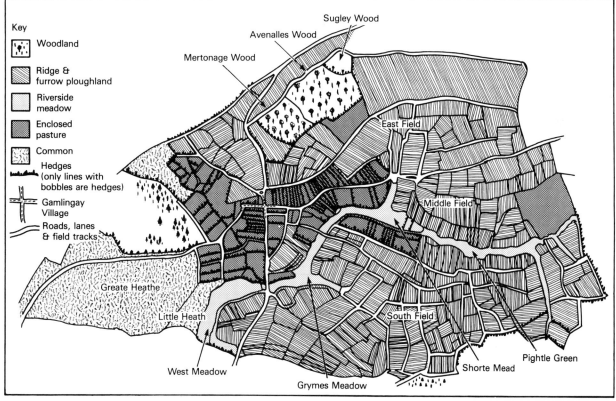

The Gamlingay map of 1601. In the adjoining drawing the different types of land-use and features are identified.

see that a hedgerow encloses a fourth component which is under plough strips. Its name 'Stock inge' or Stocking means 'land with tree stumps', and so we can be sure that this is land which has been cleared or 'assarted' from the original wood. Last but not least in this mapped inventory of the Gamlingay lands is the common, lying to the west of our map and comprising the common behind the curious clusters of closes named 'Welleses'; the vast Great Heath, and Little Heath.

The Gamlingay lands were also mapped on a larger scale, which allowed the owners or tenants of every single strip to be recorded. And here we find rich and poor, mighty and beggarly for once as neighbours. The Queen and Mrs Brudnell, Clare Hall and Abraham Jacob, Merton College and Walter Hympson all crush together cheek by jowl with at least a furrowed boundary in common.

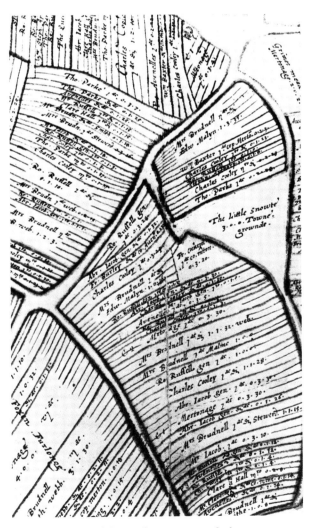

This section of the Gamlingay map records the pattern and the holders of the open field strips.

All this was to change, and later we shall return to Gamlingay and discover how. With its strips enclosed from the open fields and its deforested Stocking the map reminds us that throughout the long history of open field farming the countryside was slowly changing. The next map, showing an area around Kingston Wood, also in Cambridgeshire, was drawn in 1720 and it too underlines this point, as well as providing us with a selection of old field names. It shows how the wood itself has been eroded as assarting has bitten away at the woodland apple, creating a new little field with every bite. At the top of the illustration are old enclosures with names like Short Lays and Great Barefoot, but closer to the woodland margins is a belt of assarts running from Maudlings to Brake Close and their continuous upper boundary clearly traces the former extent of the old wood.

In the past, almost every field had a name. Many of these names are unrecorded, known only to the farmer or else forgotten, while the modern prairie fields are anonymous in every respect and quite undeserving of the dignity which a name would give. Some of the Kingston names are descriptive. The surveyor's map shows that 'Twenty Acres' – surveyed at 22 acres, 2 rods, 30 perches – was pretty well-named before the survey determined its extent, although the former owner of 'Ten Acres', measured at 7 acres, 1 rod, 11 perches, must have been an optimist. 'Brickilns' must have contained such ovens, 'Ox close' will have pastured the plough oxen; 'Three Cornered Close' is quite so, while 'Comb-grove Close' is shaped like a medieval wooden comb, and the name 'Brake Close' probably describes a break, clearing or assart in the old wood. A little manorial grouping was slotted into the diminishing wood and it comprised the moated home-stead, a few cottages or farm out-buildings and some informative field names. 'Dovehouse Close' was beside the lord's dovecote, 'Stew Pond Close' contained his little fish-rearing ponds; 'Kiln House Close' was by the kiln, and 'Hogs Piele' may be Hogs Pightle, a patch of land where the pigs were kept. 'Pound Meadow' may have held a pound where beasts which strayed on the communal fields were penned to be reclaimed by the guilty owners, but 'Harron Wood' is a puzzle and probably has nothing to do with a heron colony – no lord would have allowed these birds to roost so near to his vulnerable stew ponds. As we have shown, old maps and half-forgotten field names can tell us a great deal about the history of the countryside.

While thousands of lowland parishes resembled the Gamlingay pattern, in the English uplands, much of Scotland and parts of Wales, open field farming of this kind could not function. There the resources of good

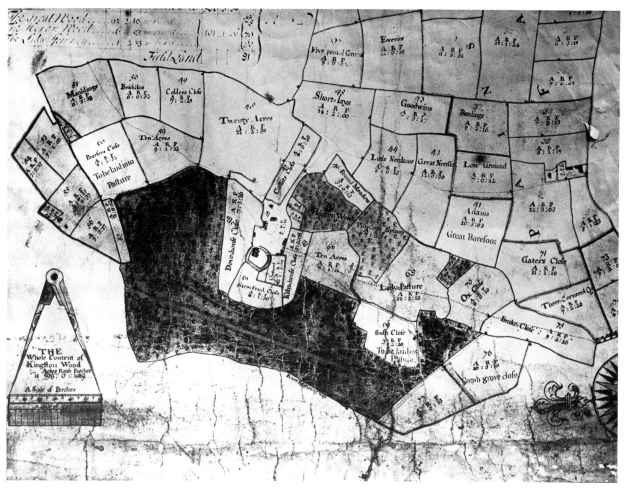

The map of Kingston Wood, showing the cleared fields of 'assarts' which have greatly reduced the extent of the woodland. Note how the fields have names – a normal feature in traditional countrysides. The figures denote the areas of the fields in acres, rods and perches.

soil and dry, sheltered land were thinly spread, the harsher environments could not sustain fat farming villages and the emphasis lay on livestock farming. In the lowland open field areas substantial portions of a parish would be devoted to ploughland and, after a couple of seasons cropping, the furlongs would be rested in turn as fallowing pastures. Muck and fallow were the essence of good farming and most open field land only improved. But in the north and uplands, variations of a different system were employed. Here the peasants ate rye bread, and oats were grown for family and for fodder. The farmstead, township and small village communities set the best pocket of ploughland aside as an 'infield'. This favoured patch received all the farmyard muck and its strips were kept in constant production. To increase the arable land, patches of 'outfield' pasture beyond might periodically be ploughed, cropped and the exhausted land then left

to recover under pasture for many years. Beyond the settlement, the infield, the low hay meadows and the hillslope pastures were the vast rough grazings of the open commons of the fell or mountain.

This form of farming, often called 'infield-outfield', existed in different forms in many different parts of Britain. It no longer exists in its traditional form, though one can often see many of its field and settlement components surviving in the living land-scape. A typical township in the Pennine Dales would control five types of land: the infield or infields which grew oats, barley or rye; the stone walled pastures above; the little gardens, paddocks, garths or 'tofts' which clustered around the dwellings; the open rough grazings of the fell; and the meadows which filled the valley bottoms. Of these components of the country-side, the little village paddocks and plots were owned by members of the community, as were most pastures.

The commons were shared by members of the neighbouring communities, although they were sometimes 'stinted' – this is to say that local rules limited the number of beasts which could be run there to prevent over-grazing. Like the infields, the meadows were divided into individual strips, here known as 'doles'. While it is easy to assume that the infield ploughstrips were the most important components of the farming scene, the commons not only supported the majority of the livestock but they also supplied peat for fuel, bracken for litter, some timber and other useful materials, while the amounts of hay cut in the meadows governed the number of beasts which could be over-wintered.

The farming landscapes of the Lake District had many similarities. At Wasdale Head near Wastwater the infield covered around 300 acres and was shared by around twenty families. Today it is partitioned by a network of stone walls, but the basin is still studded by great stone heaps, a legacy of the times when an orgy of stone-picking cleared the land for ploughing. Much of the agricultural progress in Lakeland was achieved by families of 'statesmen', independently minded peasants

and small yeomen who colonized the vast monastic sheep runs of the region following the Dissolution of the Monasteries. At Threlkeld, 'Town Field', with its eleven strips and five stripholders, survived until the middle of the nineteenth century, though in the eighteenth and early-nineteenth centuries the old village and township infields were gradually dismembered, shared out and the new divisions perpetuated by the building of stone walls. But many features of the old farming life live on, so that along the valleys and lakesides one can see the walled pastures of the 'intake' running up to the 'head dyke' which marks the junction between the land claimed from the fell and the vast commons of the open fell. The township boundaries on the fell were often marked by isolated stones, but these were often superseded by mile upon mile of stone walls. Clustered beside the farmsteads are the hay meadows of the 'inland', which were sometimes ploughed to yield a crop of oats or roots for fodder.

Over much of Scotland other versions of infield-outfield farming known as 'runrig' held sway. But while the statesmen of the Lake District were doughty, independent and occasionally quite prosperous, the

A closer view of the walls which partition the old infield at Wasdale Head. Note the stone heaps or 'clearance cairns' composed of stones gathered from the land to permit ploughing.

Scottish clansmen and tenants generally lived in abject poverty. Loose clusters of squalid shacks punctuated the infields, and the townships, known as 'clachans' in the Highlands and 'fermtouns' (farm towns) in the lower lands, were described by Sir J. Sinclair in 1831:

> The houses were not built according to any regular plan but scattered in every direction. The roads and alleys were inconceivably bad, especially in wet weather, as few of them were paved, and what added greatly to their miserable state was the abominable practice of placing the dung-hill, in which every species of filth was accumulated, before their doors.

The hardships were partly the results of life in an over-populated and impoverished landscape, but conditions were worsened by the systems of tenancy. The great lairds and chieftains sublet their domains to lesser gentry or 'tacksmen' and the tacksmen sublet to peasants who in turn subdivided the tenancies until the poorest families could be subsisting on $\frac{1}{32}$ part of a single farm unit. Meanwhile, the short-run leases discouraged the insecure peasants from making lasting improvements to the land. A typical example has been provided by the geographer R.A.Dodgshon for Sprouston Mains farm on the Roxburgh Estate. The farm was subdivided so that William Robinson rented $\frac{3}{8}$; Robert Brewhouse, $\frac{1}{4}$; John Turner, $\frac{1}{8}$, and James Waddell, $\frac{1}{4}$ of the land.

Around the infield ploughstrips of a typical township lay the poorer lands of the outfield pastures, rising up towards the peaks and plateaux where the Scottish black cattle roamed at will – and were raided by all and sundry. But in the loftier parts of Scotland, Wales and Ireland there was another facet to rural life – the seasonal migration to the high pastures that is termed 'transhumance'. In the Scottish Highlands, as the spring sunshine warmed the bleak landscape and a sweet flush of young grass greened the mountains, the cattle were driven up from the heavily grazed pastures around the clachans. The migration coincided with May Day and the not entirely forgotten pagan festival of Beltane – a key landmark in the mountain year. Then the families of clansmen lived in lofty summer settlements known as 'shielings'. Here they followed an idyllic if impoverished lifestyle in tiny stone or turf-walled huts known as 'bothies', watching over their beasts, making cheese and butter and sometimes raising a small crop of oats or rye.

In the English mountains, to the small extent that transhumance existed it seems to have died out in the Middle Ages and, as in Wales, some of the old summer settlements were replaced by single permanent farmsteads. Some similar practices survived much longer and in the early years of the nineteenth century around fifty parishes in Devon and Cornwall would despatch shepherds and flocks along the old droveways to the open summer grazings on Exmoor, where around 25,000 sheep would gather. In Wales the tradition of migrating households was active until the seventeenth century and it lingered on in the fastnesses of Snowdonia until the start of the nineteenth century. In this country the main relics of the old custom are found as place-names. *Hendref* refers to the farming base amongst the grainfields and meadows in the valley bottom; *meifod* describes a middle or May dwelling, briefly occupied as a staging post on the trek to the *hafod*, the lofty summer settlement, while some other cottages which were associated with cheese-making during the summer season were known as *lluest*. In Ireland (where transhumance was known as 'booleying' from the word *buaile*, a place where cattle were penned or milked), the tradition largely died out in the seventeenth and eighteenth centuries, although it did last until the nineteenth century in some remote places. In the Scottish Highlands the landscape is still littered with the ruins of clachans and shielings and old infields and shieling plots can still endure as patches of emerald vegetation in the duns and mauves of the moorland, while in Wales and Ireland the place-name legacy serves reminders of a lost way of life.

Before we look ahead to the eighteenth- and nineteenth-century changes to the farming landscapes we should briefly glance backwards to what were, and in some places still are, the most visually striking fields of all: 'strip lynchets'. They are seldom mentioned in popular countryside books, and where they are, they are wrongly identified as prehistoric fields or medieval vineyards. In reality, strip lynchets are medieval fields which are carved like mighty staircases into the hillslopes of both northern and southern England. Only the pressures of a swelling population and a severe shortage of untapped land resources could have impelled ploughmen to undertake such daunting efforts, and so these fields probably date to the over-populated centuries before the dreadful onslaughts of the pestilence began in 1348. Some fine flights of strip lynchets survive, as at Worth Matravers in Dorset, Coombe Bissett near Salisbury, around Challacombe on Dartmoor, Malham in the Yorkshire Dales and there are some particularly striking flights at Linton near Grassington in Yorkshire.

While all the methods of farming which we have described are dead and gone they have left many epitaphs which are still visible in the British fieldscape

Medieval strip lynchets give the slopes a stepped appearance at Winterbourne Steepleton in Dorset. They were produced by ploughing along the contours of the slopes.

Wharfedale in Yorkshire is perhaps the best place to see fields of many different kinds and ages. The snow emphasises the medieval ridge and furrow (centre) and strip lynchets (above).

as well as a rich legacy of old names. Open field strips, some a little altered, are still worked at Laxton in Nottinghamshire, Braunton Great Field in Devon, Haxey in Lincolnshire, Soham in Cambridgeshire and at Forrabury near Boscastle in Cornwall, but these are just the accidental survivors of once very widespread tradition. In Scotland the seventeenth century closed grimly with the Seven Ill Years of Famine. The demise of the old clan system on the battlefield of Culloden in 1746 and the rising tide of agricultural 'improvements' combined to condemn the old farming lifestyle. In the Highlands the clan families were evicted by their lairds to create more profitable sheep runs. Thousands emigrated and thousands were resettled in impoverished coastal crofting townships. Meanwhile, in the lower lands the old fermtouns were erased by 'improving' landlords and, while many purpose-built new villages were erected, the old infields, outfield pastures and commons were partitioned between fewer and fewer tenants as the lords created viable farms. In Wales, northern England and Ireland enclosure also removed the infields from the landscape, while in the English lowlands Parliamentary Enclosure eradicated the many lingering survivals of medieval communal farming.

'Enclosure' refers to the process of enclosing a land holding with walls, hedges or palings, and it encompasses a range of different field types. Some of the gorgeous thick-hedged pastures of southern and western England and parts of the Welsh lowlands must have been enclosed in this way since the Dark Ages. Almost as soon as open field farming was introduced, the slow process of dismantling the system will have begun in many localities. For one reason or another owners and tenants will have sometimes found it convenient to extract particular strips from the open ploughlands or to swop holdings around to obtain more compact blocks of land. Combe Martin in Devon and Castleton in Derbyshire have some fine examples of enclosed open field strips. This informal process of 'enclosure by agreement' worked so long as other members of the farming community gave their consent and it produced countless pleasant little fields whose curving walls or hedgerows still preserve the sweeping outlines of the original strip boundaries. Other 'early enclosures' consist of assarts, like the ones shown on the Kingston map.

But enclosure by agreement did not succeed in eradicating the venerable countrysides of open field farming. The old methods were productive if compli-

The thick, curving hedgrows of an 'early enclosure' landscape at Llanddewi Brefi in central Wales. Much of the best 'English' type of scenery can be found surviving in Wales.

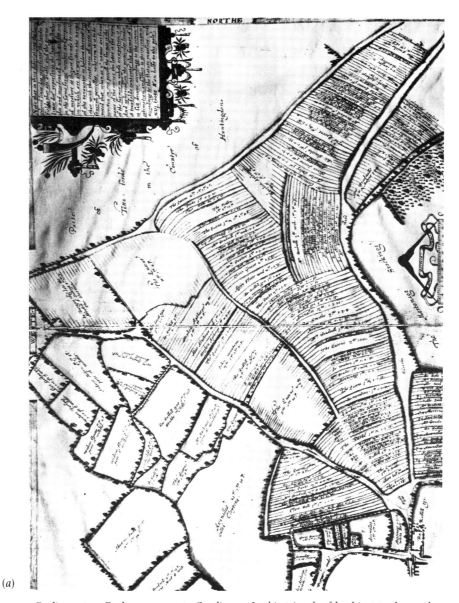

(a)

*Parliamentary Enclosure comes to Gamlingay. In this triangle of land just to the north
of the village we can compare the old strip patterns (a) with the geometrical field
patterns produced by the Enclosure of the open fields (b). Note how the little hedged
pastures of 'closes' have escaped Enclosure and preserve their old forms as they were
already privately-owned before Enclosure. Also note the two new turnpike roads which
appear on the post-Enclosure map.*

cated, while innumerable families of cottagers sub-
sisted on the varied fruits of their common rights. At
the start of the eighteenth century about half of the
English ploughland was still in open fields, while
commons of one kind or another may have covered
seven or more million acres. Yet the survival of this old
system which allowed peasant England to endure was
resented by the agricultural reformers and the avaricious masters of the countryside – who were often one
and the same. In many parishes where enclosure by

agreement had failed to dismantle the old field patterns
and ways of life, individual Parliamentary Acts were
needed to overturn the rural applecart. They could be
obtained when the leading landowners in the parish
petitioned Parliament. Until about 1750 such Acts
were relatively few, but in the century which followed
almost three thousand Acts were passed and the face of
many a parish was utterly transformed.

The appointed surveyors would plan the old arrangement and fix the outlines of the new. The old strip

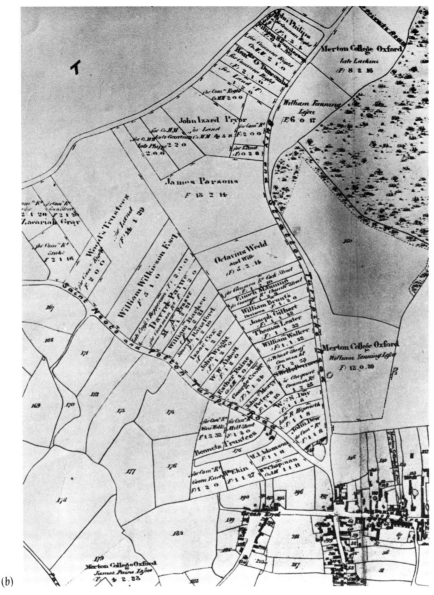

(b)

lands, meadows and common land – even including some village greens – were dismantled and repartitioned amongst individual owners. Although there was a nominal attempt to equate the proportions of land held before and after Enclosure, many cottagers who lacked a clear title to their rights were left landless and destitute, while thousands of commoners were awarded tiny, unviable holdings which could not compensate for the loss of common rights.

In Gamlingay the Enclosure Commissioners did not descend upon the village until 1844. When they arrived the landscape appeared much as it had a quarter of a millennium earlier, although two old tracks had now become improved as turnpikes. If we look at the zone of old early enclosure pastures to the left of the St Neots and Potton Turnpike in the

accompanying map we can see that a couple of meadows had merged and another had been subdivided, but the changes were quite small. Yet the names of the village landowners shown are quite different, for village society was much more mobile and changeable than we have been led to imagine. A map was drawn to depict the new arrangements at Gamlingay. Gone are the narrow, curving strips and gone are the open fields and commons. In their place is a surveyor's landscape of new, straight-edged holdings. Those in the angle of the turnpikes are smaller than most others in the revamped parish and the smallest are scarcely an acre in size. David Paine, John Dew, Zacariah Gray and Enoch Manning have been given these tiny patches in lieu of their lost common rights. It is unlikely that they were able to linger here much longer.

[27]

Parliamentary Enclosure sentenced many a peasant family to a beggarly despair. Some walked to the growing industrial towns, where drudges could earn many times the wages that the farmers paid. Others scraped together the fare to America, where they met a society free of mantraps and the humiliations of peasant life, where the poor British husbandman had more dignity and opportunities than he had ever known in his homeland. The Enclosures had robbed the poor to pay the rich, but they created attractive new countrysides. The lines drawn on the surveyor's maps swiftly materialized in the landscape as rectilinear networks of young hawthorn hedgerows or as walls which bestrode the fells, marching on beyond the lofty skyline. Georgian and Victorian England offered plenty of work for surveyors, hedgers and wallers, although often the new landowners built their own walls and set their own quickthorn hedges.

Until quite modern times the craft of hedging was earnestly practised. A robust hedgerow had to be 'laid'. Traditionally this involved splitting the growing timbers to the rootstock and bending them over to form near-horizontal layers which were then sometimes lashed to vertical hazel poles using young bramble runners as twine. Every four yards or so the hedge would be trimmed and the new growth split and laid again. Occasionally one may see similar methods still being practised, but more commonly one can recognize the handiwork of old hedgers in hedgerows which are now thin and neglected. Careful work with the razor-edged billhook is being replaced by a mechanical threshing, leaving the hedgerow tattered and short.

In the uplands, where stone was plentiful and hawthorn less vigorous, stone walls of many different kinds were built. Their form depended upon tradition, the qualities of the local stone and the tasks which a wall had to perform. Field walls were built of drystone walling and proved more robust than mortared stone

The hedgerow geometry of a typical Parliamentary Enclosure landscape, seen from the lofty chalk scarp which carries the Westbury White Horse in Wiltshire.

A long-neglected and outgrown hawthorn hedgerow at Wadenhoe in Northamptonshire. The sharp kinks in some of the lower branches were produced in the days when the hedge was layed to preserve a stock-proof barrier.

A rare sight and one which gladdens the heart of the country-lover: a newly-layed hedgerow, seen here at Barton in Cambridgeshire. Note how the hawthorn is bent over at an angle and lashed to posts.

A professional, drystone waller at work using Millstone Grit stones in the Yorkshire Dales. Note how the wall is constructed with inner and outer faces and a filling of broken rubble. The horizontal string is used to check the level.

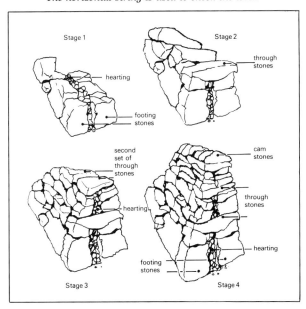

Stages in the construction of a drystone wall

since the wind could whistle through the crevices and dry the stones. The stones themselves were set with 'their tails up', slightly sloping upwards the centre of the wall, which also assisted drainage. Most walls were built with two distinct stone faces separated by an inner space packed with smaller stones. They were 'battered' or built much broader at the base than at the top, and through-stones running right through the wall helped to bond the faces, while the uppermost course was covered by a coping of capstones, 'cocks and hens' or 'bucks and does'. Occasionally, as sometimes in the Cotswolds, the jagged capstones were mortared in place to deter jumping livestock.

Fieldwalls come in many forms and not all fit this description. Around Hawkshead in Cumbria and in places on Orkney one can see walls made of vertical sheets of slabby local stone and in granite country the massive moorstone boulders contrast with the craggy chunks found in limestone lands or the slender flags of some sandstone areas. In Cornwall, where walls are known as 'hedges', the granite facings are often packed with earth and crowned with hedges and earth-packed walls are common in Wales.

Not a great deal of scholarly work has been done, but a recent survey of walls that was carried out in Holne Moor on Dartmoor, by Andrew Fleming and Nicholas Ralph, is fascinating because it shows how walls have evolved there. The oldest walls are known as 'reaves', and though sometimes re-used in medieval times, they date right back to the Bronze Age. They formed the major territorial divisions of the moor and also the shorter boundaries which defined the ancient fields. They were built with faces of drystone walling or of massive boulders or 'orthostats', but they may not be the oldest field boundaries in the area, for some were preceded by earthen banks which may have carried hedges. Some had a shallow fronting ditch and these walls were not packed with earth. 'Clearance walls' consist of elongated piles of boulders and they usually represent attempts to clear land of stones rather than to construct enclosures. Most belong to the Saxon and early-medieval period, although some could be of the Iron Age. 'Block walls', normally consisting of an alignment of large, squarish boulders, probably also date to the Saxon period although some could be older.

Barriers known as 'corn-ditches' consist of a ramp-like earthen bank, faced by a vertical drystone wall and fronted by a substantial ditch. These were built to place the obstacle of the ditch and wall in the path of deer seeking to devour the peasant crops, while the sloping earth ramp behind the wall assisted the departure of any deer which had got amongst the crops. Such walls were developed as a means of getting around Norman

In the north of England the new Parliamentary Enclosure divisions were often marked by stone walls rather than by hedgerows, as here, in upper Nidderdale near Lofthouse. In the very centre of the photograph one can just discern earthworks which seem to mark former tracks and, perhaps, a vanished farmstead.

Forest Law, which forbade the building of fences or hedges that could impede the movement of deer. The corn-ditches could therefore be dated to the Norman period; in the later medieval centuries, after the lifting of the Forest Law here around 1240, other types of boundries could be built. Some were 'wall banks', consisting of two faces of granite boulders packed with rubble or earth which sometimes carried trees or hedges. A number of old corn-ditches were superseded by wall banks or by ditched hedge banks. Finally, in nearby areas some rather ramshackle conventional walls were built in the eighteenth and nineteenth centuries when the local farmers attempted to replicate the splendid enclosure walls of the north in the uncompromising, lumpy moorstone boulders.

Field patterns and the networks of walls or hedgerows which trace out the mosaic are the essence of rural beauty. There is no single facet of the British landscape which is more valuable than this intricate tracery in grey or green. But it was estimated that between 1946 and 1974 120,000 miles of English and Welsh hedgerow were removed – a quarter of the hedgerows existing at the end of the last war. Now it is conceded that these grim figures understated the destruction. Marion Shoard has quoted the case of a single farm near the beauty spot of Sennen Cove in Cornwall where eleven miles of hedgerow disappeared in the 1970s.

Vast tracts of prairie landscape blanket East Anglia and the East Midlands, fine old southern downland pastures are now ploughed up and the bare brown patches in the countrysides of Yorkshire, Worcestershire, Devon and the Welsh and Scottish lowlands mark the change.

Farmers have responded to the government subsidies by growing cereals in fields where such crops

Each region in the stone country has its own walling tradition, and the following photographs offer a selection of walls from different parts of Britain:

Limestone country of the Yorkshire Dales; the more rounded stones may have been taken from a stream bed.

A Cotswolds type of wall at Lacock in Wiltshire, using the slabby local limestone.

The Millstone Grit country of the Yorkshire Dales.

A wall of granite or 'moorstone' blocks on Dartmoor.

A Cornish 'hedge' using massive granite boulders. Note the vegetation growing in the earth packing.

A wall of tough, ancient and angular stones on Anglesey. As with many Welsh walls a packing of earth allows a rich growth of vegetation to crown the wall.

would otherwise be uneconomic. The hedges used in the days of livestock farming have been bulldozed to give free movement to the enormous new farm machines. The landscape has also suffered from 'paddock farming'. Hedges were ripped out to create vast paddocks which were ploughed and sown with a grass monoculture, with the beasts being shifted up and down the green carpet by movable wire fences.

Wherever the hedgerows still flourish, however, and the farming habits allow wildlife to linger, the British fieldscape can still offer enormous interest to the naturalist.

The natural history of fields, walls and hedgerows

In the early-nineteenth century there were still great expanses of open commons and grasslands throughout the country which had not been ploughed for centuries. The wild beauty of these rough grasslands is reflected in the poems of the peasant poet John Clare, who so enjoyed wandering over the heaths and grasslands of the limestone country of north-eastern Northamptonshire, listening to the birds and searching for flowers.

Grasslands in Britain have always been at risk from the threat of ploughing, but in the days before mechanized agriculture, fertilizers and pesticides, it was not such a drastic treatment as it is today. Many plants were able to survive along the edges of the fields and to recolonize when pasture was re-established. Today things are very different. The original old and permanent pasture, undisturbed by man, is now a

considerable rarity. Farming today is such an efficient and highly mechanized industry, and has so many aids to suppress wild plants which are unwanted in the farming environment, that it is very difficult indeed for anything other than the chosen crop to survive. This situation applies mostly to the lowlands of England; in the north and north-west, where the weather is cooler and wetter, the growing of crops such as cereals is less profitable, and there is still an abundance of hill pastures. Such lands are better suited to the growth of grass and sheep farming than to other purposes, but it is not only the soils and the climate that affect what is grown. The farming pattern today is largely artificial so that, as previously mentioned, the economic state of the country and the high level of subsidies paid also have a considerable influence – in many areas it is much more profitable to plough up grasslands and to

In recent years the ploughing of the traditional downlands has altered the landscapes and plantlife of Wessex and in many places pasture only survives on the slopes of the steepest dry valleys or 'combes'.

Different types of grassland environment.

Hay meadows on Orkney, with plants still blossoming in the unmown margins.

Permanent pastures at Rosthwaite in Borrowdale on the low, level ground that was once part of the lake bed of a larger Derwentwater lake.

A damp meadow at Birstwith in Nidderdale which is carpeted in buttercups and daisies.

Plants which were once commonly seen in grainfields.

Oxeye daisy.

Corn marigold.

Poppies, growing here at Richborough in Kent.

Wild cornflower also found in permanent pasture on calcareous soils.

grow another crop which brings in a better cash return. This has affected certain areas more than others.

In the south of England the chalk grasslands of the Downs were one of the early victims. At the beginning of the century during a period of agricultural depression, the landscape was virtually all grassland. There were few or no fences and flocks of sheep drifted over the hills in the charge of a shepherd. The books of W. H. Hudson, who knew the downland shepherds and the hard life they led, immortalized this period of our history. The flora at this time had probably reached its optimum development and many species, now rare, were widespread in the grass turf which rolled for mile upon mile along the Downs. The early botanists thought that this vegetation was very ancient, with its many orchids, pasque flowers, cowslips, kidney vetch, horseshoe vetch, greater bird's foot trefoil and marjoram – to name but a few – and that it was probably the natural vegetation of the light chalk soils. This idea was shown to be quite mistaken when sheep farming declined and the rabbits were destroyed by myxomatosis. The rank, quick-growing grasses took over, seedling shrubs and trees appeared, and it was clear that, in time, a forest would develop.

Today the rich flora of the Downs is found only in a few places, usually on steep slopes – the only areas to escape the plough, and several such places are now protected as nature reserves. The village pond and the copse in the field corner, along with hedges and hedgerows trees are also often destroyed to accommodate present-day cumbersome farm machinery.

_____ *The decline in the grassland flora* _____

Grassland in the lowland parts of Britain is often artificial, consisting of a few species of grasses and virtually no other herbs. The old grassland was not considered productive enough and the agricultural scientist found that he could improve yields by ploughing up the old pasture and reseeding with fast-growing varieties – and indeed, who is to blame the farmer for finding the most efficient and effective way of providing food for his cattle and sheep?

The net result is that the grassland flora has declined very considerably, and many species which were common in John Clare's day are now localized or even rare. The same goes for the fauna. Permanent grassland which has been developing and growing for centuries has a thick litter layer, coarse at the top with fresh dead material but becoming finer as it breaks down to merge gradually with the soil. There is a remarkable variety of animal life in this old grassy turf, all helping to return the organic material to the soil and so maintaining its fertility. The modern grassland ley, grown from the seed of just a few species, is only allowed to remain for a few years before being ploughed up again and reseeded. No litter layer of dead vegetation close to the ground is able to develop, thus eliminating all the interesting creatures which live there.

Where the pasture is on rocky ground it is not possible to plough and reseed but it can be improved agriculturally by applying fertilizers mixed with the seed of fast-growing grasses so that the sward gradually becomes dominated by the introduced varieties. Even without additional seed, the use of artificial fertilizers is a very quick way to change the vegetation because some grasses are encouraged and grow rapidly, smothering those which do not respond so quickly. Where the old traditional method of spreading cow and horse manure on the meadows still survives, changes are much less noticeable because the release of nutrients is slower. Although there is increased growth, the composition of the grassland flora does not change significantly.

The broad river valleys of lowland England were once the home of some of our most interesting meadows. There were two types. The flood meadows were so-called because they were usually flooded in the winter, the water bringing extra nutrients which helped to stimulate a luxuriant growth in the following season. The second type, now virtually extinct, is the water meadow. Flood meadows have been used for grazing and hay making for many centuries, and have never been ploughed so that they retain their characteristic flora. Like age-old pastures elsewhere, few good examples still survive, but there are several in the Upper Thames Basin, the South Midlands and in parts of East Anglia. The flora is particularly showy, including the fritillary, or snakeshead. It was much more widespread a hundred or so years ago but has become a victim of fertilizers and herbicides. The National Nature Reserve of North Meadow, Cricklade, is one of the best surviving river valley meadows. The tradition of mowing and then grazing is still practised, and in the spring the display of fritillaries is breathtaking.

Water authorities have unwittingly contributed to the decline of flood meadows by deepening the beds of rivers and streams and so preventing annual flooding, in order to make it possible for farmers to plough up these meadows for cereal growing.

The wide alluvial plain of the River Arun north of Amberley in Sussex has a different valley meadow, in the remarkable Amberley Wild Brooks. These grass-

*Ploughing-up old meadow land in Nidderdale, Yorkshire. Note the flocks of seagulls
which suddenly materialize when soil fauna are exposed by ploughing.*

lands lie in a wide shallow basin and are often wet for much of the year because of poor drainage, vast lakes sometimes forming in the winter. In recent years, an expensive drainage scheme was planned to rid the meadows of water so that local farmers would be able to plough the land and grow more profitable crops. This brought a great outcry from conservationists and much publicity in the press because the importance of the Wild Brooks as a wildfowl wintering area would be destroyed. Its chief feature is the flocks of Bewick swans as well as many species of duck. After much discussion and a public inquiry an area has been saved but we have yet to see whether its wildlife interest has been diminished. Other unspoilt flood meadows are still under threat – schemes have recently been developed to prevent flooding in the Soar valley, Leicestershire, and the Nene valley in Northamptonshire. Neither is of national importance because so much has been lost,

but this author remembers many happy hours bird-watching in the Loughborough Great Meadow of the Soar valley, and now lives by what is probably the largest surviving unspoilt meadow in the Nene valley.

The second type of valley grassland, which is known as a water meadow and was irrigated from the nearby river, has virtually disappeared from this country, although it too was once widespread. Water was diverted onto the meadow by a system of weirs, artificial water courses and earthworks, a practice which was recorded as far back as the beginning of the sixteenth century. The meadows were flooded regularly during the winter until late spring through a network of narrow channels, the water entering at one end and rejoining the river after circulating throughout the system. This treatment prevented the meadow from freezing in the late winter and so enabled the grass to start its spring growth about three weeks earlier

Some plants which can be found in grasslands of different types.

*Fritillaries are found on river valley meadows but they are
often the victims of modern pest control.*

A species of Crepis.

*Common teazel, widely distributed in the south often on dry
soils, found also in open woods, stream banks, waysides
and grasslands.*

*Great mullein, a stately plant of dry grasslands,
open woodlands, waysides and hedge banks.*

*Yellow rattle, formerly very common in grasslands
and well-drained soils, especially hay meadows, now less so
due to ploughing of grasslands.*

The autumn crocus or meadow saffron is a threatened plant
due to the draining of damp meadows, its typical habitat.

Eyebright; this plant, which is parasitic upon the roots of
others is a widely distributed plant found on short grassland.

Common ragwort, a frequently abundant plant on well-drained
soils but much disliked by the farmer because it is poisonous
to cattle.

Bistort, a common plant of hay meadows in the north,
is sometimes grown in gardens.

The beautiful wild pansy or heartsease is widespread in many
types of grassland, woodland edges and waste ground.
It is variable in colour and growth form.

than elsewhere. The water meadow was, unfortunately, labour-intensive, in the sense that a large workforce was required to keep the channels open, earth up the banks, and attend to the sluices. Nowadays this would be far too expensive. Although the last meadows were abandoned in the years between the two wars, some can still be recognized today by the shallow depressions where the water channels used to be, for example in the valley of the Hampshire Avon. Plantations of poplars now grow on many former water meadows.

Some ancient meadows have developed on land which was once ploughed. The centuries-old ridge and furrow can be recognized quite clearly, although the grassland remained untouched apart from grazing over a very long period. As the abandoned ploughland slowly reverted to pasture, plants formerly much more widespread were able to colonize, and the grassland gradually acquired a rich flora. Relics of this type have survived only because the farmers have retained the traditional way of life handed down from their fathers and grandfathers. These meadows are often on heavy clay soils; one of the most interesting is the Upwood Meadows National Nature Reserve in Cambridgeshire, where there is documentary evidence that the grassland has not been disturbed by ploughing since the beginning of the eighteenth century, but the S-shaped curves of the ridge and furrow suggest it may be much earlier. The larger of the two fields in this nature reserve is full of cowslips and has a large population of the green-winged orchid, formerly much more widespread in the grasslands of lowland England but now rather rare. The adder's tongue fern is easily missed in the tall grass; other plants to search for are the curious dyer's greenweed, from which a blue dye called dyer's woad was obtained in the past, the rare sulphur clover, pepper saxifrage, dropwort and sawwort – in fact about 170 flowering plants have been recorded on this relatively small reserve.

Monewden Meadow in Suffolk has a similar history but is one of the few grasslands on which autumn crocus (*Colchicum*) still survives, together with fritillaries, green-winged and early purple orchids. As usual the meadow is cut for hay and the autumn crocus leaves, which are poisonous when green, become harmless in the dried hay. After the hay has been cut cattle can be safely grazed on the aftermath. The flowers which appear later in the autumn are not poisonous. The effect of mowing this sort of meadow is demonstrated most dramatically in the southern Alps, where some of the mountain meadows are mauve with *Colchicum* after the hay has been cut for the second or third time, but in the uncut grasslands it is quite scarce.

Upland pastures and stone walls

A definition of 'upland' is not easy, but generally biologists take it to be land between about 800 and 1800 feet altitude. The vegetation within this range is different from that in lowlands or in the higher mountains, a great deal consisting of dwarf scrub, particularly heather, whortleberry, cowberry, which together with other plants make up 'moorland'. Upland grassland is therefore only one type of vegetation found in this altitudinal range. Whether grassland or moorland is likely to occur in any one place depends on latitude, temperature, rainfall, soils and exposure. For instance, the vegetation at 800 feet on Ronas Hill, the highest point in Shetland at 1460 feet, is similar to that in the central Highlands at an altitude of about 2000 feet. And as one goes further west in the wet uplands of Ireland, the vegetation changes yet again. Management will also influence the vegetation. On the Pennine Hills of England and in Scotland a dwarf shrub community of plants consisting mainly of heather is maintained by careful burning at regular intervals in order to produce new shoots as food for grouse. On the other hand, if such an area is grazed intensively by sheep or, if at not too high an altitude, by cattle, then the heather may be gradually killed off and replaced in part by grassland. This has even happened on a lowland nature reserve where heather growing on an acid peat was destroyed by overgrazing and trampling by cattle and replaced by purple moor grass. Even after some twenty years there was no sign of the heather being able to re-establish itself.

Many of the upland grasslands have developed from areas which were formerly forested. We can assume that in primeval times forests extended to about 2000 feet in Britain, although the tree limit would be lower at the higher latitudes. On the more calcareous soils the clearance of trees resulted in a mixed grassland, but on neutral and acid soils heather and other dwarf shrubs would have dominated and it was only later when man's domestic animals began to graze these areas that changes took place. Persistent overgrazing seems to have caused changes which altered the composition of the flora in such a way that it is difficult to reverse. For example, mat grass, which forms dense and tough tussocks unpalatable to sheep except when very young, is extremely widespread in upland regions. It is rare in natural forests and must have been very localized before man began to fell trees to create grassy clearings for his animals. The heath rush is another plant which is very resistant to trampling and grazing and consequently spreads rapidly. It has a very squat and tough rosette of leaves and an erect flowering stem, the whole plant being unpalatable to sheep. As these two plants spread, the more palatable species become less common or even die out.

The uplands are the home of many interesting birds – in the summer the courtship calls and remarkable display flight of the common curlew are unforgettable to anyone roaming the hills, as much part of the upland scene as the wind, rain and wide, brilliant skies. The wheatear bobs his white tail on the rock, meadow pipits are everywhere, and above we hear the fluting whistle of the golden plover. On the heather moors of the Pennines and in Scotland it is the red grouse that is the most characteristic bird.

Probably the most remarkable upland area in the Pennines is Teesdale, in County Durham. It has been visited by botanists since the beginning of the nineteenth century and still has more rare plants than any comparable region in Britain, most of them arctic species which are believed to have established after the last Ice Age ten thousand or so years ago. It is a wild, windswept moor reaching altitudes of over 2930 feet, although most is in the region of 1500 to 1900 feet. By British standards the altitude is rather high, so that the climate is characterized by low temperatures, a high rainfall, a good deal of snow in the winter, and a short growing season for plants. Today Teesdale has no trees and it is hard to imagine that they could ever have grown there. Yet wood remains have been found up to 2430 feet and are thought to be relics of forests which grew between 7500 and 5000 years ago. At that time the weather was slightly warmer than it is today so that conditions would have been just that little bit more favourable for tree growth. Nevertheless the forest must have been an open one with grassy areas between the trees, otherwise the rare Teesdale flowers would probably not have survived.

The soils of Teesdale are derived from rocks of the lower Carboniferous age, some of it limestone, sandstone or shale, or harder rock known as Quartz Dolerite, which forms the magnificent feature of the Great Whin Sill. On the more acid soils heather may be abundant together with such attractive plants as bilberry, cowberry, bell heather and, in some places, the crowberry. Where grazing is heavy the vegetation may change from shrubby heaths to a grassland with sheep's fescue, common bent, and the wavy hairgrass, and, as the Teesdale rainfall is high, mat grass is very widespread and often dominant. The frequent wet places have many interesting plants: deer sedge, bog asphodel, round-leaved sundew and many different species of moss, particularly sphagnum mosses.

Nevertheless the most famous Teesdale plants grow on the Carboniferous Limestone rocks and are often associated with the so-called Sugar Limestone. This is soft and crumbly because of the great heat to which it was subjected millions of years ago. It is quite widespread in Teesdale, having been dispersed by the movement of glacial material. The Sugar Limestone vegetation of grasses and herbs stands out bright green against the mostly dark grey colouring of the numerous sedges and shrubby heaths on the non-calcareous soils. The grasses include sheep's fescue, blue *Sesleria* (very typical of the unaltered Carboniferous Limestone), quaking grass, crested hairgrass, carnation grass (which is actually a sedge), and common plants such as harebell, eyebright, purging flax, wild thyme and the common dog's violet. The areas most frequented by botanists are Widdy Bank and Cronckley Fells, where the great rarities occur. These include the alpine bistort, mountain everlasting, alpine cinquefoil – often grown in gardens – lesser clubmoss, a number of sedges, some of which are tiny but very rare, and more striking plants such as the bird's eye primrose, kidney vetch, dark red helleborine, and horseshoe vetch.

In the high valley farms of Teesdale the enclosed grasslands produce some of the most picturesque hay meadows anywhere in Britain. The most conspicuous plants of the hay meadows are the globe flower, the wood cranesbill, melancholy thistle, meadowsweet, valerian, angelica, hogweed, sorrel, oxeye daisy, earthnut, meadow buttercup, water avens, great burnett, hedge woundwort, vetches, and several species of the delicate lady's mantle. Orchids are also common, particularly the spotted, early purple, fragrant and frog orchids, and the twayblade.

In Co. Clare, Western Ireland, there is an equally remarkable limestone area, the Burren. The name means the Great Rock, and aptly describes the bare rounded hills and terraces of hard limestone – a very different landscape from that in Teesdale. The vegetation is so sparse that it scarcely warrants the name 'grassland', but a host of plants grow in the deep cracks and crevices of the limestone, including a curious mixture of southern, northern and montane species often growing at sea level or just above. There seems little doubt that the Burren flora is a relic of earlier times, as is Teesdale, but why mountain species should mix with others more typical of southern Europe is not known. The white flowers of mountain avens spread over the rock surfaces and even by some of the Burren's dirt roads – surely one of the most unusual wayside plants. The vivid red flowers of the bloody cranesbill fill the rock crevices and spatter their colour over the flat terraces wherever the plant roots can anchor in a crack, however small. The shrubby cinquefoil is well

*The following plants can be seen on undisturbed chalk downlands
in the southern parts of England.*

Carline thistle (in seed).

Cypress spurge, a plant of calcareous grasslands.

*Wild rose, the commonest in the north.
The leaves are softly downy and the hips globular.*

*Sweet briar found on the chalk and limestone of the south,
has sweet smelling leaves and egg-shaped hips.*

*The bird's foot trefoil (yellow) and black medick.
found on light soils especially chalk and limestone.*

*The rough hawkbit and carline thistle, two common
plants of grasslands on calcareous soils.*

Hedgerow fruits help to sustain wildlife through the winter.
Here is a selection.

Hawthorn or quickthorn, for centuries widely planted
as a hedgerow plant.

Blackthorn or sloe, a common hedgerow plant
with rich insect fauna.

White bryony found in hedgerows and scrubby places.
Avoided by rabbits (berries poisonous).

Rose hips, a valuable source of vitamin C
and also as a favourite food of small mammals.

Woody nightshade or bittersweet (poisonous)
is a common hedgerow plant but not to be confused with
its very poisonous cousin, deadly nightshade.

Guelder rose a characteristic plant of chalk soils.

A parched limestone pavement in the Burren, Co. Clare. Ivy and juniper are growing in the deep fissures.

established as in Teesdale, and the hillsides of Black Head are dotted with the blue of the spring gentian. Here too there is much heather and the long creeping stems of bearberry. The animal life is not so remarkable but a fine moth, the Burren green, is much sought after by entomologists as it occurs nowhere else in Ireland or Britain, although it is well known on the Continent. The Burren is also the only place in Ireland where the pearl-bordered fritillary butterfly breeds and in open spaces in the hazel scrub many woodwhites fly leisurely by.

In our survey of British grasslands we must not forget the famous Machair, particularly that on the west coast of the Outer Hebrides. The name machair is a Gaelic word for grassy coastal dunes. In most instances the sands are quite flat, without the familiar dune hills of other coasts. The coarse sand is made up of tiny fragments of sea shells, and so is very calcareous, and the vegetation resembles that of limestone and chalk soils in southern England but also of course includes northern species. In some parts of the Outer Hebrides the grassy plains may extend more than one-and-a-quarter miles inland from the shore. It is not surprising therefore that the machair is of considerable importance agriculturally and for centuries has formed excellent grazing for sheep and cattle.

Walls

The uplands are well known for their stone walls: pale grey in the Carboniferous Limestone country, dark grey where there is granite and a rich warm colour in the Cotswolds. The stone wall is an ideal habitat for many animals, even in exposed altitudes. It provides shelter from winter storms, food in the plant life growing in the crevices, and a safe breeding site. It is a favourite nesting place for the wheatear, pied wagtail, redstart and even enables the common starling to penetrate into the treeless higher latitudes, as, for instance on Orkney and Shetland, by using crevices in dry stone walls for its nest. Snails, woodlice, silverfish, beetles and many others are common, particularly where there is limestone, while certain spiders are characteristic of the stone wall habitat. One species, *Textrix*, with an attractive patterned abdomen, is one of the best-known.

Hedges

Today nearly all grasslands in the lowlands are enclosed in some way either by fences (whether wooden, wire or stones) or by hedges. Those long lines of shrubs and trees, white with may or sloe in the spring and summer and berried in the winter, are the essence of the British countryside. 'They enclose but don't oppress', as a foreign visitor put it in the eighteenth century. Their charm lies in the varying shapes, sizes and colours, and curious patterns created as they wind over the hills and valleys, and along the streams, eventually meeting on the horizon to give the impression of a never-ending 'forest'.

The usual method of beginning a hedge was to dig out a ditch in order to build up an earth bank. Woody plants were set on top, mostly hawthorn but sometimes any young shrubs and cuttings that came to hand. In the course of time a thick hedge formed and the bank sides were clothed in grasses and hedgerow plants. In the west and south-west, where drystone walls were preferred as field boundaries, the usual practice was to cap them with turf. After a few years the seeds of hawthorn, sloe, elder and other woody shrubs would be transferred in bird droppings and a hedge begin to form. While this process was going on the grass on the top would spread down the sides, other plants take a hold in the rock crevices, and soon the stonework would be almost completely hidden, and in time difficult to distinguish from hedge-topped earth banks. When really mature they are very colourful in the spring with bluebells, cowslips, white campion, ferns and many other plants.

The Enclosure Acts of the seventeenth and eighteenth centuries greatly increased the rate of hedge planting. Hedges were sometimes planted around the new boundaries of the enclosed land, but in other cases they separated the limits of the field furlongs of the previous open-field system of cultivation, so that the ancient pattern is still visible.

In the eighteenth and nineteenth centuries, when a shortage of home-grown timber was becoming acute, many farmers realized that hedgerow trees could be a valuable source of timber. They planted oak, ash, elm and other trees with this in mind. Elm was a popular tree because the timber did not rot when immersed in water for use as culverts, drains and posts. It was the commonest of hedgerow trees before the dreaded Dutch elm disease reached Britain – a new virulent strain which was on timber imported from America – and killed over 80 per cent of them. Most of the dead trees have been felled but in many places vigorous new shoots from the old stumps are rising above the hedgerows. In those places where the chain saw has not yet been, ivy scrambles over the dead trees, hiding the timber, providing food and shelter for insects and a nesting place for the wren, goldfinch and spotted flycatcher.

In 1951 a survey by the Forestry Commission showed that the most abundant hedgerow tree was oak, closely followed by elm, ash and various other deciduous trees. Beech and sycamore were both quite common and there were some conifers. Apart from trees, the hedgerows themselves gradually acquired a variety of shrubs and woody climbers – the older the hedgerow the larger the number of species of these plants to be found. Hawthorn was almost always the favoured hedging species, being quick to grow into a thorny, stock-proof barrier. But hawthorn will not keep its monopoly forever. Gradually new seedlings like the blackthorn, spindle tree, holly, sycamore, field maple, oak, bramble, hazel or elder will secure a toe-hold in the hedgerow, and this slow process of diversification has provided the basis for the modern craft or science of hedgerow dating. Nobody seems to know exactly why it should be so, but pioneering work by Max Hooper and W. G. Hoskins seems to show that each species of tree or shrub which is present in a typical 30 metre (approximately 33 yards) hedgerow stretch represents 100 years in the life of that hedge. In Wiltshire a hedge which was known to have existed in Saxon times (it was mentioned in a Saxon charter) now has hazel, oak, two species of wild rose, field maple, hawthorn, dogwood, crabapple and sallow – all reasonably common without one species being dominant. Some old hedgerows have as many as twelve species dating from Saxon or Norman times – though a thousand years of life in the landscape endows a rich old hedgerow with not an ounce of official protection. In comparison the more recent hedges, Parliamentary Enclosure hedges and those of eighteenth- or nineteenth-century origin, have only two or three species, of which hawthorn is by far the commonest, followed by blackthorn. Elder also gets in rapidly because as soon as there is perching space for birds, the seeds are deposited in the bird droppings.

Hedges which were formed by leaving the shrubs and trees along a wood edge while clearing the rest for agriculture are of special interest to botanists. As might be expected, they have a wide range of tree and shrub

Hedgerows are most attractive when in blossom. Here is a selection.

Elder, both flowers and berries are used for wine making.

Mountain ash or rowan, most commonly seen as a solitary tree of the uplands.

Old man's beard, our only wild clematis. Especially common on calcareous soils where it festoons the hedgerows.

Bramble or blackberry, one of the best loved of wild fruits. Does best in overgrown hedges.

Hedge bindweed, sometimes a very persistent weed in gardens. The nectar of the flowers is much sought after by insects.

Honeysuckle, the food plant of the white admiral butterfly.

species and woodland plants, bluebells, wood anemones and mercury, which reveal their past history. Several examples of this type of hedge have been discovered by examining aerial photographs because they clearly show the outline of the ancient wood, with curving lines rather than the symmetrical shape of hedgerows planted along open-field boundaries. Monks Wood Experimental Station (when it was part of the Nature Conservancy) studied this type of hedge in some detail and showed that certain species of shrubs and plants could be used as indicators of the hedge's origin. For example, thirty-three relic wood-edge hedges in Huntingdonshire had elder, rose, ash, blackthorn, oak, privet, maple, dogwood, spindle and hazel, all being well represented although blackthorn was the most numerous. Maple, dogwood, spindle and hazel are all strongly associated with relic woodland hedges. This relationship with the past is what we now call ecological history, a fascinating new subject which is

giving us much valuable information. In this survey the principal species that are planted in hedgerows – hawthorn and elm – were excluded in order to ensure that only natural colonization was being considered. The herbaceous plants which are good indicators of a relic wood-edge hedge are all well-known woodland plants, and in addition to wood anemone, bluebell and mercury (the most common plants) there are wood melick, crested cow-wheat and yellow archangel.

Hedge removal started quite early on in the nineteenth century. Where the main occupation was sheep grazing, large fields were still preferred because a good deal of open land was needed. The process of hedge destruction accelerated in the inter-war periods of the twentieth century and was given a tremendous boost by the drive for more efficient farming during the last war and afterwards. All country lovers are aware that hedges are still disappearing at a fast rate, especially in some parts of the Midland plain of England, and particularly in East Anglia.

But how much hedgerow do we have in Britain? It is very difficult to estimate and some of the early attempts were far from accurate. A careful estimate made in the 1960s suggested that we had something like 500,000 miles of hedgerow in England and Wales. This is only a guess but a good starting point from which to estimate the rate of destruction. Again this is difficult to calculate and one can only take samples from different parts of the country and use them for a generalized estimate for the whole of Britain. One of the first studies used a selected area on which an aerial photograph of 1946 showed there to be seventy-one miles of hedgerow. In 1963 a similar photograph showed that it had fallen to forty-six miles, in 1965 there was a drop to twenty miles, and a year later it was down to sixteen miles. This shows a decline of about 65.5 per cent of hedgerow mileage in a period of twenty years. Later surveys over a greater area suggested a loss per annum of about 5000 miles of hedgerow in England and Wales from 1946 to 1963. It is clear from this work, however, that hedgerow removal was far greater in the east and south of England and much less in many parts of the west, south-west and north. These regional differences are consistent with a greater hedge loss in arable areas, and a smaller one where there is grassland. In the former the loss from 1947 to 1969 was 23.2 per cent of all hedgerows, and in the latter in the same period only 8.4 per cent.

But why are hedgerows so important for wildlife? Perhaps the finest account of the hedgerow harvest of fruits, nuts and berries was written by Richard Jefferies in 1878. He wrote of the hawthorn berries (peggles) so loved by thrush and blackbird, the hazel nuts, elderberries, the blue-black sloes with a bloom like the grape, the red or green berries of the white bryony, whose root is supposed to be a powerful ingredient of love potions, gooseberry and currant bushes spread by birds taking the fruit from nearby gardens, the brilliant red hips of the wild rose, and of course the ubiquitous blackberry. Then there are acorns, chestnuts, ash keys, and crabapples.

The greater the variety of plants and shrubs in the hedgerow, the greater the number of insects. Common plants such as nettles, usually regarded as weeds elsewhere, nurture some of our finest butterflies; the umbellifers – hedge parsley, cow parsley, and hogweed – have flowers whose nectar is much sought after by hoverflies – 'natural fuelling stations', as that great pioneer of animal ecology, Charles Elton, once called them. The wealth of plant-feeding insects attracts many predators, mainly bugs, beetles, spiders, wasps and parasitic hymenoptera, all of which are potentially useful in nearby crops for reducing pests.

A hedge also provides shelter for birds' nests, especially if it is untrimmed; rabbits burrow in the hedge bank, the hedgehog hibernates among the dead leaves, and finds slugs, snails, a nest of mice, beetles, and caterpillars to eat in summer. Weazels, stoats and foxes hunt for prey, while above in the hedgerow trees wood pigeons and jackdaws nest and occasionally an owl or a kestrel find a safe hole for breeding. A large number of birds have been recorded using hedges of one type or another either for feeding, shelter or nesting. Without trees the bird list is much reduced and if the hedge is trimmed low and kept narrow by ploughing up to it, then again fewer birds are seen. Where a road or a track runs along a grass field, the hedges are often cut less frequently and are usually bordered by a grassy verge and bank. The ideal hedge, which is broad and tall, with flowery banks and numerous trees for hole-nesting birds, is really quite rare, and is disliked by most farmers. Even if tolerated such a hedge would suffer in arable country from spray drift and by scorching during stubble burning.

Although trees and tall hedges are much sought after by cattle and sheep, for shade in the heat of the summer and shelter from the icy winds in winter, some farmers do not appear to think this important. Some years ago during a hot summer, this writer saw a herd of bullocks in a field which was completely devoid of shade. A furniture van came along the road and parked on the grass verge, casting a broad shadow over part of the field. A nearby bullock moved into this cool haven, quickly followed by others, and soon the entire herd was crowded into the small patch of shade. What a difference a tall hedge or a few trees would have made to them! The hedge is a windbreak, slowing down the force of gales particularly in the winter when light soils are easily blown away. In the peat fens of East Anglia hedges are rare and anyone who has seen the immense storms of brown dust billowing over the lands and roads in the strong March winds, taking with them the newly sown seeds of the summer crop, will realize the extent of this destructive force. The Breckland heaths were once open sandy plains and frequent dust storms built up inland dunes which were never stabilized by vegetation. Then in the eighteenth and nineteenth centuries windbreaks of Scots pine were planted until they criss-crossed the landscape. Gradually the land was brought into cultivation or planted with trees. The old pine hedges can still be seen in many places; they have done their job and although formerly 'laid', they have for long been allowed to grow into trees.

— 2 —

DOWN IN THE GREENWOOD

*This pollarded oak in Sherwood Forest must be three or more
centuries old and in old age is a wonderful habitat
for birds and insects.*

Of all the components in the green mosaic of the British countryside, woodland is probably the most misunderstood. Many people regard woods as the last fragments of the primeval wildscape, while only in this age of synthetics could we look upon woodland as a sort of wasteground. It may be a kind of battlefield – a place where the battered forces of conservation skirmish with the forces of destruction in the campaigns which are leading towards the countryside Armageddon – but woodland was never wasteground. The misconceptions are rooted in the now untenable view that on the eve of the Saxon settlement these islands lay shaded by the canopy of a vast and virgin wildwood. The subsequent history of the landscape was perceived as a triumphal pioneering epic in which resourceful Saxon and medieval settlers rolled back the leafy counterpane. Also misleading was the medieval description of woodland and common as 'waste'. In its earlier meaning, 'waste' did not denote wild, unwanted ground, for the woods, commons and marshes each played a vital role in local subsistence. There will also be many people who quite literally fail to see the wood for the trees and forget that woods have histories as well as species. And so we begin this chapter with a brief history of the woodlands before taking a more detailed look at their natural history.

Man has been master of his setting for a very long time, and so woodland should not be regarded as the last frontier of untrammelled Nature, but as a useful resource that is a blend of the natural and man-made worlds. As a resource, it was, until modern times, carefully managed and regulated, while the traditions of woodmanship must be very ancient. The pioneering phase of wildwood clearance belonged not to the Saxon era but to the Neolithic and Bronze Age periods. The prehistoric people had it in their power to remove the British woodland completely had they wished to do so. But like their medieval successors, they needed suitable timber in enormous quantities, as fuel, game cover, for home-building, fortifications, fencing, for hafting tools and weapons and, in the Ages of Bronze and Iron, for smelting. Expanses of woodland must have been managed according to various systems to produce timber in different sizes and qualities to serve different purposes. It is doubtful if natural woodland could ever have provided evenly-sized timbers in the sufficient quantities needed to build timber trackways like those excavated in the Somerset levels, or to revet and reinforce the ramparts of the massive hillforts. At some times, the pressures of a rising population must have pressed back the woodland margins, while at others, land exhausted by over-farming will have surrendered to rough pasture and woodland.

Following exhaustive surveys of prehistoric settlement traces in Northamptonshire, Cambridgeshire and Dorset, the archaeologist Christopher Taylor has concluded that by Roman times the English countryside was probably less wooded than it is today. Sometimes the relics of ancient settlements and fields can be discovered in places that were later to be wooded in medieval times. The great medieval forest of Rockingham in Northamptonshire covered an area which must previously have been open farmland and which included at least ten small Roman settlements. But the medieval landscape was also not as heavily wooded as people imagine, and the woodland historian Oliver Rackham has discovered that, for example, Cambridgeshire carried less woodland in the mid-thirteenth century than it does today. Although a remarkably large proportion of our surviving woods still sit exactly within their medieval boundaries, there are numerous places where the distinctive corrugations of medieval ridge-and-furrow ploughland can be recognized on what is today a woodland floor.

Clearly we are meeting factors which are much more complicated than the old idea of a great Saxon assault on the virgin wildwood that was carried to its completion in the medieval centuries. Rather, we must imagine a successive rolling back and forth of the woodland frontiers. During times of ancient colonization when rising populations had outstripped the contemporary farming resources, then packages of valuable woodland would be surrendered to agriculture. At other times, woods would be ardently protected for the cornucopia of useful resources which they stored, while at other times still, when there was

Woodland returned to Britain after the close of the last Ice Age. Gradually deciduous trees displaced pioneering species like the pine and birch from the more favourable environments and deciduous woodland blanketed most but the loftiest hills in England, Wales and Ireland. This oak is growing on the crags above Derwentwater in Cumbria.

plague, famine, war, land exhaustion, economic collapse and decay, the advancing woodland tide would reclaim the derelict and depopulated farmlands.

There certainly was a good measure of woodland clearance or assarting in late-Saxon and early-medieval times. But much of this woodland had overgrown the villas and native farmsteads of the Roman era – and so it could not have been primeval. It must have been established in the centuries of pestilence, strife and commercial chaos which began with the waning of Roman power.

A good deal is known about the medieval practices of woodmanship. If we think of the woods of the Middle Ages only as hunting reserves then we overlook the enormous demand for timber which existed at these times. There were various kinds of woods, like deer parks, the wooded portions of the royal hunting forests, or woods which were cropped to furnish specialized timber for particular industries and markets, and woods which were integral members of the monastic and manorial empires. Any small manor house or farmstead would consume spinneys of oak or black poplar needed for heavy framing timbers, perhaps a cluster of elms for boards or poles, while a coppice might be cleared to provide all the light timber like hazel needed for the wattle panels and for the sways which pegged down the thatch. More light timber would be devoured for hurdle-making and fencing materials, and coppices also yielded the copious supplies of fuel needed for charcoal-based smelting and glass-making. Massive oaken timbers were used in shipbuilding; masons needed scaffolding; armies required great siege engines, arrows, spears and shields, while transport required carts and wagons of oak, ash and elm. Lacking diesel or gas and seldom having access to coal shipments, the towns were warmed by convoys of firewood. Countryfolk were more self-sufficient, and while peasants were forbidden to fell trees they were generally allowed to gather dead wood as fuel and to take timber for essential purposes such as house-building and the construction of gates, carts and ploughs. Woodland was an essential component of local subsistence and some seventeen parishes had rights in the woods and commons of Tiptree Heath.

While it was sometimes practical to import European timber, the forests of Britain met almost all the demands. Medieval people were ingenious in the ways that they were able to harness resources and mesh together a variety of activities. In order to obtain regular supplies of timber of different grades, the larger woods were subdivided into managed units which were harvested by felling according to different

Although sights such as this are very rare today, scores of managed medieval woods will have looked like Wolves Wood near Hadleigh in Suffolk, with tall trees grown as 'standards' standing over the coppiced underwood.

rotations. Some areas were regularly coppiced (periodically cut) to produce light timber, others were felled only once a generation to yield heavy constructional beams, while the two activities were often integrated in places where tall, well-spaced and infrequently felled 'standards' grew above a coppiced underwood. Many woods were highly valued as grazings for pigs, cattle and horses, but browsing livestock could not be allowed amongst the lush shoots of a coppice. In wood pastures the beasts grazed amongst well-spaced standards or amongst trees which were pollarded (to produce a rounded head of young branches) above the reach of browsers and which produced crops of poles from the regularly shaved crown. Some of the old woodland grazing customs must have been very old and many of the old roads and trackways of the Weald seem, according to recent work by T. Tatton-Brown, to have originated from prehistoric paths used in moving pigs from the settlements of north Kent to the hamlets which nestled in the wooded swine pastures of the

Weald. Commoners' rights of pig-grazing or 'pannage' were jealously guarded in many medieval communities.

Woods were valuable assets and were protected against unlawful pillaging. Most medieval woods were hemmed by ditched 'wood banks' which clearly marked the property boundary and which kept livestock out of the tender coppices, while internal banks could be built to mark the manorial boundaries in shared woods. Many such woodbanks survive as degraded but clearly recognizable earthworks and they often demonstrate the medieval pedigree of a particular wood.

But not all our woods are a legacy of medieval times. In 1664, the courtier John Evelyn published his *Sylva* in which he bemoaned the neglect and removal of the woods and forests which 'our more prudent ancestors left standing for the ornament and service of their country'. The book was a hit, and the inspiration of many new plantations. Each subsequent generation has, for better or for worse, produced its plantations and they can often be distinguished from older woods by their geometrical boundaries, the dominance of the one chosen tree species and, often and most easily, by their 'plantation' names. At first the plantations produced the traditional hardwoods for the traditional uses. In the eighteenth century the European larch and the Scots pine began to be introduced in commercial plantations, and in more recent times many good old countrysides have surrendered to the dark anonymity of marshalled armies of Corsican pine, Sitka spruce, lodgepole pine and the like.

The Scots pine is an attractive tree and is indigenous to Scotland and the Lake District, but England and Wales are essentially hardwood countries where lime, oak, elm, ash, alder, hazel, birch, the evergreen yew,

Hazel coppice in Wolves Wood.

Beautiful pollarded beeches at Knightwood Oak.

The drab landscape of commercially-grown conifers can be compared to the attractive beech pollards which survive just a few yards away and are shown in the previous photograph.

The lime is a very graceful tree, whether grown as a standard, or as coppice timber as in this wood at Wandlebury in Cambridgeshire. The lime was very numerous in the ancient wildwood.

the hornbeam and, in the southern chalklands, the beech, have in their different ecological combinations, competed for space, light and niches since the days when farming began. It was less than two centuries ago that the ancient woodland crafts, which had kept our woodlands fruitful and healthy, began their decline. Cheap imported and home-grown softwoods displaced the slow-maturing hardwoods from the timber markets. New ships of coke-smelted iron, houses of brick and utensils of steel and plastic propelled the deciduous woodlands into commercial obsolescence. Then the rise of forms of farming which were capital-rather than labour-intensive and the growth of new outlooks on the land encouraged the pursuit of short-term profits needed to pay off interest on borrowings. Few farmers and estate owners were prepared to wait for a crop which would take a generation or more to mature.

A medieval wood bank still marks the edge of Hayley Wood in Cambridgeshire. Many old woods which still survive have their boundaries marked by such venerable earthworks.

Today most woods are far from being the 'Merrie Greenwoodes' of times past. Outgrown coppices and pollards contort in grotesque forms while the once majestic standards stand neglected and decaying as the deathly flotillas of bulldozers advance. Before exploring the natural wonders of the woods which survive, mention must be made of the place-names which have long fascinated those interested in woodland history. Many names tell us about the trees which grew in a locality during Dark Age or medieval times when the names were given, and Ashwell in Hertfordshire still has ash growing around its well. There are hundreds of place-names containing Old English elements which either refer to trees, like 'holt', or to areas cleared of trees, like 'stubbing'. They include ridding, field, ley, wood, stock, dene and hurst. But we must always be very wary of place-names. A modern family living in the depths of surburbia might choose to call their house 'The Elms'. This does not mean that the home lay in a great forest of elms, but that the couple of elms at the end of their garden were unusual, noteworthy and therefore prominent features of the local landscape, and so worthy of being adopted for naming purposes. The evidence contained in our many 'woodland' place-names has still to be deciphered, but names which mention a particular species of tree are usually trustworthy. They include Ackton, with its oaks, or Accrington with its acorns; Birkenhead, once a birch-grown promontory; Aldershot and Aldergrove, quite different today; Ashfield; Ashton and Ashstead; Haughley, with its hawthorns; and all other thorny places like Thornbrough, Thornby, Thornton le Moor and Childer Thornton.

Each wood has its history of service to mankind, but for most country-lovers the surviving woodlands are, above all, reservoirs of plants and wildlife.

Forests and wildlife

Today only about 8 per cent of Britain is tree-covered, one of the smallest totals for any country in Europe. The great forests have gone and although the largest remaining area, the New Forest, is protected, a great deal of it is not covered by trees. As our population grows and industrialization develops, the demand for timber increases and today production only meets a little more than 8 per cent of all our total requirements of timber, pulp and paper.

In spite of this it has at times been suggested that timber was an outdated commodity, and that commercial forestry would come to an end. In 1862, when the Royal Navy decided to build its ships with metal hulls instead of wood, there was great concern about the loss of markets for timber, and in recent years the prediction has been that when energy is really cheap and all materials are synthetically produced, timber will no longer be required and the world's forests will be allowed to grow again. But there is unfortunately no sign of this happening, rather the shortage of timber gets worse.

Concern over the timber supply prompted the government to create the Forestry Commission in 1919, and since then it has encouraged tree planting by acquiring land or making covenants with private owners to allow the Commission to manage their forests. Nevertheless since 1919 the Commission has been a charge on the Exchequer, never yet having produced an overall profit in spite of its growing income from sales. On the credit side, it has made extensive contributions to our knowledge of tree growing and also to applied research on subjects such as timber treatment and control of timber pests.

The Forestry Commission's official remit is simply to grow trees and produce more timber. It has no other function in the eyes of the government, but in the last twenty or thirty years it has responded to the increasing public interest in woodlands for amenity and wildlife by providing picnic sites, nature trails and information centres for visitors who like to walk through their plantations. Perhaps the best known example is Grisedale Forest in the Lake District, where it is even possible to go deer hunting on payment of a fee. The early experiments have proved so popular that the Commission now fully recognizes amenity and conservation as major activities in addition to its main function. A number of forest nature reserves have also been created, and some small woodlands which the Commission has found uneconomic to run by their own staff have been sold off to County Conservation

Decaying tree stumps are havens for many forms of invertebrate wildlife and plants.

Trusts as nature reserves.

This part of the Commission's work is non-productive in a commercial sense, adding somewhat to their total expenses, and it has been suggested that a charge for admission to Commission forests should be made. Although this may not be welcomed, entomologists already pay a fee for their permits to collect insects in areas such as the New Forest.

Much of the Forestry Commission planting has been to reafforest land which was formerly wooded or scrub-covered, or not used for agricultural purposes. In some parts of the country, notably in East Anglia, forests have been planted on land on which trees have never grown in historic times, for example the 25,000 acre Thetford Chase in Norfolk and Suffolk. Here trees were planted on land which at the time was considered too poor for agriculture. Today modern agricultural methods would have enabled the farmer to grow crops

profitably. This great forest was originally planted to supply pit props for the coal mines, but by the time the trees had grown, modern mining methods had changed and timber was no longer needed for this purpose. It is now used mainly for chipboard and other synthetic wood products. The trees in Thetford Chase have not grown as fast as was originally expected and some foresters believe that this is because the sandy soil and low rainfall restrict their development.

Nearly all plantings by the Commission are of coniferous trees. The timber is generally known as softwood, and is more valuable commercially than the slower-growing hardwoods. There has been much opposition in the past to these dark blocks of coniferous plantations, like ink stains on the landscape. Their sudden appearance in a pleasant landscape of rounded green hills offends the eye, particularly in National Parks such as the Lake District and other areas of

Some creatures of the woodland.

*New Forest ponies are probably descended from stock introduced many centuries ago.
Today there are so many that they overgraze the heaths and grasslands.*

The tawny owl.

The fox, our largest mammal predator and one which has adapted very successfully to the man-made landscape.

The blackbird is one of our commonest birds found from urban gardens to mountain valleys.

upland country. The Commission has recognized this and has attempted, in recent years, to plant their forests so that they follow the contours of the land and blend in with the local topography which is their setting and background.

Plantations of pine, spruce, larch, Douglas fir and other conifers established by the Forestry Commission during the last sixty years make up a large proportion of the high forest (that is, mature woodland with a closed canopy) in the lowland parts of England and Wales and dominate in the mountains of the west and north. Where a coniferous plantation replaces deciduous trees it inevitably results in a much poorer fauna and flora. All the ground flora disappears under the dense canopy, although some of the original plants may persist along the rides. The insect life is devastated, and the same can probably be said for the birds, although a few other species appear which were previously absent or rare. Where the forest was planted on land which was rough hill grazing or sandy heathland, there may be a number of gains in the fauna. In Norfolk and Suffolk the populations of red and roe deer have increased considerably in the coniferous forests, and are tolerated as long as they do not do too much damage, since there is an income from deer shooting. Sparrowhawks and innumerable wood pigeons build their nests in the dark forests, thrushes and blackbirds are found on the fringes but do not often penetrate deep into the plantations. Coal tits and goldcrests are often heard but the common warblers are virtually absent. In the Breckland plantations crossbills are sometimes seen but they seem to prefer isolated groups of pines as nest sites. In the Kings Forest conifer plantation in Suffolk stone curlews nested on the woodland rides for a number of years because the trees were planted on the heathlands which were their traditional breeding territory. This has probably now ceased as the birds would tend to move elsewhere when the trees grew taller.

The management system of clear-felling and replanting creates a new habitat for a time. While the ground is still open in a felled Breckland plantation, woodlarks may breed for a year or two and then willow warblers, grasshopper warblers and whitethroats colonize as scrubby trees take a hold. When the ground vegetation is suppressed by the spreading canopies, these birds disappear. In many parts of Europe the crested tit readily colonizes new conifer plantations when the trees are twenty to twenty-five feet tall. But they need holes in old fence posts and decayed trees for nesting and also some ground vegetation for feeding. In Scotland, however, this charming bird has tended to remain in its old native pine forests, its traditional

breeding territory. Maybe the population has been small and isolated for so long that the urge to find new places is not so well developed as in its continental cousins. Nest boxes placed in the new plantations might help in encouraging the crested tit because many man-made forests throughout the country, both north and south, appear to be suitable for it. It might even succeed in Thetford Chase, where the light sandy soils are similar to those of the dune conifer plantations established on the west coast of France. These dune forests are very varied, intermingled with open grassy places, and it may be that the regimented stands of trees in some of the British plantations are too uniform for the crested tit to prosper.

Since the Forestry Commission plants few hardwoods for commercial purposes, most of the deciduous woods that remain in Britain are in private ownership. The Commission does, however, often plant deciduous trees as a roadside fringe to a large conifer plantation. This practice has three important functions. It makes the roadside much more attractive to look at; it creates a habitat for wildlife; and it reduces the risk of fire by screening the conifers from the lighted matches and cigarette ends thrown out from passing vehicles. The Commission is also responsible for a certain amount of deciduous woodland in places such as the New Forest and the Forest of Dean but much of this is now regarded more as amenity than commercial forest.

The privately owned woodlands are generally rather small, and used for a variety of purposes. Game preservation, particularly pheasant breeding, is common while other forests are maintained for forest produce, fox coverts, family investment, or purely for pleasure. Work at Cambridge University has shown that many such woods have retained their boundaries, as they are today, for several centuries. As the human population grew, more land was needed for growing food but some woodland was always essential to rural communities in the period before the Industrial Revolution. The poorer people often had the right in certain woodlands to collect dead wood, kindling, nuts, fruits, fungi, honey, and sometimes to graze domestic stock. Timber became a valuable commodity and was put to a great many uses which today have been mostly forgotten. The older trees provided large pieces of timber such as gate posts and material required for building and the smaller saplings would be made into

Woodland soils are usually rather poor, but the autumn leaf fall in deciduous woods helps to maintain the levels of fertility.

fence posts. Coppice timber had many uses. Depending on the length of the coppice cycle, the thicker wood would be used as fuel, the thinner as fencing materials, for making hurdles, baskets, handles, and even for some domestic utensils. Hazel was the main source of coppice timber but oak regrowth was also treated in the same way when the standards were felled, and the bark was useful as a source of tannin.

The commonest tree in these forests was the good old British oak. There are two species in this country, and both are common. The pedunculate oak, which prefers heavy soils, clays and loams, is more frequent in the southern half of England, and the dermast or sessile oak, which prefers acid soils, is the characteristic oak further north. The separation between them is not sharp, both species being found together, and they hybridize freely. The beech, one of our finest trees, is also common in deciduous high forest, but is most characteristic of the chalk downs in the south, where beech plantations can form commercial crops.

Sweet chestnut also produces a valuable coppice. This tree was introduced by the Romans – it is common in Italy – so that they could still eat the familiar chestnuts they had at home, although the climate in this country today is not really good enough to produce ample crops every year. The chestnut has a strong durable timber and trees grow to a considerable size. Unfortunately the trunks are susceptible to what is called the 'shakes', that is cracks which follow the line of the grain, and so in general the timber is unsuitable for large pieces of wood such as planks. The chestnut coppice is still used in south-east England, cut on a twelve-year rotation when the stems have developed into poles. These are then sawn into measured lengths and split, forming the familiar chestnut pales which are bound together with wire to make fencing. There are perhaps many other cheaper forms of fencing nowadays but chestnut pale fencing is attractive and very long-lasting.

The ash is another very useful timber tree. It has the advantage of regenerating abundantly in woodlands and also grows to a considerable height and forms a tree of some size. The timber is not very hard but is excellent for fencing and as material such as for the handles of axes, hammers and hay rakes.

Outside mature woodland, the most familiar trees of the countryside after oak are ash, sycamore, and until recently different species of elm. This is true in the writer's own parish, but we can also add willow, alders (because we are in a river valley), limes which are planted as avenues or in big gardens, and varieties of poplars. Elsewhere of course other trees may be more common – hornbeam, yew or holly, or even pine.

Woodland nature reserves

Although not much coppicing is done today for commercial purposes, this form of management persists in certain woodland nature reserves because without regular cutting certain plants would either disappear or become much more rare. The reason is that the coppice cycle creates an exposed forest floor every few years, just after the coppice has been taken, so that the sunlight and air is able to reach the ground, which before was heavily shaded. The light immediately stimulates certain plants to grow, particularly bluebells, primroses and violets, which in the first two seasons after coppicing make a dense splash of colour in the spring. Others decline in the greater light intensity, particularly dog's mercury.

In Hayley Wood, Cambridgeshire, there is a very special reason for continuing the coppice cycle. This wood is one of the few still left in England where the oxlip grows in abundance. It flowers in profusion in the season after the coppice has been cut, and it is essential for the Cambridgeshire Naturalists' Trust, which owns the wood, to manage it on the old traditional system of coppice rotation. Hayley is a remarkable wood because, although only 122 acres, it has been so well researched historically that we know a great deal about it from the middle of the thirteenth century to the present day. Throughout these 700 years its boundary has more or less remained as it is today, apart from an odd corner of $3\frac{1}{2}$ acres cut off when the railway was built in 1864. In 1251 it was owned by the Bishop of Ely and there is some evidence that it may well have been the same size and shape for many years earlier than this.

Surviving documents show that the main value of Hayley Wood was for the production of timber and coppice. This continued throughout the centuries until the latter half of the nineteenth century, when the market for this type of timber began to diminish and Hayley became more valuable for its game. Although deer graze in the wood, there is no evidence that from 1251 to the present day grazing by domestic stock was ever practised, except for a reference in the Domesday Book of 1086, which may mean that pigs were taken into the wood to eat acorns. Throughout the second half of the nineteenth, and well into the twentieth century it was strictly keepered, with the public not admitted, its owners using it as a fox covert and for hunting pheasants and deer. Equally remarkable, it does not appear to have had any buildings erected in it – apart from a gamekeeper's cottage in the centre of the wood – or suffered any other major disturbance. On this evidence Hayley Wood is probably an indirect survival of primeval forest in that there has been a

Oxlips growing in Haley Wood, Cambridgeshire.

continuous cover of trees, although modified in many ways throughout its long history. Supporting biological evidence is that all the tree species now growing in Hayley are known from pollen records to have occurred in the same geographical region 3000 years ago.

Hayley Wood also has a number of herbaceous plants, such as the oxlip, which are now known to be indicators of ancient woodland. Some of these, for example dog's mercury, herb paris, and the grass *Millium effusum*, are all characteristic of closed woodland. On the other hand, plants that are good indicators of secondary woodland – that is, forest which has developed on land which previously had no trees – such as keck, spurge laurel, and ivy, do not grow there. It is probable that dead wood, rotten trees

his purpose. Because it was so durable, oak provided strong, big timber for buildings and ships, and the preponderance of oak in lowland deciduous woods may therefore be an artefact due to continued selection of the most useful tree.

One often finds that the leaves of the oak are almost eaten away by caterpillars in the spring. These may be geometrid moths, winter moths, or mottle umber moths, and especially the oak roller moth, which sometimes is so abundant on oak trees that they are totally defoliated. The trees usually manage to recover and produce a second set of leaves later on in the summer, but in Hayley Wood as many as one in four oaks died after a spectacular caterpillar plague between 1916 and 1925. Defoliation was repeated so often that the trees were weakened and many died. A dead oak may stand for as many as thirty years before it falls but although the wood above the ground remains hard and dry the roots eventually decay. The fallen tree lying on the forest floor is in contact with moisture so that decay is accelerated by fungi and bacteria followed by insects burrowing into the timber. It may take another twenty years before there is a significant effect on the trunk. And it may be as much as 100 years before the whole tree disappears and is incorporated back into the soil. For other species of tree the time period may be different: for elm and ash it is shorter, though perhaps with hawthorn and yew it may be longer.

The abundant acorns which fall from the oaks in many woods seldom seem to regenerate and in spite of research we do not yet know all the factors responsible. However, there is no doubt that herbivores such as mice, squirrels, jays and magpies all eat the seed, and if the acorn does manage to germinate and send up a shoot, it is likely to be eaten off by rabbits, hares or deer. This means that woodlands which are predominantly oak at the present time will not always be dominated by this species; in the next few hundred years our woodland nature reserves will gradually change, perhaps to an ash-dominated community, or even elm, if Dutch elm disease does not once more take a hold and devastate the new trees.

Spring time in coppiced woods attracts many visitors. The annual pilgrimage to see the flowers is akin to the mushroom or bilberry gatherers on the Continent, with a single-minded goal: to see – and we hope not to pick – the bluebells, primroses and violets, or in the case of a few select woods in the southern part of East Anglia, the oxlip. This plant occurs only in a very localized area in Cambridgeshire, Essex and Sussex but sometimes, as in Hayley Wood, it is very abundant. On the Continent of Europe the oxlip is widespread, occurring commonly in mountain pas-

and fallen branches were removed for firewood well into the twentieth century and it is only now, as a nature reserve, that decayed timber is allowed to remain on the forest floor. This long history of removal of dead wood may possibly have made a considerable difference to the composition of the invertebrate fauna of Hayley Wood, although we do not know as much about the insects and other invertebrates as we do of its history and vegetation.

Oak is the commonest tree in Hayley, as it is in most surviving woodlands throughout lowland England. But this does not mean that oak forest is the natural climax that would have occurred without the intervention of man. Throughout the centuries when man was dependent on the forest for essential materials for everyday life, he would obviously select the best tree for

There is much more to the plantlife of woodlands than the trees.
This is a selection of woodland plants.

Primrose, now much less common, found mainly in woods and hedge banks but in open grassy places in the west.

Hart's-tongue fern, commonest in the west, especially in rocky woodland and shaded hedge banks.

Ripening berries of lords and ladies.

Livelong or orpine. A local plant of woodland edges and hedge banks.

Woodland Creatures.

The grey squirrel, introduced from North America and now common throughout lowland England.

A red deer suckling its fawn.

A red deer fawn.

tures and in wooded areas into Italy and down the Appenines. It is not a characteristically woodland species as it is in Britain. In Britain it always occurs in chalky boulder clay woodlands, of which Hayley is a good example. It is a tall plant, reaching 11 inches, and is very similar to the primrose in that its flowers are the same pale yellow colour, but they are grouped together at the head of a single stalk, and tend to droop, whereas the primrose normally produces single flowers on individual stalks from the centre of the leafy rosette. The leaves of the oxlip are also different – longer and not so crinkly as the primrose and a slightly paler green. One must be careful, however, not to confuse the oxlip with the hybrid between the cowslip and the primrose, which is often very similar but never occurs in large numbers as does the true oxlip. The hybrid can also be distinguished by orange streaks within the throat of the corolla tube – proof of its cowslip connections. If a wood has oxlips, it does not usually also have primroses, or they are very scarce. In other woods, for instance the Monks Wood National Nature Reserve, the primrose is abundant where there is more light, particularly after coppicing. The cowslip, however, occurs only on the woodland fringe and is typically a grassland plant. The primrose/cowslip hybrid is seen in Monks Wood from time to time but usually not more than one or two plants together.

In some years the spring flowering of the oxlip in Hayley Wood is very disappointing, and visitors come away thinking it must be dying out. The villains are the fallow deer which roam the wood and the neighbouring area. They have a special liking for oxlips and nip off the flowering stems leaving stumps, and sometimes denude a considerable area. By erecting a deer-proof fence around a small area within the wood it was found that the number of flowering oxlips per unit area may be nine times as great as that outside the exclosure. Oxlips which are repeatedly defoliated by deer cannot set seed and although the individual plants are long-lived there is no doubt that the numbers have declined in the last twenty years. The deer seem to have colonized the wood some time in the 1930s, and between 1960 and 1970 the population estimates varied between twenty and sixty. Visitors to nature reserves love to see large mammals such as deer. Unlike the fox and badger which are generally secretive, deer are usually easy to watch as they become accustomed to people when not molested. The reluctance of reserve or park managers to reduce their numbers often allows the population to grow too large for the food resources, and very considerable damage may be done to the vegetation. The only answer would seem to be an annual cull to keep the population down to a reasonable level.

Butterflies, birds and spiders

Everyone who likes the open air enjoys woodland walks, but not any woodland will do. Dark silent woods are rather forbidding, unfriendly, and sometimes even frightening. The woods we like best have dappled light, colour, sunlit glades, logs to picnic on, and the broad canopy of mature trees to shelter us from the wind and rain. The appeal of this sort of wood may be an emotional one, but it also makes good ecological sense. The human eye likes variety in the landscape; a constantly changing scene is more interesting than the sameness of a conifer plantation. The shapes of trees are also important, the rounded outline of the oak or mature Scots pine is more pleasing than the crowded pyramids of firs. Variety of habitat ensures that there will be a rich flora and fauna. In the woodland context the presence of trees of all ages and of different species, dead wood, both standing and on the ground, open grassy glades, a shrubby under-storey, and places where there is a colourful herb layer of woodland flowers, is the ideal. As we walk through this type of wood there is something new every few yards, every turn of the path a different scene and additional interest. This is also the woodland preferred by most forest butterflies, though it is in the southern half of England where most species occur. The first warm days of spring bring out the winter hibernators, peacocks, tortoiseshells, and the bright yellow brimstone – perhaps the first to be called a 'butter' fly. The first two feed on nettles, but the last is a shrub feeder and lays its eggs on the leaves of the common buckthorn. More rarely the large tortoiseshell may be seen in a few of the deciduous woods of south-east England, where its larvae feed on the elm and willow. Perhaps the demise of the elm has contributed to its decline; one has only to cross the Channel to find it commonly in the woods of the Ardennes, and it is widespread throughout the Continent.

Butterflies are not really numerous until high summer – June to August – when the speckled wood, hedge brown, ringlet, small and large skippers, and green-veined white will often be commonly seen along woodland rides. Others such as the purple hairstreak, which feeds on oak, are much less common than one might expect. The green hairstreak, feeding on leguminous herbs and shrubs, also tends to be local. Some butterflies go through periods of extreme scarcity and then after the lean years their numbers increase and they appear in places where they have not been seen for a long time. The comma, a cosmopolitan feeder on plants ranging from nettles to various trees, goes through these cycles of scarcity and abundance, and at

The changing seasons in an old beechwood plantation
(Wandlebury in Cambridgeshire).

the time of writing is reasonably frequent. The white admiral is similar, and in this writer's home county of Northamptonshire was seen in many localities during 1982. It feeds on honeysuckle but prefers to lay its eggs on the rather straggly plants growing in the woodland shade rather than on the high, sweetly scented banks of honeysuckle along the sunny woodland edge. The black and brown hairstreaks both feed on the common shrub blackthorn, or sloe, but they are choosy – the former occurs in a few woods in the southern Midlands while the latter, although widespread, is not often seen in numbers.

If you ask butterfly enthusiasts which species they would most like to find, the majority will almost certainly decide on the purple emperor. It is one of the largest species breeding regularly in Britain, although it is confined to the southern half of the country, excluding the south-west. It is often difficult to find even in woods where it is known to occur, but the flash of purple with some white and orange as it suddenly appears in a sunny glade is a moment never to be forgotten. It seems to prefer fairly open oakwoods, although the main food plant is the goat willow, a common woodland shrub or small tree. It overwinters as a small larva, begins to feed again in the spring and eventually emerges as the perfect insect in July. Some entomologists believe that the purple emperor is more widespread than most of us realize. This is because it seems to have the ability to breed in a particular wood for some years without being discovered. A surprising number of people like to collect the eggs, rear the insects in captivity and then liberate the butterflies when they emerge in the following summer. The captive population is thus protected from predators throughout the egg and larva stage and perhaps the combined effort of these entomologists results in an increased population in certain parts of the country.

While walking through our ideal wood on a summer's day looking for butterflies, there will be bird song all around us. Woodland birds are heard rather than seen, so there is no problem in combining the two activities. Most people will know the songs of the song thrush and blackbird because they are so familiar in gardens. The same applies to the blue and great tits, both of which will be common in our ideal wood. Perhaps slightly less familiar is the willow warbler, a small greeny-brown leaf warbler, whose song is a fragile, high-pitched falling trill, and the chiff-chaff, which is identical in appearance but is immediately identifiable because it calls its name. The chaffinch, robin and wren are all familiar woodland birds almost anywhere in the country and in the winter help to enliven the otherwise silent woods. The finest of our

woodland singers, the nightingale, is confined to the southern half of England but is also absent from the extreme south-west. In my experience it has declined appreciably in recent years, although its numbers may fluctuate because it is certainly present in considerable numbers in its favourite haunts. The nightingale, blackcap and garden warbler all like a woodland with a well-developed undergrowth in which to construct their nests, but the chiff-chaff and its less common cousin the wood warbler build their nests on the ground, very cleverly weaving them into the grass, sometimes in parts of the wood where to the human eye there seems to be very little cover. The wood warbler is associated in this writer's mind with the pied flycatcher and the common redstart, because in my formative years as a bird-watcher I visited the oak forests in the Llandovery valley of mid-Wales and these three birds were my constant companions whilst walking through the woods.

Of our three British woodpeckers the greater spotted is the only one which can be called a truly woodland bird. The green woodpecker, although often heard or seen in woodlands, prefers to feed in open grassy areas, where it finds its choicest food, ants. Near this writer's home village the green woodpecker is quite frequent, although there is no real forest. It often feeds on the grassy slope of our garden, digging vigorously into the turf. A neighbour has complained that it attacks his beehives, drilling holes through the wood in order to feed on the larvae. His hives are now patched with pieces of wood in many different places but thankfully he is more interested in trying to photograph the bird at work rather than do it harm. On two occasions a pair of green woodpeckers have brought their young into our garden and boldly come onto the terrace close to the lounge window. The third British woodpecker, the lesser spotted, or barred, as some prefer to call it, is about the size of a sparrow but has a distinctive, loud call which is unmistakable. It is also seen frequently in woodlands but seems to prefer to nest in orchards, groups of old willows, and even in hedgerow trees.

The birds of the twilight and dark hours of the night are not obvious and will only be seen by the dedicated. Only two of our native owls spend most of their time in woodlands, nesting and hunting there – the tawny, which is probably our commonest owl, and the long-eared, which is widespread but less often seen. Unlike the tawny, little and barn owls, the long-eared is not a hole nester but selects the old nest of a magpie, crow, wood pigeon or sparrowhawk, or a squirrel drey, in which to lay its eggs. It is also mainly a bird of coniferous forest in Britain, perhaps because it is ousted by the tawny, which is *the* owl of deciduous woods.

This is borne out by the fact that in Ireland and the Isle of Man, where there are no tawnys, the long-eared occurs equally commonly in all types of woodland. Both of these owls catch birds, mice, voles, rats, and also insects as food, but recent research has shown that the tawny's commonest food is earthworms! Nevertheless rodents must be particularly important because when they are scarce tawny numbers fall and they fail to breed successfully.

The careful naturalist, treading quietly along a woodland path, may disturb our only woodland wader, the woodcock. It flies very silently, darting from side to side between the trees. Its nest is usually in a dry place where the ground vegetation is sparse, as the woodcock relies on its superb camouflage to escape detection. When this writer was a boy woods were shot over more frequently than today and the woodcock was not often seen, but today it can be found much more easily in the many forest nature reserves. In the spring evenings during the twilight hours it makes its roding courtship flight, on owl-like wing beats, along the edge of the woodland.

While the woodcock has increased, its crepuscular neighbour, the nightjar, has disappeared from many of its old haunts. Although found in open woodland, it is not really a forest bird, but it is worth exploring for it in cleared areas in coniferous forest or where a young plantation is in its early years. If it is present, the distinctive churring note, which may continue for several minutes and can be heard over a long distance, will immediately identify it.

The less-known woodland creatures, which are hardly noticed by most of us, include that not very popular group, the spiders. A great many species live in woodlands, from the tops of trees throughout the canopy to the shrub layer, from the bark of tree trunks down to the forest floor, in the grass, under rotten wood, and in fact in almost every conceivable place. When picnickers spread their tablecloth over the grass and dead leaves of a sunlit glade, they will probably cover between 400 and 500 spiders – but they are very tiny and will only crawl deeper into the litter. Like other groups of invertebrate animals, different species inhabit different types of wood. A coniferous plantation has a much poorer and usually different fauna from that in a deciduous wood. Occasionally certain rare species are associated with one type of tree or shrub, as for example a rare spider, *Uloborus*, which occurs mainly on box. Similarly, there is a great difference in the spider fauna of the woods in the south of England and those in Scotland. In Scotland, if you see a wood ant dangling from a thread of silk on the bark of an old pine tree, you are likely to be near one of the rare species of *Dipoena*

known only from forests in central Scotland. It hides in bark crevices and feeds on wood ants which are caught on sticky threads as they climb the trees in search of prey.

More widespread in the forests, both deciduous and coniferous, of England, Wales and Ireland, is a much larger spider which is never very common but is quite thrilling to find. This bright emerald green spider is over an inch long and the adult female is so fat and rounded that it looks quite impressive. It does not have a common name and is known to arachnologists as *Micrommata virescens*. The male is only half the size and less frequently seen because male spiders have a much shorter life than females, but if you find one there is no mistaking its identity. Its green colour has a yellowish tint and the abdomen is decorated with three longitudinal vivid scarlet bands. The contrast of red and green makes it very conspicuous to the human eye, but in the light and shade of a leafy environment it conceals itself very successfully. It is more common in the south of England than anywhere else and widespread in the forests of central Europe. In Ireland I have seen it in hazel scrub in the Burren of Co. Clare and also in Glengarriff Forest, Co. Cork, where it was remarkably abundant in a small grassy clearing hidden among coniferous plantations.

A great many animals which are associated with woods are not entirely confined to this habitat. If they were, their chances of survival would be reduced as forested land gets less or is altered by management. Through the course of history those species which have managed to maintain their numbers in spite of the great changes man has made to the landscape are obviously well adapted to a range of different conditions. On the other hand rare species are usually more specialized and can only exist in a particular type of environment. Several examples are to be found in wood pastures (see Chapter 7), where certain species cannot survive in the absence of ancient decayed trees and consequently are now very rare. Perhaps in primeval times there were many more highly specialized species which became extinct as man cleared the forests, ploughed the grassland and drained the marshes. In order to ensure that our present-day woodland fauna continues to thrive, new mixed deciduous woods should be planted. Very little of this is being done. The County Conservation Trusts, the National Trust and the Nature Conservancy Council are helping to preserve what little we still have, but only the Woodland Trust and Men of the Trees seem to be actually creating new woodlands for the future. Other preservation bodies should be urged to do the same.

A few of the many different species of fungi found in the British Isles.

The shaggy pholiota grows in thick, large clusters at the base of deciduous trees or on tree stumps. The flesh is yellow and has a radish smell with sharp taste. The young caps are edible but the large ones are best avoided.

Phebia radiata *is a common woodland fungus growing on fallen branches in damp woodland from August to December. It also causes white rot and damages stored timber.*

Coriolus versicolor *is the most common polypore bracket fungus in Britain. It grows on dead tree branches and stumps in tight clusters of brown velvety fruit bodies with a white margin. It is not edible.*

The fly agaric is one of our most attractive woodland fungi, the dappled sunlight making its cap a fiery red. It is the typical toadstool of children's books and Christmas cards, but as it is poisonous it would perhaps be better not to give it this publicity.

Pleurotus sapidus *is locally common in woodlands growing on dead and dying elms and other trees. It is related to the oyster fungus which is very palatable and sometimes cultivated for culinary use.*

The honey fungus is so named because the young fruiting bodies are a honey yellow with a brownish tinge. It is one of the most destructive fungi in forested land, killing a wide variety of trees both coniferous and deciduous. The mycelium spreads through the soil so that nearby trees may be affected.

Fungi

In the British Isles there are at least 10,000 different species of fungi. Most of these are very small and inconspicuous, living in the soil or anywhere where there is organic matter for them to feed on. Some can be very harmful to our crops, animals or even to humans but the vast majority are not pests and play a very important role in the break down of organic matter. Unlike green plants, which create nourishment from water, carbon dioxide and light by photosynthesis, fungi must find their sustenance from other material, plant or animal. The most familiar fungi have a 'toadstool' shape or form a 'bracket' on a dead tree or rotten log. These, however, are only the fruiting bodies; the plant itself consists of finely ramifying threads, called hyphae, which forms a network – the mycelium.

The gill fungi, as the toadstool and bracket species are called, include many which are palatable and nutritious. Others are poisonous and a much larger number are simply inedible. In most countries in continental Europe mushroom picking is a favourite pastime of thousands of people who have a remarkable knowledge of the species, such as which are best to eat or to dry for use as food flavouring. In Britain relatively few people know the edible species, apart from the wild mushroom which is much sought after. If you want to learn about other tasty species consult an expert and never eat a fungus which you have not positively identified.

— 3 —

COUNTRY ROADS

Most country roads are almost impossible to date. Here the lane which forks to the left may be extremely old, for it runs towards the ancient stone circle of Swinside in Cumbria.

An attractive pack-horse bridge over the Derwent near Rosthwaite in Borrowdale, Cumbria.

Walking along a quiet country lane or footpath, the rambler can sense the presence of history. He walks in the footsteps of long-forgotten tramps, peasants and traders – perhaps in those of monks and friars, pilgrims and mercenaries, robbers and drovers, or even those of legionaries from the far-flung corners of the Roman Empire too. Townsfolk may zip across the landscapes of Britain on bustling made-up roads, but from the lay-by or verge they enter the gentler corners of the country-side via paths, tracks and byways which are the enduring fragments of many old networks of transport, all once useful and all developed for a reason. Now, when these hardening little arteries meander narrowly before melting away into the embracing greenery, they may seem aimless and devoid of destinations. And so it is important to remember that every one of them was useful to a community of travellers. Each one was once a practical little routeway, engraved into the country-side by the day-to-day business of getting people and their possessions to wherever they were needed or wanted to be. Some routes were always humble, never more than farm and field tracks. Others are the distressed gentlefolk of the landscape, lively long-distance routeways which have decayed and fragmented. Others still have risen from rustic oblivion and now exist as clamorous thoroughfares. Communications are ever in flux and every byway has its own special story.

Aware of this, the rambler may find that these little corridors are as fascinating as the countryside which surrounds them and will want to know when a lane or track was forged; where it originally went; why, and the sorts of people that used it. Sometimes the answers to these questions are evident in the landscape itself. Often they can be gleaned from historical research, but often too the origins of a routeway recede beyond the horizons of retrievable history.

The oldest trackways of all – those used by our hunting and foraging predecessors – are not readily apparent in the landscape. Some will have followed animal migration trails of prey like the reindeer and red deer, and these old routes have long since evaporated from the scene. There are some routes, however, which are clearly determined by topography and which must have been used by our distant forbears. Where rivers have held to their ancient courses rather than mean-dering and side-stepping across flat flood plains, the riverside paths will probably have been used since at least Mesolithic times, while mountain pass routeways, like the rather frightening Hard Knott and gentler Honister passes in the Lake District, have surely been used since before the dawn of farming.

We know that in Neolithic times, in addition to the labyrinths of farm, field and forest tracks which must have existed, a number of long-distance routeways came into existence. Sometimes the peasant families of this period may have attended ceremonies at local tombs and temples, while hunters must have travelled many miles in pursuit of game. On the whole, though, it seems unlikely that longer journeys were generally contemplated. But the people of the Neolithic period were consumers, and happy to trade for the axes of flint and polished stone or the well-made pots brought by itinerant merchants. They arrived at the farmsteads, hamlets and market sites via seaways and trackways like those used to transport East Anglian and Sussex flints to Wessex or Lakeland axes to the communities of eastern England. The land routes were not made-up roads, but consisted of braided networks of little trackways which tangled through long 'zones of movement' like the cords in a frayed rope. Often these zones of movement followed the dry scarp crests and watersheds which rose above the zones of arable farming and provided sweeping panoramas of the surrounding countryside. In the lowland areas, the ancient routeways have often vanished or become disguised by the modern routes which must often trace their courses. Some of the Neolithic routes can still be recognized, like the Icknield Way and the more famous Wessex Ridgeway, which linked to connect East Anglia, the Chilterns and the Wessex downlands. Such trackways are identified by the Neolithic monuments and axe discoveries which regularly punctuate their alignments, but there are other so-called ancient trackways, like the 'Jurassic Way' of the Midlands limestone scarp, whose credentials seem very dubious.

Abandoned roads can be recognized as rounded troughs or 'holloways'. Here, in the area between the Lake District and the Pennines near Crosby Ravensworth we can see a very interesting set of holloways. The holloway of a Roman road runs from lower right towards the left centre of the photograph and it is crossed by the holloways of several other trackways which are running upwards across an old common.

The prehistoric era continued until the Roman invasion of AD 43, and in the course of the successive Ages of Stone, Bronze and Iron, the countryside became purposefully organized and populous. Field tracks, lanes and grander thoroughfares ran hither and thither, with each one surviving in use so long as there were people eager to use it. Just how many of our enduring country lanes are a part of this inheritance we shall never know, but in many parts of the countryside it seems likely that most of the lane network already existed by Roman times, imposing a framework for parochial movement which subsequent generations were pleased to perpetuate. The country-side can be a very conservative place – one where

changes cause expense and disruption and where new ideas are sniffed, pondered and then often forgotten.

Before the Roman conquest there had been nobody in England with either the power or the inclination to appraise the existing road system or assess the trans-port needs of the country. Britain was partitioned between sets of fluctuating and generally hostile tribal territories and most or all of the unimproved trackways which criss-crossed the countryside arose spon-taneously as peasants sought the most convenient routes from hamlet to hamlet, farmstead to fields or village to market. In time, the most useful of these tracks were engraved into the landscape as hollowed furrows worn down by the passage of hooves, feet and light farm carts. In counties like Cornwall, most of the trench-like roads which we travel today were probably already well-hollowed by Roman times.

The Romans, however, saw the country through quite different eyes. They were less concerned with parochial commerce and provincial rivalries than with the need to move armies over long distances at speed, to police the backwaters, support the new towns and markets, extract the produce of the subject territories and exploit the demand for imperial products. Roman roads like Watling Street, Dere Street and Ermine Street, initially provided as highways for military conquest, are well known, while other important routes led to Channel ports. Despite the passage of almost two millennia, the map of Roman main routes has a surprisingly modern look. It depicts a well thought-out national *system* of long-distance route-ways which radiate outwards from London. Most of the more important Roman routes were new creations, built by ordinary legionaries who were trained as competent road-builders. But in a few places, the Romans seem to have taken over pre-existing routes, like High Street, which meanders along a high Lakeland watershed, while the more Roman-looking Ped-

An old Roman road existing as a quiet pathway, the so-called Via Devana near Cambridge which ran from Cambridge to Colchester.

dars Way in Norfolk is thought to result from the consolidation and upgrading of ancient trackways.

In some cases, the remnants of Roman handiwork can still be glimpsed, as on Wheeldale Moor above Pickering, where the rubble foundations of the minor road are exposed, or the so-called 'via Devana', south-east of Cambridge, where the characteristic ditch-flanked raised roadbed or 'agger' is plainly seen. Very occasionally, the identity of a Roman road will be proclaimed by a still-surviving milestone, like the trio found on the road between Ty'n-y-groes and Aber near Conwy. In many places, the Roman routes have virtually disappeared, but in many others they are preserved as straight stretches of road which might easily be mistaken for eighteenth- or nineteenth century parochial Parliamentary Enclosure roads (see below). Very commonly, a Roman road will survive in fragments of straight trackway which suddenly appear and just as suddenly fade into a faint holloway or vanish completely, only to re-emerge a mile or so further on as another straight lane or minor road. This hyphenated appearance results from the decay of some stretches of the old alignment, while other stretches have lived on as country tracks or have been absorbed into the network of cross-country roads.

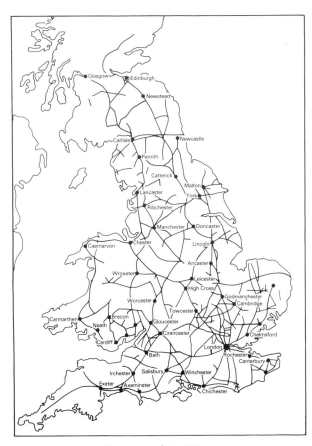

Roman Roads in Britain

A few Roman milestones can still be found in, or close to, their original positions; this example at Middleton near Kirkby Lonsdale was moved 200 yards from its original position in 1836. The inscription shown records this move, but there is also a brief Roman inscription 'MP LIII' denoting 53 miles to Carlisle.

One quite typical stretch of hyphenated Roman road can be seen to the west of Buckingham. It approaches Finmere village in the guise of the A421, but leaves the settlement as a humble village lane and then evaporates, though its course is clear on the map, for it survives as the Buckinghamshire/Oxfordshire county boundary. After about a mile, it crosses the Great Ouse and immediately becomes visible, this time as the main street of Water Stratford. It then briefly carries a minor road, loses it, guides the boundary alignment of Stowe Park, trends northwards to head for the town of *Lactodorum* (Towcester), but can scarcely be discerned until it surfaces as a tiny stretch of farm track. Its arrival in Towcester is not apparent, yet here it joined a Roman road which survives in a completely different form: Watling Street appears here as the thunderous A5(T).

The Roman standard in road planning and building was not really matched until the motorway era, and for centuries the essentially Roman framework of roads, subject to piecemeal modifications, provided England's basic transport system. It is clear that this network was vital in Saxon times, even if its maintenance was neglected. One section of Dere Street – here now the B6275 – provides delightful cameos of the Roman legacy. The village of Piercebridge stands in the confines of a Roman fort which overlooked the bridged crossing of the Tees, while just to the north of the village, Legs Cross, which is probably a Saxon monument, guards the spot where a local road crosses the old Roman routeway. The Roman roads did not meet all the needs of the Dark Age communities. Some stretches became abandoned and overgrown, while new ribbons of unmade track would loop-off from the Roman routes

Many sections of Roman road survive within the living transport network. Here we see the country road running from near North Carlton to Sutton in Lincolnshire picking-up a long straight section of Roman routeway.

to reach settlements which had appeared in the centuries following the Roman collapse.

While salt had been produced in considerable quantities in Roman times by evaporating brine at coastal saltings, many of the roads and tracks known as 'saltways' seem to have developed in Saxon and early-medieval times. In the days before the arrival of oriental spices or refrigeration, salt was essential to the preservation of hides, meat and fish, while the general shortages of winter fodder often made it necessary for beasts to be slaughtered and salted-down as winter approached. Salt, from the seaside hamlets of the Cheshire salt workings, was perhaps the most common commodity in Dark Age trade and Sussex alone had some 294 saltings at the end of the Saxon period. The whole of mainland Britain must have been crisscrossed by tracks which were forged or used by salters taking their vital goods to the villages and towns of the interior. Just like all the other old roads, these saltways can vanish or survive in a variety of different guises. Often they can only be discovered from the evidence of surviving 'salt' place-names, with Abbots Salford and Salford Priors in Warwickshire, Salterford in Nottinghamshire and Salterforth in West Yorkshire, indicating the fords used by the sellers of salt. Salcott in Essex, Saltcoats near Ayr and Salthouse in Norfolk were places with warehouses for salt and most of the 'salt' names tell us about the trade in salt, though a few must derive from the Old English *salh-* a willow.

The Romans had an effective transport policy, but it has been said that the roads of the Saxon and medieval periods 'made themselves'. New unplanned and unsurfaced roads would appear simply as the result of the natural growth in traffic between places. Although causeways were built to link the Fenland island of Ely to dry land while the roads leading into Wales were improved during the campaigns of Edward I, very few new roads were deliberately engineered during the Middle Ages, and those which made themselves were often poorly maintained. Even so, the roads of the realm tended to be heavily used: by peasants moving from village to field or market; pilgrims en route to the numerous and extremely popular shrines at places like Glastonbury, Canterbury and Walsingham; merchants plying between market and fair; the administrators of great estates riding from manor to manor, and by the king with his vast retinue in tow as they moved from one royal manor to another like a swarm of hungry locusts.

Hosts of roads which were vital highways in medieval times have tumbled into the ranks of the humble country lanes and byways, like some stretches of the old Banbury Lane between Banbury and Northamp-

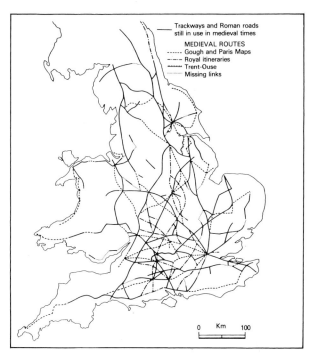

Known Medieval Routes

ton. One of countless such denoted roads is the old route, now a minor road, from Liskeard to Bodmin in Cornwall, via St Neot. It was superseded by the A38(T), and like most medieval and older roads it would be very hard to date; but the lovely Panters Bridge, just eight-and-a-half feet wide, is known to be a fifteenth-century replacement for an older bridge, Pontiesu or Jesus Bridge, which was mentioned in 1241. Of course, the road is likely to be far older than the first appearance of its bridge in the records.

Although the medieval roads carried considerable traffic, they were generally too poor to allow the haulage of heavy goods over long distances. Rivers were preferred for this function and many country lanes were developed as feeder routes to the river transport system, ending at lively little river ports which, today, may survive as sleepy villages like Nun Monkton in Yorkshire and Reach in Cambridgeshire. The medieval roads existed more as rights of way than as fixed and made-up routes. After intensive use, such a road could become deeply hollowed into the countryside, furrowed by ruts and impassable in wet weather, when ponds would form in its gullies. As likely as not, the route would then divert around the more difficult stretches, even if this involved trampling crops and breaking hedgerows. The local countryfolk, meanwhile, would often grab a little extra land by allowing their farming and buildings to encroach upon the highways. Even so, the roads were important in local

Many drove road inns still survive. This one, between Ripley and Fountains Abbey in Yorkshire, stands beside a section of Enclosure road which superseded an older road and droving route.

trading and many new villages were established beside the highways, enticed by the prospect of market commerce. In other ways, the attitudes to the roads were more lackadaisical. The historian B. P. Hindle has noted how, in 1386, the Abbot of Chertsey allowed two wells to exist in the road from Egham to Staines. When a traveller fell into a well and drowned, the Abbot heaped insult on injury by claiming his goods. It was not unknown for muckheaps or even cesspits to trespass upon the highway.

In the rolling uplands of Britain, where livestock farming was always predominant, the rivers tended to run swiftly over treacherous rapids. But while the prospects for river transport were much poorer, the cattle and sheep produced in these areas could be walked to the lowland markets. In the course of the medieval period, vast branching networks of drove roads developed. Initially, the drovers must have exploited the existing patterns of lanes and byways which were linked together to form the long droving routeways. From the Welsh uplands, for example, scores of medieval drove roads funnelled into Montgomery and Bishops Castle. Then, the open upland commons of the Long Mynd beckoned and the cattle were driven up and over the swelling mountain along the Port Way, pausing to graze along the hillcrest before being driven down to the great market at Shrewsbury.

It was probably in the latter part of the medieval period that a trade in walking the black and Highland cattle of the Scottish Highlands and Islands down to English markets developed. The Highland drove roads also made themselves and must have incorporated useful stretches of existing track as well as the paths used from driving stock from the winter valley grazings up to the high summer pastures. Fattened on these upland grazings, in the weeks between midsummer and autumn the herds began their trek southwards, moving along the glens and straths to the great fairs or 'trysts' held at collection centres like Crieff, Falkirk and Dumfries, where they were bought by English drovers. At Crieff in 1725, some 30,000 cattle are known to have been sold to English dealers in the course of a few days, while even in 1663 around 20,000 cattle passed through Carlisle in the course of the annual droves. The routes which the drovers took to reach the trysts will have depended upon the state of the weather and also that of law and order. In wet seasons the clansmen chose routeways overlooking the sodden valley and cascading burns, while in dry years they sought the lusher grazings of the glens. Since cattle rustling was the national pastime of the Highlands, areas known to be dangerous were avoided where possible, although the surviving track up from Aviemore to Glen Feshie in the Cairngorms was a drove road with a Celtic name meaning 'Thieves' Road'.

The drove trade gained momentum in the eighteenth and early-nineteenth century and some of the broad green roads leading down into England became deeply grooved into the landscape by the passage of herds. These were usually about forty strong and accompanied by the drover, his lad and a couple of dogs, although larger herds that numbered several hundred beasts were also moved. The cattle were shod

for their journey and a blacksmith specializing in bovine footwear is known to have worked at Grassington in the Pennines. From the Scottish trysts, the herds arrived at collection centres in the north of England like Skipton, Ripon, Masham and Malham. A vast pasture at Malham might have held some 5000 cattle at any one time in the late-eighteenth century, while a Skipton grazier, a Mr Birtwhistle, often had 10,000 cattle on the drove roads. At the northern fairs, the cattle were resold to graziers for a season's fattening and then despatched to local butchers or to southern English markets.

The arrival of the railways killed the centuries-old droving trade stone dead, but the old drove roads are still vital features in many countrysides. Sometimes they are masked by modern roads, have become no more than faint green troughs or are fragmented into stretches of farm track. But in other places they are still obvious as broad, walled green lanes or appear as deeply-worn holloways, gouged and smoothed into the upland passes. One fine stretch of former drove road running into Bradwell in Derbyshire has been hollowed into the hillside to a depth of ten feet.

Sometimes the drove roads coincided with the contemporary pack-horse roads used by convoys of pack ponies and the tough 'jaggers' who led them,

Jagger Ponies from an old illustration by W. Gilbert Foster.

An abandoned pack-horse lane at Birstwith in Nidderdale.

although the directions of cattle droving and pack trading in goods like salt, iron, coal and textiles did not always coincide. Trading by pack-horse was surely older than recorded history; it survived the canal age, but gradually declined in the face of competition from the railways. The sturdy pack ponies often bred from the *Jaeger* stock of Germany, could carry their panniers over difficult ground where carts and wagons could not pass and the pack-horse roads, which are found in one form or another throughout Britain, tend to endure in their most inviting forms in the hilly regions. In the lower-lying areas, they may live on as metalled roads, or else endure only in secret fragments – like the once-busy medieval pack-horse road from Otley to Knaresborough which was superseded by the A658, but which surfaces as an overgrown section of flag-stone paved route in Riffa Wood near Huby. This route can only be pieced together from a study of old documents, but in many other places old pack-horse alignments can be reconstructed on Ordnance Survey maps by linking up stretches of footpath, farm track

and surviving road.

Interested readers might like to experiment by recreating the old pack-horse track used to carry coal mined at Ingleton (a few miles north-west of Settle in Yorkshire) to customers in Pateley Bridge and Ripon. It ran eastwards across the moors near Malham Tarn via the now remote hamlet of Bordley to Skythorns and Greenhow Hill. Parts are now made-up and drivable, other stretches appear as hollowed trackways with old names like Thwaite Lane, Moor Head Lane and (part of) Mastiles Lane. Many of the old pack-horse trails are surely inherited from very ancient routes, and this track is flanked by the probably Bronze Age stones of the 'Druid Altar' which stands above Skythorns.

One of the delights of the old pack-horse roads are the dainty but rugged pack-horse bridges. A very small proportion of these bridges, like the lovely fifteenth-century example by the green at Moulton in Suffolk, belong to the medieval period, but most, while seeming ancient, date from the eighteenth and early-nineteenth centuries. At this time, the pack-horse traffic increased, when a rapidly growing population and the stirrings of the Industrial Revolution invigorated the traffic on roads carrying coal to towns and villages, textiles from weavers' cottages to market and manufacturers from the mills to ports and cities. The tough little Lakeland bridges, the slender stone bows of the Yorkshire Dales and the slab-on-boulder 'clapper bridges' of the West Country, Cotswolds and Pennines each have a special charm.

The bridges apart, the medieval reliance on roads that made themselves continued long after the close of the Middle Ages, and lasted until the turnpike era of 1663–1895. Medieval peasants were sometimes coerced into repairing stretches of highway, while merchants and landowners – either from frustration or benevolence – would occasionally donate funds for maintenance and bridge-building. In 1555 the Highways Act required householders to work for four days each year on road maintenance, but the task was often shirked. In many villages it was probably cannily realized that to improve a road would only bring an increase in the amount of traffic using it, and so lead to extra demands for road works.

In both Scotland and Ireland roads were the spontaneous creations of traffic, so that most journeys were

A graceful little pack-horse bridge at Wasdale Head in Cumbria.

made by following difficult stretches of farm lane, market road, drove road and more ancient trackway. In both these countries the provision of some better, more purposeful thoroughfares was one of the happier products of English domination. In Scotland, although the Act of Union was accomplished in 1707, support for the Jacobite cause produced an uprising in 1715

The fifteenth-century pack-horse bridge at Moulton in Suffolk. Note the slightly pointed arches, a feature of many medieval bridges.

and various local rebellions. In 1724 an Irish General, George Wade, became commander-in-chief in the Highlands. Following a survey of his command, he proposed the construction of 250 miles of military road and the building of forty bridges – all needed to allow his garrisons to police and pacify the region. By 1736 the network of military roads which still provides the skeleton of the Highlands' transport system was complete and Governor Caulfield was able to proclaim:

Had you seen these roads before they were made,
You'd lift up your hands and bless General Wade.

Perhaps so, although it has been pointed out that what the Roman army achieved in two years in northern England, took the British army some seventy years in the Scottish Highlands, for more much-needed military roads were built after the uprising of 1745, while the standard of the new Highlands roads was often poor. Most of the military network of narrow, stone-kerbed road does not endure in its original form, but lies beneath modern metalled road, although at places along the rather frightening A93 Devil's Elbow road south of Braemar the modern and military roads diverge, allowing fragments of the eighteenth-century work to be explored.

The road network of Ireland was also greatly improved in the eighteenth and nineteenth centuries. The most impressive of the new works was the military road built through the lofty core of the Wicklow Mountains after the rebellion of 1798, and now a popular scenic route for tourists. Numerous straight turnpikes were built in Ireland during the eighteenth century, helping to quicken the commercial life of the towns and countryside. Here, the English estate owners were powerful, the labour force cowed and abundant, and supplies of stone for road building plentiful.

In England too the turnpikes brought a welcome alternative to the muddy, rutted lanes which had been standard fare for travellers for over a millennium. The turnpikes of the coaching age were constructed by the appointed local Turnpike Trusts financed (hopefully) by tolls and they were generally created by improvements to existing routeways. Although the first turnpike had appeared in 1663, the movement did not gain momentum until the following century, when hundreds of these roads were built. They became the main roads that were associated with the glamorous if often arduous mail coach traffic, for in 1784 one John Palmer began the practice of carrying the mail in enclosed passenger coaches drawn by four horses and protected by a guard armed with a blunderbuss.

Hundreds of these turnpikes endure as useful modern roads and often the fact that an A or B road is a

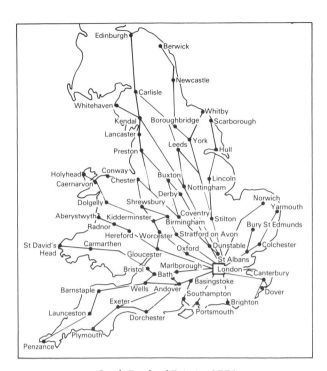

Coach Roads of Britain, 1771

former turnpike is only apparent from the wayside toll houses which dot its route. Most such houses survive as private dwellings, but their origins may be betrayed by the projecting three-sided bow frontage which allowed the toll collected to observe the approaching traffic and by the blocked or altered ticket window contained in the frontage. The turnpikes themselves took their name from the pivoting pole barrier which barred the road beside the toll house. A few old turnpikes have declined in competition with other routeways and have descended into the ranks of the country lanes, but they tend to be rare. Thus all of the nine turnpikes which converged on Northampton endure today as modern A roads with just one exception, the B526. In due course the turnpikes were taken over by public authorities and the last trust was disbanded in 1895. But while the turnpikes themselves do not often survive as humble lanes and tracks, they did cause the decline of other roads in their vicinities. Some decayed by natural processes as traffic gravitated to the improved routeway, while other competing roads and lanes which might be exploited by toll-dodgers were deliberately barred and closed. One fine example of a formerly important routeway is the Old Bath Road which survives as a rutted track to the east of the great stone circle of Avebury on Fyfield Down. It could have been an important prehistoric routeway and existed as a herepath in Saxon times, becoming a part of the medieval Great West Road between London and Bath.

However, following the turnpiking of the present A4 route westwards, this section of the Old Bath Road was closed in 1815.

Not all the roads built in the period 1750–1850 were long- and middle-distance turnpikes, and many miles of local road were created as parts of a Parliamentary Enclosure package (see p. 25). Since most Enclosure Acts were confined to single parishes, the new farm and field access roads which they created often failed to link up with those of neighbouring parishes, where the Enclosure would have arrived at a different date, or not at all. These roads were usually short, narrow and as straight as the topography allowed, and in this tidying-up of the parish plan, many of the old lanes and field tracks which had threaded between the medieval open fields became redundant, although some endured as public footpaths.

The most recent chapter in the saga of our country byways has sadly involved the closing of many public footpaths which are so valued as a means of exploring countrysides in which 'No Trespassing' signs proliferate as never before.

Threatened and vanishing from the countryside, along with other features of the heritage like hedgerows, woods and wetlands, are many of the old

An attractive old milestone at Hadleigh in Suffolk.

footpaths which provide country-lovers with their link and passport to the rural world. Hard statistical facts about these rights of way are strangely difficult to obtain, although recent work by the Ramblers' Association and Open Spaces Society has been published in the book *Rights of Way: A Guide to Law and Practice*. In Scotland, paths have not been recorded, but here, fortunately for the innocent rambler, the law of trespass is vague and chaotic. The information relating to England and Wales shows a most remarkable inequality in the provision of footpaths. Data compiled on the basis of the old administrative counties and dating from 1973 show that Gloucestershire comes bottom of the rambling league, with only 0.1 miles of footpath or bridleway per square mile of territory. Cambridge and the Isle of Ely, the parts of Holland and Lindsey in Lincolnshire, Norfolk, the East Riding of Yorkshire and Merioneth are all very poorly endowed, with 1 or less miles per square mile. Top of the league of honour came the old county of Cardigan, with 10.1 miles; second was Worcestershire, with 4.9 miles, while Buckinghamshire, Derbyshire, Kent, Somerset, Surrey, the Isle of Wight, Anglesey, Flint and Montgomery all tempted the visitor with more than 3 miles of footpath or bridleway per square mile.

A cheering factor, but one which by no means compensates for the loss of public footpaths in recent years, has been the creation of several new long-distance footpaths. In 1965 the Pennine Way, running from Edale in Derbyshire to Kirk Yetholm in Scotland, was opened as a 250-mile routeway which linked up dozens of old trackways. It was followed by the 95-mile Cleveland Way on the North Yorkshire Moors and coast, the Offa's Dyke Path and the North Downs Way. Several other long-distance footpaths have been created and the current position is summarized in the map 'Planning for Leisure' (see Appendices). Other similar routes are delayed as a result of opposition from local landowners. We hope to have shown that the lanes, tracks and footpaths of Britain have a wide variety of ages and had many different origins and uses. Some readers may have a favourite byway that they would like to know better – so how does one explore the history of a little routeway? Because many of the lanes and footpaths of Britain are so very old, one will often be unable to discover the origins of a route, but one may often be able to learn a surprising amount about its history. The prehistoric credentials of long-distance routeways can be hard to establish; the Old Bath Road mentioned above leads to the great late-Neolithic temple of Avebury and is a possible ancient routeway – although costly excavations would be needed to establish its prehistoric claims.

The Dorset coast path as it descends towards Lulworth Cove.

If a country route is perfectly straight then it is almost certainly either a Roman alignment, or a much more recent creation which reflects the eighteenth- and early-nineteenth-century passion for geometry and order in the landscape: probably a Parliamentary Enclosure road but perhaps a relic of estate or park improvement and planning. If one can link up sections of straight lane, road and pathway to produce a long-distance alignment extending for several miles across the landscape, then the stretches concerned are almost certainly Roman – particularly if the alignment points to a known Roman town or fort. (No track, straight or otherwise, should ever be assumed to be a 'leyline', for these notorious 'old straight tracks' have no reality in the landscape.)

Medieval lanes and tracks, on the other hand, tend to weave and kink in a seemingly haphazard way. This is not because the peasants, pilgrims and nobles liked to prolong their journeys, but because as these routeways developed, they had to take account of other features of the landscape which had already come into existence. The medieval roads linked villages, curved around dwellings and churches and, most particularly, they followed the boundaries of fields and furlongs. Sometimes this need to pick a way through a village field system would produce a road composed of successive dog-legs as the route followed the corners of the furlong blocks of strips. And so an enduring country road may bend and twine across the countryside because it is preserving the outlines of long-extinguished fields –

but whether this knowledge will console the frustrated driver who is trapped on such a road behind a rumbling tractor is another question.

Surviving documents seldom allow one to date the origins of a medieval road exactly, although one may sometimes be able to date the abandonment of a road and its decay to become an overgrown holloway. Many a pasture is grooved by the lanes which radiated from villages that are now deserted, and sometimes the demise of the village can be dated. Thus, the deeply hollowed track running through the waterlogged pastures below Cublington village in Buckinghamshire was the main street of old Cublington, abandoned when the already ailing village surrendered to the Black Death, around 1350.

Only a minority of roads were created to serve a single narrow purpose, so that most drove and pack-horse roads were cobbled together from existing stretches of trackway, while many of them endure or survive in parts as modern metalled roads. A worn lane which ends abruptly at a farmstead and which cannot be extended to link up with other stretches of routeway may never have been anything more than a farm access track. But it could still be very old, for many farms, particularly those of upland areas and the West Country, can be found to stand on the sites of their Dark Age predecessors.

As with the Roman roads, one can often reconstruct drove and pack-horse roads by linking together the sections of road, track and holloway which mark the former route, and often the old documents and maps will serve to confirm the alignment. Punctuating the routes are pack-horse bridges, too steeply-arched and narrow ever to have carried wheeled traffic, and the old droving inns, some decaying but others converted or surviving. Several are still called The Drovers, while others, like The Feathers at Ledbury, formerly flourished on the droving trade. Old maps are particularly useful to anyone who seeks to rediscover the history of a routeway and one may recognize the once-lively through-routes which are now mere lanes or track-ways or the humble byways improved and elevated as turnpikes, as well as the scores of old village-to-field tracks which may now exist as threatened public footpaths.

Most country lanes, even the humblest, have names, although a name may not be the original one and it may only be preserved in old maps and documents. Some of the names are very informative. Harepaths or 'herepaths' seem to have been used as military routes during the Dark Ages; 'ways' often follow Saxon township and parish boundaries, while 'mere' lane names are also often associated with Saxon boundaries

and mere lanes may still be flanked by the massive hedgebanks established in Saxon times. Although place-names can sometimes be very deceptive, they may tell one where a lane was going long after the destination has been abandoned. Mill and Ford lane names are obvious, while 'Stockbridge' was a bridge of logs, 'Trowbridge' one of trees and 'Stanbridge' one of stone. Stiles, which looked much like their modern equivalents, being simple ladders or flat-topped upright logs, existed in the Middle Ages. Sometimes they can be located in medieval documents, where they often appear as *steile* or as the Latin *scalarium*, a ladder. Occasionally, a 'stile' place-name will survive to show where a footpath crossed a hedge or wall. The common 'Lidgate' place-name refers to Saxon or medieval swing gates used to control the movements of livestock, and lidgates were often placed across the roads at the boundaries of township lands or on the edges of villages and hamlets (though some 'gate' place-names in Scotland and the north of England derive from a Danish word for 'street').

River crossings are also preserved in many place-names. The several Stapleford names seem to denote difficult fords that were marked by posts, 'Borth' place-names in Wales can refer to ferries, while the Gaelic 'stair' describes stepping stones. Both place-names and old documents can tell us about former roadside features. The detailed West Yorkshire Archaeological Survey seems to show that roadsigns were very uncommon in medieval times; wayside inns and taverns far fewer than today, while hermitages, chantry chapels and brothels were quite numerous, detailing the roadside scene in their very different ways.

So far, we have said little about the nature of transport itself. Horses and ponies have been used for riding and draught in Britain since at least the Iron Age. In the east of Yorkshire, chariot burials of Iron Age warriors covered by square barrows have been excavated and the traces of vehicles were discovered. These were not heavy, scythe-hubbed chariots of the kind depicted in some old schoolbooks, but light carts, probably little different from those used by the farmers of the time. The Romans introduced a broad range of two-wheeled carts and four-wheeled wagons and mail coaches, and the new surfaced roads were level enough to permit the use of heavier vehicles. In Saxon and medieval times, the gradual decay of the Roman road surfaces and the emphasis on river transport must have diminished the role of road vehicles and many thoroughfares and bridges were only suitable for pack ponies. Carts and wagons were used where the roads allowed and our best impressions of these medieval vehicles come from contemporary illustrations. One depicts a rather rickety predecessor of the covered wagons of the Wild West movies, but had wickerwork sides, iron-studded wheels and a canopy that was perhaps of leather or felt. Such wagons would have been used on the well-organized monastic estates, in the baggage trains of armies, by bishops for the collection of their tithes or to gather the products of the great feudal estates.

Improvement in wagon design came gradually, but in the post-medieval period continental innovations were adopted in East Englia and Lincolnshire and filtered into the interior counties. Carriers' wagons, looking quite similar to the covered wagons of the old West, became the ancestors of various types of improved farm wagons and by the nineteenth century a series of elegant and sophisticated designs had evolved, each one tailored to the terrain and tastes of the different provinces. The carts and wagons which now rumbled along the turnpikes or creaked and groaned on the winding, rutted lanes announced the perfection of the wheelwright's craft, while pride in ownership was proclaimed in the brilliant details of their paint-work.

Two-wheeled vehicles – the low-bodied wains or harvest carts with lines as rakish as any corvette, the plank-sided tipping muck carts, and the spring carts with bump-dampening springs which were favoured by village carriers – could operate on narrow, hilly lanes which the wagons could not negotiate, and so they were particularly favoured in rugged areas like Cornwall, the Cotswolds, Scotland and Wales. In the middle of the nineteenth century the craftsman-built carts or 'tumbrils' were joined by the 'Scotch carts' which were built in various Scottish factories and perhaps introduced to the eastern counties of England by immigrant Scottish farmers. They were simplified for factory production methods, yet though bound with bolts and filled with cast iron hubs, the Scotch carts were often embellished with the seemingly pagan device of a pair of eyes painted on the frontboard. These eyes could spy for danger or counter the 'evil eye'.

The improved carriers' wagons of the sixteenth century had spawned a series of variants by the eighteenth century and these were further refined in the nineteenth century, until the less elaborate factory designs began to compete with the products of the village workshops. Massive 'box wagons', some equipped with double shafts, were favoured in the flat and bountiful grain country of East Anglia, while smaller, shallow-sided 'bow wagons' were better adapted to the rolling terrain of the counties further west. In the second half of the nineteenth century the plank-sided 'barge wagons' and the 'boat wagons',

One of the many old waggons preserved in a museum of rural life at Stowmarket in Suffolk.

which had sloping sides and fully underlocking front wheels, arrived as cheaper factory-built products which lacked the elegant frills of the wheelwrights' designs.

In order to lighten the craftsman-built wagons, all the timber supports were shaved and chamfered into gracefully faceted forms which invited the painter to pick out the details in brightly contrasting hues. In one of the most delightful expressions of British regionalism, each province developed its own distinctive colour scheme. Wheels were usually red, while a bright blue was widely favoured for cart and wagon bodies, particularly in counties like Derbyshire, Sussex, Staffordshire, Wiltshire, Dorset and those of East Anglia, although Norfolk farmers sometimes favoured buff or white. Other examples included orange in Northamptonshire, yellow in Buckinghamshire and Shropshire, brown in Bedfordshire and Hertfordshire, dark blue in Devon, buff in Kent and red or brown in Yorkshire.

During the twentieth century the manufacture of carts and wagons diminished as tractors replaced horses, while craftsmanship became a costly commodity. The factory-built vehicles had also undermined the trade of the village wheelwrights, although a few workshops endured into the 1930s. But of all the village craftsmen, the wheelwright or cartwright had surely been the king. His product was the epitome of functional art and the wheel itself blended precision engineering with a profound understanding of materials. The hub or 'nave' was cut from an elm log which had seasoned for at least a decade, while the spokes were cleft from oak heartwood and the 'felloes', which combined to form the rim, were of ash, or occasionally of beech, oak or elm. When the blacksmith arrived to fit the red-hot iron tyre, the contraction of the cooling hoop rammed thirty or so separate joints tightly into place.

Like many of the most wholesome and appealing features of the countryside, the swaying carts and wagons have departed, along with the heavy horses which drew them. A few roadside examples remain, generally poorly maintained and badly painted, to lend an aura of old world charm to the adjacent pubs, but fortunately the recent upsurge of interest in the dying rural heritage has resulted in the restoration of these noble vehicles. Many restored examples can be seen at rural life museums and farm parks like those at

Drusillas near Alfriston, Upper Dicker and Sedlescombe in Sussex, Stowmarket in Suffolk, Mawthorpe in Lincolnshire, Tilford in Surrey, Wolvesnewton in Gwent, Oakham in Leicestershire, Lincoln, Reading University and several other places (see Appendices).

As the carts and wagons became larger and more numerous, so their grinding wheels intensified the age-old problem of the rutting of the road surface. During the sixteenth and seventeenth centuries, the authorities attempted to ban wagons because it was thought that the lighter carts with only two wheels caused less damage to the road surface. Attempts were also made to increase the width of wheels to reduce the cutting and rutting effect and an Act of 1662 prescribed a minimum width of four inches and this was increased by subsequent Acts. It is unlikely that the legislation was taken very seriously. With the arrival of the turnpikes, lower tolls were levied against the wider-wheeled vehicles, while those with enormous wheels that were some sixteen inches broad were freed from tolls for a year in 1753.

An old Scotch cart rotting in a Cambridgeshire field. Note the eyes on the board above the shafts, a traditional motif intended to deflect the evil eye or to see the devil.

The effective answer to the problem only came with the introduction of new types of road surface. During the first half of the nineteenth century, John Loudon Macadam's method of road surfacing won great popularity. It involved laying a six- to twelve-inch road bed of small, broken stones which was then covered by a layer of angular gravel that was bedded-down by the passage of vehicles. This produced a much smoother and more durable surface than the old method of building a road of river-rounded stones or shingle bedded in a matrix of earth and clay, and it was less expensive than Thomas Telford's technique of laying a coating of gravel on a six-inch layer of stones spread upon a bed of large stone blocks.

Most of the broader country roads now have a surface which is durable, dependable and not particularly interesting. In complete contrast, their verges are both fascinating and fragile and they often provide a last refuge for plants and animals evicted from the surrounding fields by modern farming practices.

Nature on the roadside

Roadside verges have a long history. The Icknield Way, a prehistoric trackway which runs along chalk ridges between Wiltshire and Norfolk, is one of the oldest. It was used not only by travellers but for driving cattle and sheep to and from market. So it was wide where plenty of land was available and narrow if confined to a ridge. Another ancient route, the Singing Way in Oxfordshire, follows a narrow limestone ridge and is so named after the pilgrims who chanted as they walked along. It was during the Roman occupation that man-made roads following fixed routes were built for the first time, but the verge was still the natural vegetation which extended on either side. As cultivation spread over much of the countryside, the grass verge remained as the only land that was not ploughed. The undisturbed roadside is today more important than ever before for wildlife – a green ribbon of hedge and verge, the only sanctuary for plants and animals in a biological desert.

Many of our rural roads follow the same route as they did when first used hundreds of years ago and in some areas the verges were kept wide to accommodate the farm stock as well as horse and carriage. In Cambridgeshire these wide verges are found by roads which cross the ancient sheep walks on the chalk soils and they are common in east Leicestershire, which was traditional cattle country. Today they are appreciated by the hiker and naturalist, if not lost to road widening and soil dumping. The winding country road with hedgerow and grass verge still provides pleasure for the cyclist and motorist who is not in a hurry, and long may they survive, without the hedges being cut down and the corners straightened. Roadworks cause considerable disturbance; where the road is widened the vegetation will be destroyed and the new verge must be sown with grass seed and regularly cut to prevent the growth of tall weeds.

In an ideal situation, where a long verge passes over several different soil types, some wet, some dry, with shady and sunny patches, the habitat variety will encourage different types of vegetation to grow and the animal life will also be more varied. When verges are not sprayed we can still find plants that previously lived in the meadows on the other side of the fence – the buttercups and oxeye daisies of the 1930s, now swept away by herbicides. Just as the farmer was quick to use selective herbicides to improve his crops, so were the County Council road engineers to control verge vegetation. Until the last war road verges were cut with mechanical mowers or even a scythe in some rural areas. The herbicide promised more effective and long-lasting vegetation control along our roads and also at a lower cost. It caught on quickly and spread over most of the country. Only in areas like the uplands, the A93, for instance, which crosses the Grampians and reaches a height of over 2000 feet, is the naturally short roadside vegetation left untouched, and remains the same as the surrounding moors. Road maintenance engineers found that one or two applications a year of a herbicide, sometimes mixed with a growth retardant chemical in an attempt to keep the vegetation permanently short, was adequate for most purposes.

This sort of 'convenience' management did not quite work out as the road engineers hoped; the public was soon offended by the sight of mile after mile of dying

A wonderful flush of scentless mayweed on the unsprayed roadside of the Cairn mon earn road in north-east Scotland.

A selection of roadside plants.

Cow parsley, one of the commonest meadow and wayside plants
on lowland England.

Foxgloves beside a steep lane in Millstone Grit country near
Smelthouses in Yorkshire. This plant prefers acidic soils.

Green alkanet (blue) and greater stitchwort (white)
growing beside a lane at Polyphant in Cornwall.

Meadow cranesbill can be found on roadsides in the limestone
regions of the Pennines, but is generally common elsewhere.

Rose bay flowering on a roadside near Aysgarth in Yorkshire, a common plant of disturbed ground.

Bluebells growing beside the old track leading to the Pentre Ifan prehistoric tomb near Fishguard in Wales. In the moister west and south-west the bluebell grows in many open areas, often by roadsides, but in the east it is confined to woodlands.

The large campanula or giant bellflower, a handsome wild flower of woods and hedgebanks. It is widely distributed in Britain but much commoner in the north. This specimen was photographed on a roadside near Aysgarth in Yorkshire.

vegetation. Public reaction, together with concern for the less common plants by conservationists, and the increasing need for economies in road maintenance, gradually reversed this trend and today few verges are sprayed or even cut, except at corners where visibility is reduced by the growth of tall plants in the summer. In fact mowing and spraying ceased in many areas in 1975 following a Ministry of the Environment directive in an effort to save money.

It has been estimated that there are just under half a million acres of verge in England and Wales, about half as much again as the total area of land in our National Nature Reserves for the whole of Great Britain. According to another estimate, about 50 per cent of this land is managed as grassland, which until 1975 was mown, or in some cases sprayed at least once a year. This has influenced roadside verges in different ways, some not entirely favourable. In the lowlands, where a vigorous growth of tall plants is typical of roadside verges, less common plants may in some instances be suppressed. Some plants prefer open disturbed ground, as in the East Anglian Breckland, where there are sandy roadsides which provide the best habitats for rare species of *Veronica*, rather tiny plants which only the expert is likely to notice, and for the creeping glabrous rupture-wort. Both of these are eliminated when smothered by taller plants but there is some evidence that their seed will survive for a long time in the soil. When the right conditions are restored the seed germinates and the plants are able to flower again. Sometimes disturbance may be very frequent where there is cable laying and maintenance of sewers and gas mains, but this is more likely on verges close to urban areas than in the countryside. In general the richer and most interesting roadside floras are where the verge has not been disturbed, just as the oldest permanent grassland is richer in plants than in more recent swards.

Studies by the Nature Conservancy Council have shown that about 870 species of plants, mostly native, are associated with road verges. This is a high proportion of the approximately 2080 species found in Britain and includes thirty-five which have been classified as nationally rare. For some of these a roadside is the last remaining locality and if this habitat were destroyed it would become extinct. This happened in the case of the sickle-leaved hare's ear, a tall plant belonging to the carrot family which was associated with arable cultivation at a time when agricultural methods were primitive. As weed control in crops became more efficient this species declined until only one locality was still known – a single roadside in Essex. In 1955, after roadworks in this area, it disappeared and now no longer exists in the wild in this country. Another plant,

the great fen ragwort, was once widespread in the East Anglian fens but declined as marshes were drained and reclaimed. For a time it was thought to be extinct but in the early 1960s a small colony was found on a Cambridgeshire roadside which is now protected. On a verge of the Icknield Way, Cambridgeshire, the perennial flax reaches its southern limit in Britain and not far away is another colony on the Via Devana Roman road which passes by the famous Gog Magog hills. In Lincolnshire it is entirely a roadside plant, especially by Roman roads. The spring cinquefoil, a creeping plant with bright yellow flowers which prefers stony limestone soils where there is not too much competition with other plants, is also a roadside rarity.

Most of the Breckland sandy heaths have been reclaimed and cultivated since the last war and apart from the nature reserves, the road verges are almost the only alternative habitats for wildlife. In addition to the annuals already mentioned, two perennial plants, the Spanish catchfly and the field wormwood, neither of which is known outside Breckland, have been found on verges. Both species are very palatable to rabbits and rarely flower where they are persistently grazed. However, roadsides are generally lightly grazed because the rabbits are continually disturbed by traffic, enabling these plants to flower and set seed.

In 1980 there were 6210 miles of trunk roads in England including 1335 miles of motorway. The latter are fairly recent in construction so that the verges have been developed from freshly deposited soil. Motorway verges have several useful functions. They accommodate road signs and notices, store grit for winter use and provide space for snow which has been cleared in bad weather. They must therefore be part of the road design and not made solely for amenity and landscaping. On dual carriageways and two-lane single highways, the verge width is between eleven and twelve feet but where the road is built up or where it cuts through higher ground, large areas of soil, rock, or in some cases chalk, are laid bare. These exposed banks are not left to develop their own vegetation because they would only provide a bed for agricultural weeds. Where there is soil selected grass seed mixtures are sprayed on in a sticky solution which adheres to steep slopes and provides the seeds with nutrients when they germinate. Trees and shrubs are planted on verges in many places to improve the motorway landscape and, in general, the arrangements of bushes and trees are well thought out. On banks of bare chalk the road engineers have sometimes used the seed of typical chalk-loving plants mixed with the grass seed. This is a great improvement on the usual uniform green cover of grass; the commonest wild flower seed is bird's foot trefoil, and its bright yellow flowers, densely packed in small patches, are reminiscent of the meadows on the chalk downs. The seeds of other plants eventually reach the new verges and observant travellers will notice cowslips, primroses, cow parsley, oxeye daisy and, of course, dandelions.

Motorway verges in England are usually sown with a mixture of ryegrass, red fescue, smooth-stalked meadow grass, and crested dog's tail. The only non-grass species is white clover. Clover has been shown to be one of the most attractive plants for foraging hive bees and particularly for bumble bees, whose longer tongues are more effective in reaching the nectar and as a result pollination and seed production are very high. White clover is not only useful to the apiarist by providing food for his bees; it is also beneficial to the vegetation by enriching the soil with nitrogen. This is because bacteria which live in small nodules on the roots make nitrogenous compounds by 'fixing' atmospheric nitrogen. Some of this is liberated into the soil so that the plants living with the clover are able to benefit.

It is only during the last few years that it has been possible to buy the seed of common grassland plants and several commercial firms now offer different mixtures to meet individual requirements. These wild plant mixtures are used in parks, in amenity grass-lands, and also on new road verges. Road verges with short grass, longer grass, shrubs and even trees, as are often to be seen bordering motorways, provide an interesting range of habitats which can be exploited by many insects, birds and small mammals. This type of linear habitat, which has length but little breadth, acts as a dispersal corridor and enables species to move to new areas and reinvade where there have been local extinctions. The modern landscape is full of man-made barriers, arable fields, coniferous plantations and wide roads, all obstacles to movements by our common species of plants and animals. Continuity of roadside verge vegetation is therefore valuable in maintaining mobility of wildlife.

But living by a roadside is full of hazards. In the summer, road surfaces get much hotter than the adjacent vegetation and in the winter very much colder. No doubt some animals are deterred from crossing roads but when others do they face the hazard of motor traffic – we have all seen dead foxes, badgers, hedgehogs, hares, stoats and many birds which have failed to cross to the other side. In parts of central Europe even tortoises are road casualties. In the days when the frog was common, the annual spring migration to the breeding haunts was accompanied by an immense slaughter on the roads. This still happens in a few places and groups of local people have banded together to keep watch and help the frogs in danger.

Counts have been made of the number of bird and animal casualties on particular stretches of road and the totals recorded are quite frightening. In the Netherlands a recent estimate for the whole country was about 653,000 birds and 159,000 mammals killed on the roads every year. Dead animals on the road attract predators and these also risk being killed by the traffic. In Wales polecats are road victims, in Shetland it may be otters, and in Kent badgers, although the last is a fairly common casualty in many parts of the country.

The value of the wayside hedge for birdlife is well known, but very few studies have been made of the herbaceous verge as a bird habitat. A detailed study in Denmark showed that because of traffic disturbance very few birds spent much time on the grass verge, but skylarks bathed in loose sand on some verges and the linnet and greenfinch came to feed on the seeds of knot grass and the ubiquitous dandelion. The ground-nesting birds recorded in this survey showed that the skylark was by far the most common and only two other species bred within the study plots, one nest each of the whinchat and the partridge. A few of the skylark nests were destroyed by summer mowing but most were further away from the road edge in the longer grass which was not cut.

The invertebrate fauna of roadsides, on which not much work has been done, depends to a great extent on the width of the verge, that is, size of habitat, and its floristic richness. Where the traffic is busy, the two to three feet nearest the road must be excluded because the splash zone on the verge is contaminated with mud, dirt and salt. There the vegetation growth is different and few invertebrate animals live there permanently. The more plants there are on which larvae can feed, the more beetles, flies and hymenoptera will be found; and the more varied the structure of the habitat, the greater will be the number of spiders, particularly web-spinners. Common flowering plants provide nectar and pollen for adult insects, including common butterflies. For example, the most northerly locality for the chalk hill blue butterfly is on a calcareous road verge in Lincolnshire.

Road verges are not the only wayside reservoirs of wildlife, railways also have deep cuttings with relatively undisturbed floras. It has been estimated that there are about 135,000 acres of land on railway embankments, enough to include some valuable nature reserves. In the days of steam, hand labour was used to control vegetation close to the line, although sparks from the engines frequently burnt dry material such as bracken, and in drought years fires caused by steam engines occasionally spread to farmland and caused considerable damage. With the change from steam to diesel, fires mostly ceased and the railways soon found that the cost of keeping embankments clear of encroaching scrub and tall plants could be reduced by using herbicides. The spray was applied only to nine or ten feet outwards from the line on each side and the rest of the embankment was allowed to develop naturally. In the last few years this has allowed a considerable growth of tall vegetation, scrub and even trees on some embankments. Recent surveys by the Institute of Terrestrial Ecology for the Nature Conservancy Council have illustrated the trends and variations in vegetation from place to place and also in some of the animal life. For example, foxes are now using the scrub for breeding.

Of more interest to the conservationist is the railway line which is now disused, the lines and sleepers removed, leaving the firm gravel track as an excellent path. Scrub and trees grow up to form a broad deep hedge which is both picturesque and valuable for wildlife. Some disused tracks have been bought by County Trusts for Nature Conservation. More often the neighbouring farmer has incorporated the land into his farm. Nevertheless there are still many which have become pleasant country walks: the old single line between Blythburgh and Southwold in Suffolk is the best vantage point for bird-watching in the Blyth estuary; the line on the north side of Hayley Wood nature reserve in Cambridgeshire is now a quiet sunny track; and the long-extinct railway between Oundle and Thrapston in Northamptonshire has fine overgrown hedges always full of birds.

Although thousands of people pass by road verges every day, they are mostly in cars and have their eyes on the road so that they scarcely notice the roadside flora. Consequently the animals and plants are not as well known as they ought to be. We should encourage amateur naturalists and ramblers to inform their local natural history society or county trust of any interesting features they note during their walks. We also know comparatively little of how best to manage roadside verges which are of natural history interest, bearing in mind the other uses to which they must be put by the road engineer and the disturbance they must suffer from time to time. This is an essential part of understanding how conservation works and professional ecologists should look at this question more closely to find out whether the advice to road maintenance engineers can be improved, with the result that verges become an even more interesting and attractive part of the countryside amenities.

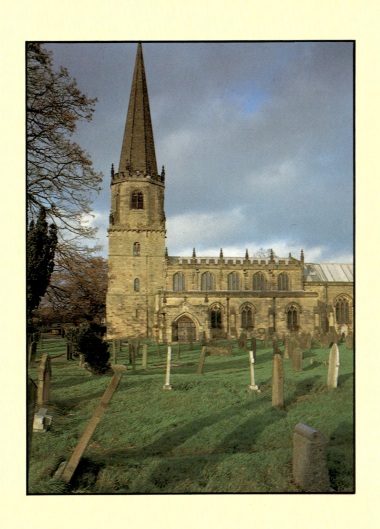

— 4 —

THE VILLAGE CHURCH

Churches have histories rather than dates. A ruined Saxon cross stands beside the church at Masham in Yorkshire, the base of the tower is early Norman work and a sequence of medieval alterations and enlargements can be traced in the fabric of the building.

The village church is a living monument to its own little patch of the countryside. Almost invariably it is a building which echoes the changing ideas about communal worship, as well as one that displays the architectural tastes and achievements of successive ages. It is also likely to be the focus and highlight of any excursion around the visual charms and historical features of a chosen village. Some visitors will mount a serious campaign of exploration and seek to piece together an understanding of the evolution of a building, allocating dates to different bits of masonry and appraising the tombs and other monuments contained. Others will simply be attracted to the mellowed, friendly building by the loveliness of its architecture, the gentle calm of its setting and the majestic silence of the interior, while others still, those of a more spiritual nature, will be drawn like latterday pilgrims to experience a new place for communal worship. The village church is many things to many people, but its magnetism reaches across religious boundaries; it is loved in many different ways, but only the strangest and most soulless of people can resist its quiet allure.

Not surprisingly, the village church has become the subject of a mountainous literature and we cannot hope to be even vaguely original if we follow the well-worn descriptive paths. The traditional approach to the church begins with an outline of Saxon architectural features and proceeds, via the temporal stepping stones of the Norman, Early English, Decorated, Perpendicular and neo-Classical styles, to culminate in an appraisal of Gothic Revival buildings.

Rather than embark on this overcrowded routeway, the photographs accompanying this chapter represent features of churches from the different ages of church building and we suggest some other approaches to the village church. Most of the more studious church visits begin and end with attempts to give dates to the various architectural components, and so a more basic question is often overlooked: why is the building where it is? Having explored the wherefores of the church, we then look at the whys, and describe how the church may mirror the changing fortunes and ideas of the com-

munity which it served. Then we locate the building in its countryside capsule of building traditions and explore the ways in which the use of local resources and the pursuit of particular provincial fancies created such a wonderful heritage of regional styles, so that the churches of Norfolk and Cumbria or Dorset and Grampian are so distinctive and different. Finally, we examine the churchyard setting of the church, both as a rewarding source of historical evidence and as a little haven for wildlife.

To begin to understand why many churches are where they are, we must go back in time a thousand years, perhaps a little more, to one of the most mysterious but formative eras in the creation of the countryside. In the first few centuries after the conversion of the pagan Dark Age kingdoms of Britain, village churches will scarcely have existed and Christian worship was brought to most rural communities by priests who were based in monasteries or minster churches and who regularly set forth to preach in the surrounding localities. It is often difficult to identify the old minster churches. Sometimes the ancient minster function is preserved in the name of a place, as at Wimborne Minster in Dorset. In other cases the site of a minster church may be marked only by a modest and much later successor church, as at Horningsea in Cambridgeshire. The minsters could be sited in lands donated by a ruler, on a long-hallowed site or in settlement places inherited from Roman civilization. They can be suspected where a substantial church occupies a large island in the heart of a settlement, as at the shrunken village of Stow in Lincolnshire, where the minster was built beside a Roman road.

Here, the main elements in the story are known. Blocks of building stone lying in the churchyard are the only obvious relics of Roman settlement nearby, but we know that around 975 Bishop Aelnoth built a church here to serve as the main minster of his diocese. This building burned – molten lead from the roof has been found under the church floor – and the building was rebuilt by Bishop Eadnoth around 1034-1050, and then improved and endowed by Earl Leofric of Mercia and his celebrated spouse, Godiva. Much of the surviv-

A sequence of pagan religions existed in Britain before the introduction of Christianity.
One of the earliest was associated with the magnificent stone circles of the
late-Neolithic to early-Bronze Age period. Sunset at Castlerigg stone circle in Cumbria.

ing fabric dates from the years around the Norman Conquest, but in 1073 the see was moved to Lincoln. Stow briefly survived as a Benedictine Abbey, but then began its long career as an unusually imposing parish church. The minster function seems to have enhanced Stow's importance as market centre, but after the see was moved, trade deteriorated and the markets were shifted to Marton, while the village or townlet declined.

In other places still, the only surviving hint of the former existence of a minster may be found where a group of village churches serve, or formerly served, as parochial chapelries of a single member of the cluster. In this way, the Fenland church at Doddington seems to have been the minster of a vast original parish in which subordinate chapels developed.

Before village churches were provided, the priests would often preach to a local congregation at a place marked and hallowed by a cross. Some of these crosses survive, but they have often been moved a little way from their original positions, while it is not easy to distinguish between the crosses which marked open air preaching sites and others erected in the yards of

existing Dark Age churches. Good examples of these stone crosses include the trio gathered together in the ancient Roman fort which is now a churchyard at Ilkley, those erected in the market square at Sandbach in Cheshire, the two in the yard at Bakewell in Derbyshire, the cross with its lofty tapered shaft at Gosforth in Cumbria and the broader but finely carved example at Irton, a few miles away. All are beautiful, but none can quite equal the masterly carving of the crosses seen at some Irish monastic sites like Monasterbois or Clonmacnois.

In the middle and later centuries of the Saxon era in England, the minster churches were gradually superseded by 'field' churches which were built in large numbers to serve the local rural communities. Hundreds, probably thousands, of village churches will trace their ancestry back to a field church founded in Saxon times, though usually all traces of the original Saxon architecture have been removed. Normally, these churches would have been younger than the parishes which they came to serve, for most parishes seem to be old estate and communal territories which

The medieval church at Nevern near Fishguard has many associations with early Christian worship.

predate the Christian era. The field churches were provided both by landowners and by religious communities, but in looking at the relationship between a village and its church we are generally faced with a 'chicken and egg' situation. Both the first truly permanent English villages and the original field churches seem to have appeared at about the same time, around the eighth, ninth and tenth centuries, so that one seldom knows which came first. In some cases, a secular or ecclesiastical patron will have furnished an existing village community with its church. In others, a village will have developed at the hamlet site or uninhabited setting where a church had already been erected. A high proportion of the field churches were originally built beside solitary manor houses to serve

the spiritual needs of the Saxon lord, his family and retainers and recent archaeological work suggests that this 'proprietorial' origin was the most common. It is hard to generalize about anything as diverse as the British church, but in England at least, the 'typical' village church would seem to originate as a humble timber chapel built beside the manor house of its Saxon proprietor. Now, after a millennium or more of change, churches and manor houses are still close neighbours in scores of villages.

Whatever their origins, villages and churches would soon develop together so that while isolated churches are quite common countryside features, in the great majority of cases they mark the sites of deserted villages. But there were some churches which were not established in the places that were most convenient to their patrons or congregations, but were built at anciently sacred places inherited from the dead or dying pagan religions. The most frequently quoted

The Bronze Age standing stone in the churchyard at Rudston near Bridlington.

A Celtic cross standing in the churchyard at Altarnun in Cornwall. The beautiful medieval granite building is known as 'the cathedral of the moors'.

Ornate carving on the shaft of the ruined Saxon cross which stands in front of the church at Masham.

example is that of Knowlton in Dorset, where the (now ruinous) church stood isolated from its village in the encircling earthworks of an ancient henge.

Country folklore is full of tales of how the Devil frustrated church building work or how stones were miraculously moved to the sites favoured by God. Though often featuring in the weird and sensational books which masquerade on the 'non-fiction' shelves, such tales have little if any historical worth. The tale of migrating building stones features at Godshill on the Isle of Wight, where the fourteenth-century building occupies a late-Saxon church site. The suggestive name did not, however, originally mean 'the hill of God'; the hill could have belonged to a Saxon with a name like Godhelm, Godmund or Godwin, though it might be translated as 'the hill of the idol', suggesting a church site inherited from that of a Celtic or Saxon pagan shrine.

There are several churches which stand on or beside seemingly artifical mounds, some of which may be ancient pagan burial barrows. They include the famous Saxon church at Barton-on-Humber and Maxey church near the Cambridgeshire–Lincolnshire border, while mounds lie close to such churches as Tidenham in Gloucestershire, Taplow in Buckinghamshire and Wickham St Paul in Essex. Other churches, many of which are now village churches, were attracted to holy wells, some of which could have been revered since Iron Age or even Later Bronze Age times. Wells Cathedral may be the grandest example; here a Roman settlement had its mausoleum close to a holy well and was succeeded by a Saxon cemetery, burial chapel and minster and, by 909, St Andrew's Cathedral. At the humbler level, one may find holy wells inside a church, as at Marden in Herefordshire, in the churchyard, as at Holywell in Cambridgeshire; in the churchyard wall, as at Stevington in Bedfordshire, or just outside the churchyard as at Eskdale in Cumbria.

It is easy to assume that if the oldest recognizable architecture in a church dates from (say) the Norman period, then the church is a Norman foundation. An assumption like this would probably be quite wrong, and it has often been said that churches have *history* rather than *dates*. And so a chancel might display windows in the Decorated style of around 1300, but this does not show that its foundations or walls were built then – a point easily appreciated if the reader thinks of all the old houses in a neighbourhood which have had fashionable double-glazed windows fitted. At Rivenhall in Essex, the church excavated by Warwick Rodwell was assumed to date from a rebuilding of 1838–1839 until the Saxon fabric was found almost intact beneath the nineteenth-century stucco. In the few cases where churches have been expertly excavated, such as at Rivenhall, Hadstock in the same county, Barton-on-Humber or Deerhurst in Gloucestershire, all sorts of unsuspected rebuildings have been exposed. We now know that it was quite typical for a church to begin as a humble two-celled timber building and go through two, three or more rebuildings before the Saxon period was even over, while all the older masonry could disappear in the course of the Middle Ages as towers, side aisles, clerestories and new chancels were acquired. Far more churches existed at the end of the Saxon era than ever found their way into the famous Domesday survey.

Occasionally the antiquity of a church is betrayed by Dark Age relics like crosses or tomb slabs which have been incorporated into the fabric in the course of later rebuilding works. One extremely fine example is the church of St Brynach at Nevern near Fishguard and it is festooned with relics. The tower is Norman, the remainder mainly of the fifteenth century, and the whole restored in 1864 and 1952. The dedication to St Brynach, however, suggests a very early date, for the saint died around 570. Built into the windowsills of the transeptal chapel are two ancient stones, discovered in the priest's chamber in 1906. One is a most unusual cross slab, the other has a bilingual inscription in Latin and the Irish *ogham* alphabet which commemorates 'Maglocunus (Maelgwn) son of Clutorius' and it may date to the fifth century AD. Outside the church, just east of the porch, stands a bilingual monument to Vitalianus which could be of similar age. Far more imposing is the great cross nearby, a magnificently carved monument of around 1000. Built into the north wall of the church is a recut stone with a Latin inscription which may date back to the Roman occupation, while a consecration cross of uncertain but great antiquity is built into the east wall of one chapel.

Without the evidence of these relics, one might assume that the church originated when the Normans occupied the area at the end of the eleventh century. But the invaders simply inherited an ancient foundation and territory. A British fortification crowns a nearby hill and was probably the base of the chieftain Clechre who, according to the *Life of St Brynach*, granted the church site to this Irish missionary. This would have been quite early in the sixth century, for a further grant of land was made by Maelgwn Gwynedd who is known to have died in 547. 'Llan', referring to a piece of holy ground, is a common element in Welsh place-names, and at Nevern the situation seems to have been quite typical. The boundary of the Llan which the chieftain granted to the missionary was marked by a stream – the Caman brook – which pro-

vided a division between the sacred and secular ground and whose waters could be used in the holy rites. Nevern is only really unusual in that so much of the ancient evidence has endured, with its hints of nearby Roman buildings and strong implications of an early, sixth-century origin.

Where, as is often the case, a church lies not at the heart of a village, but rather out on a limb, it is not easy to know whether the church was placed in this eccentric position because the site was a noble and prominent one, whether the lands donated for the building just happened to be a bit peripheral, whether the site was chosen for its ancient sanctity rather than its centrality – as may be the case with the wonderful Fenland church at March – or whether the village has drifted away from its ecclesiastical anchor. We know of many cases of villages which have slipped their moorings, including Castle Camps and Caxton in Cambridgeshire.

Occasionally, a village will be found which boasts more than one old church and Beachamwell in Norfolk, now served only by its glorious Saxon foundation, once had three churches and the village is made up of at least two components. A few over-churched villages are declined market townlets, but often the duality of churches testifies to the merging of hitherto separate settlements, as at Duxford in Cambridgeshire. Very rarely, the two churches will reflect jealous rivalries between different patrons, as at Swaffham Prior also in Cambridgeshire, where the two establishments actually share the same churchyard. The churches serving Alvingham and Cockerington in Lincolnshire cohabit in the same yard. At Aldwincle in Northamptonshire, manorial proprieties were involved: one of the two manors provided the church of All Saints in the south-east of the village, while the second church, dedicated to St Peter, was provided by Peterborough Abbey which owned the other manor. The parishes were united in 1879.

Many villages were built as new planned settlements in the Middle Ages and many others are the results of the re-planning of older originals. In such places one can often see that the church is one of the planned components. At Castle Donington in Leicestershire the church sits neatly in its rectangular property block, overlooked by the medieval castle mound. There are scores of other places where the church plot is plainly one component in a medieval master plan, normally

The little-known but delightful Saxon church at Little Ouseburn in Yorkshire has its tower built of masonry pillaged from abandoned Roman buildings nearby.

the brainchild of the local manorial lord.

The church was an essential facet of medieval village life and it was usually provided by the local lord or lords. It was almost invariably the most costly and durable building in the neighbourhood and was generally designed by one of the many now anonymous master masons, a man appointed by the patron to guide and oversee a labour force of itinerant artisans who worked as stone cutters and layers, carvers of wood or stone and carpenters. The styles in masonry and carpentry which were expounded in village churches were usually derived and simplified from those displayed in the latest great cathedral-building enterprises. Occasionally, however, the craftsmen working in village churches may have been the innovators of new techniques while some of their craftsmanship was equal to that which could be found in the finest cathedrals. This is true of the wonderful Norman stone carving in churches like Barfreston in

Two churches served separate congregations but shared the same churchyard at Swaffham Prior in Cambridgeshire.

Churches with two towers are very seldom seen. At Wymondham in Norfolk a priory was founded in 1107 and became an abbey in 1448. The octagonal tower was originally a central crossing tower but a dispute between the monks and the villagers of Wymondham resulted in the physical division of the shared church and after the Dissolution the monk's portion of the church, lying beyond the octagonal tower, was destroyed, while the building used by the village was preserved.

Kent or Kilpeck in Herefordshire, while the church at Patrington in Humberside is a palatial expression of the Decorated ideal.

Churches were ever being improved, enlarged, embellished or else reduced according to the whims and fortunes of patrons and the rise or fall of communal prosperity. Consequently, it can be very difficult to find churches which are pure and complete expressions of a single architectural style. Perhaps the least altered Saxon example is the church of St Lawrence at Bradford-on-Avon. The grandest Saxon church, and also one of the oldest, is the magnificent building at Brixworth in Northamptonshire. Dating from the seventh or eighth century, it is still a very impressive building despite the loss of much Saxon masonry and the gaining of a quite incongruous spire. The most attractive Saxon towers are those at Earls Barton in Northamptonshire and Barton-on-Humber, while the

celebrated and much-altered church at Greensted-juxta-Ongar in Essex is the sole survivor of the once widespead Saxon timber church tradition. It would be unwise to compare the calm simplicity of Saxon village churches with the ornate splendours of those of the High Middle Ages. They are more aptly seen as symbols of progress and a determination to advance towards the first home-grown English civilization.

To see a reconstruction of the sort of church which might have been built in the Dark Ages in the Celtic uplands, one must go to St Non's chapel and holy well near St David's. Here, close to the ancient religious foci the chapel overlooking the headland and bay dates only from 1934, but is built in the manner of 1000 years before.

There are hundreds of village churches which are substantially Norman and most are much more oppressive and austere than the bijou buildings at Barfreston and Kilpeck. The church at Melbourne in Derbyshire is a remarkably large and impressive example, Stow in Lincolnshire has a merging of Saxon and Norman influences, while Stewkley in Buckinghamshire has a good example of a typical Norman village church. The Early English style of the thirteenth century is seen in its most inspiring forms in the great new cathedrals and abbeys of the period, but it is also well represented in some village churches, like the one at Skelton in North Yorkshire. Scores of small Welsh communities gained their first durable church at this time and the country contains many simple, towerless and unadorned buildings of the twelfth and thirteenth centuries, many of which were built in places sanctified by early Christian worship. Llanhowel church in the Preseli Hills is a small and rugged but captivating building of the twelfth and thirteenth centuries and it stands on a reputed sixth-century Christian site. Llangelynin church, which perches on the cliffs between Tywyn and Barmouth, is truly memorable: a nuggety rough stone building of the twelfth century with a humble bell tower and it stands alone on a seventh-century Christian site.

The Decorated style of the late-thirteenth and early-fourteenth centuries is well represented in the village churches of Britain, particularly in their windows, for many old buildings were 'refenestrated' with the elaborate curving tracery of this style. The most lavish and breathtaking expressions can be seen in cathedrals like Wells, although we have already mentioned the glories of Patrington village church, where the final stages in the work employed the later Perpendicular style. The lovely and imposing church at Ashwell in Hertfordshire retains much of its fourteenth-century integrity and here, the end of both the Decorated style and the days of an overcrowded medieval countryside is marked by the graffiti on the inner face of the tower which describes the onslaughts of the great pestilence, the Black Death. The victims of this terrible disease are buried beside the path which leads to fine and rare fifteenth-century double lich gates.

The Perpendicular style, which was adopted in the years following the arrival of the Pestilence in 1348, is displayed in thousands of village churches. Few entirely new churches were built during the long currency of this style, but innumerable buildings were rebuilt or had their window spaces enlarged to accept the fashionable tracery with its flattened arches and groves of slender mullions. Even the most splendid Perpendicular village churches, like North Petherton in Somerset or Titchmarsh in Northamptonshire, usually contain at least some fragments of a less majestic older building.

The church was a versatile and adaptable building which echoed the changing fortunes and ideals of its

Breamore church contains some of the most appealing Saxon architecture – note the characteristic 'long-and-short work' in the quoins of the transept. The porch is Norman and the building employs local flint with stone in the quoins and details.

patrons and congregations, so that few of the enduring structures bear much resemblance to the original. It would grow to match the needs of a swelling congregation, but when a community perished or was removed, then the church might crumble or else be pillaged for materials for the local lord's new mansion. If a community gradually withered, then the church might shrink with it. The evidence of decline can be found at scores of sites in Norfolk, where the collapse of a very heavily populated medieval countryside was particularly severe. At Bayfield, the church is known to have been functioning in 1603, but the decay of the congregation clearly caused a reduction of the building; the chancel arch was walled-up leaving a small entrance so that services could be held in the chancel while the nave was abandoned, but during the eighteenth century the building became no more than a romantic ruin in the park of Bayfield Hall. At Glandford nearby, services ended at the start of the eighteenth century and the building was left to decay until 1875

when the ruined chancel was partly restored to allow Sunday services to be held. In 1882 the burial ground was reopened, while between 1899 and 1906 Sir Alfred Jodrell had the church completely restored as a monument to his mother.

At Stow, the old minster which serves the shrunken village is still a mighty cruciform building, but the majestic Early English building at the village of Llanddewi Brefi near Lampeter has lost its great transepts. Here as elsewhere, the reduction of the building to match a diminishing station or congregation is marked by scars or 'roof creases' on the fabric which mark the positions of the lost components. But an old roof crease scar on the tower of a church does not always show the reduction of a building and will often reflect the desire for a brighter interior which developed during the medieval centuries. The earlier medieval churches tended to have steeply pitched roofs and narrow lancet windows producing gloomy, oppresive conditions inside. Such churches were often better illuminated by lowering the pitch of the roof, inserting a high level clerestorey of windows and widening the building by the addition of side aisles with large window openings. The effect was to produce a wider, slightly lower and much brighter building.

In its attempts to meet the religious needs of the nation, the medieval church tended to be autocratic and rather mystifying; debate and the interpretation of the scriptures was not encouraged, while few peasants will have understood the full meaning of the Latin rituals. Brilliant decorations, spectacular ceremonials and eye-catching symbolism, however, must have made an enormous mark on the senses of the congregation, for the great majority of its members lived out lives of drudgery in dim, squalid hovels. Meanwhile, the church was often also a powerful, rich and avaricious owner of land and collector of dues. And yet, the village church was an absolute communal focus. It not only served as a temple but also as an often boisterous social centre and business forum. On market

days the trading might spill over into the churchyard, while by hallowing the communal boundaries and blessing the plough, the church intervened to buttress the livelihood and security of the congregation. Not surprisingly, centuries of local history as well as the shifting currents of national political and religious outlooks can be found encapsulated in the fabric of many village churches.

Many facets of social evolution also became petrified in the building of the village church. In the earlier medieval centuries, the wealthy had tended to express their piety or hopes for salvation by generous bequests to monastic foundations. Later, they tended to seek more personalized epitaphs, often in the form of bequests for family chantry chapels or other splendid additions. Particularly anxious to proclaim their wealth and status in durable and impressive forms were the members of the rising trading dynasties. The famous church at Lavenham was partly provided by the Springs, a rich family of local clothiers – and no

Norman carving of exceptional quality is displayed above the doorways in the small church at Barfreston in Kent.

Ashwell church in Hertfordshire is a fine building in the Decorated style.

opportunity to announce their benevolence in the building display was missed – while at Fairford in Gloucestershire the church was rebuilt by the cloth merchant John Tame. At Cirencester and several other places, the wool merchants provided chantry chapels where masses were sung for the souls of the donors. Trading guilds provided such additions in scores of market town churches, while smaller guilds were also active in a number of villages. At Cawston in Norfolk the plough screen is a reminder of the medieval ploughman's guild, while a number of timber-framed guildhalls, like the one at Whittlesford in Cambridge-shire, were provided by village guilds associated with maintaining and improving the local church.

It is difficult now to imagine the colour and opulence of the pre-Reformation church and the pageants of painting and imagery which persisted in the course of

Llangelynin church, typical of Welsh church architecture in the twelfth century, stands on a site associated with Christianity since the seventh century.

the Reformation and the violent Commonwealth purges. While the Roman rituals may often have seemed remote and mysterious, the church was also emblazoned with simpler messages, sometimes in the form of doom paintings spread across the chancel arch to proclaim the fates awaiting sinners. Examples survive at Chaldon in Surrey and Long Coombe in Oxfordshire. Thousands of these paintings disappeared beneath coats of Protestant whitewash, although a number have been rediscovered and restored. In the course of the post-Reformation assaults on what was unfairly regarded as 'idolatory', images were broken, crosses torn down, painted glass smashed and the rood screens, which marked the mystical division between the nave and choir, were sawn from their mountings. One of the finest rood screens and galleries, acquired from a nearby religious house, can be seen in the village church at Llanegryn near Dolgellau.

The traumas of the Reformation long passed, the church in England tended to subside into a rather sanctimonious torpor in which the needs of the

Fine carving in the Decorated style in the splendid church at Patrington in Humberside.

underprivileged were overlooked in a slavish movement to enshrine the values of the governing establishment. The spectacular if obscure Catholic rituals were
replaced by an emphasis on long and thunderous
sermons, and many a village church acquired its lofty,
overbearing pulpit in the seventeenth or eighteenth
century. Wooden pulpits began to appear in the
fifteenth century and excellent late-medieval examples
are found at Rossington in Yorkshire or Ipplepen in
Devon; Croscombe in Somerset has a fine Jacobean
specimen but the culmination of the preaching vogue
was marked by the eruption of the daunting three-
decker pulpits. The 'ground floor' was represented by a
desk from which the congregation was led in responses.
Above was another desk from which the parson read
the service, while crowning the edifice, like the poop
deck of an old warship, was the pulpit itself, from which
the sermon was released on the timorous if drowsy
assembly. There are good examples of these pulpits at
St Mary's in Whitby, Sall in Norfolk and Cottesbrooke
in Northamptonshire.

The eighteenth-century church in England being so
thoroughly and unhealthily wedded to the prevailing
social order, the hierarchical divisions of society
became fossilized in the structure of the church. At
Cottesbrooke and several other churches, the family of
the squire not only had its own special pew, but also a
private fireplace. Pews began to be provided in parish
churches in the later medieval centuries and they
proliferated after the Reformation, when they began to
express the intense territorial instincts of the members
of the congregation. They were occupied according to a
family's status in the community, or more particularly,
according to the house that they occupied – and
Christian charity was unlikely to extend to the inter-
loper who usurped a cherished position in church. And
so it is not surprising that when Richard Gough began
his history of the parish of Myddle in Shropshire around
1700, he described the local families in order according
to their positions in the seating plan of the church: even
at worship, each bottom was placed according to
property and pedigree. Meanwhile, the tombs of the
aristocracy, ever grander and more melodramatic,
increased to hem in the congregations at scores of

*Although the tower is relatively modern the famous wool church at Long Melford is
one of the finest examples of Perpendicular church architecture. Note the use of
flushwork of flint panels defined by stone.*

village churches so that the proverbial Martian visitor might have thought he had entered a family shrine rather than the church of God. In many a kowtowing parish he would probably have been right.

As the memories of the conflict and turmoil of the Reformation and Commonwealth faded, the nineteenth-century church was freer to adopt features from the glittering Gothic heritage. Some parishes took the 'high road' and some the 'low' and this was again reflected in the building, so that trimmings like communion rails, screens, gaudy glass and other ornate fittings were commonest in churches tending to the higher persuasion. At the same time, many of the more intense eighteenth- and nineteenth-century worshippers came to feel that the established church was losing sight of its crusading Christian mission and they sought the simpler, more independent values of the nonconformist sects.

Countryside explorers who flock to the village churches will often not give the nearby chapel a second glance, yet this generally much younger building can be just as much a part of the living communal history. Restricted funds and the general nonconformist wish to shun ostentation tended to produce bleak, seemingly uninviting exteriors – but chapels should always be experienced from the inside. Many contain the most elegant woodwork. Their internal arrangements usually reflect the close bonds between the congregation and their minister or lay preachers, with a simplification of the traditional nave, chancel, aisle,

transept and tower layout of the traditional churches. In many villages the forerunner of the local chapel – a private dwelling where religious meetings were held until the community could afford to build its chapel – will still survive. The chapel was often financed by the wealthier middle-class members of the nonconformist congregation, such as farmers and small industrialists. Though generally modestly endowed, many of the buildings, particularly the Welsh ones, are surprisingly large and barn-like and this in part reflects the original high hopes of recruitment. But in scores of communities, the multiplication of nonconformist chapels tells of the factional quest to establish the 'ideal' form of worship and also of the local squabbles and rivalries within the congregation. In several Welsh villages and townlets the streets seem to be lined with chapels dispensing competing and only marginally different forms of Christian worship, and clearly the intensity of devotion and the emphasis on its tiny details has produced heavy bills for the upkeep of

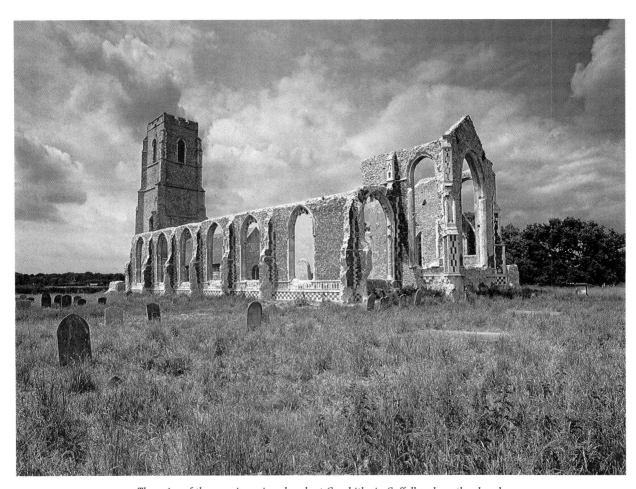

The ruins of the once-imposing church at Covehithe in Suffolk, where the church decayed along with the community.

half-empty buildings.

We have glimpsed country churches as monuments to the history of their communities, but they also embody the physical qualities and architectural fancies of their regions. While successive architectural fashions lapped across the landscape, each province had its own resource of building materials, its own traditions and its own ideas about how a church should look. Local wealth or poverty, possession or lack of good stone, the skills and preferences of the local schools of masons and the inexplicable regional tastes in proportions and decoration all governed the character of clusters of parish churches. So far as good stone was concerned, some places had it and other did not. Builders in the have-not locations could make do with whatever flints, river cobbles or low-grade rubble were to hand or else the patrons would accept the high costs of importing a decent limestone or sandstone. The quality stone could either be used for the entire building or it might be used to build 'quoins' or corners, tracery, lintels and other structural details.

Best from the points of view of the masons and cognoscenti were the fine-grained golden, cream or silvery 'oolitic' limestones of counties like Northamptonshire, Oxfordshire, Gloucestershire and parts of Somerset. It could be sawn into perfect blocks to form buildings with a smooth or 'ashlar' surface or it could be finely carved for decorative work. There were a few other top class stones, like the milky Magnesian Limestones of central Yorkshire or the Tunbridge Wells Sandstone of Kent. A wide variety of other stones were employed according to local convenience, ranging from the tough granites of Cornwall, the soft Red Sandstones of the west Midlands, the Millstone Grit of the Pennines to humble but passable products like the slatey rocks of Wales and Cumbria, the Greensand of the south east and the modest sandstones of the east Midlands. Although the limestones of the oolite belt were supreme in every respect, the portfolio of British churches would be far less enticing without the motley majority of rough-textured buildings composed of rubble hewn from a humble local quarry. As it is, the buildings echo the hues and textures of their local settings, for few patrons could contemplate the fearful costs of buying in stone from a renowned but distant source. In the chalklands, the Fens and the clay vales, however, such purchases were sometimes essential. The chalk seldom yielded beds tough enough to be used for external masonry. Flints gathered in nearby fields were often used for walling but good stone like the Barnack rag of north Cambridgeshire were needed for corners and windows. Celebrated quarries like Barnack, Weldon, Ketton and Doulton exported their lovely products by river and

Remarkable carving decorates the medieval bench ends at Altarnun.

cart to the stone-starved areas lying miles away.

The delightful regional variations in the stone fabric of the British churches is easily explained in this way, but much harder to interpret are the provincial enthusiasms for different architectural forms. The most celebrated, of course, is the glorious quiver of mid Anglian and southern Midlands broach spires – a regional fancy which was developed to perfection. But there were many other variations. The Saxon and Norman flint round towers of East Anglia may simply reflect the impossibility of building corners in flint, but the blunt pyramids of 'Sussex caps' seen on some Sussex towers, the tower-topping leaded *flèches* or Hertfordshire spirelets, the tiny pinnacles gracing many Yorkshire towers or the massive stair turrets favoured in Devon all represent particular regional fancies which seem little related to the building resources of their regions.

Then there are the imposing churches which tell of periods of regional prosperity. Most of these buildings are found in areas which flourished on the late-medieval wool and textile industry, and the magnificent Perpendicular wool churches of East Anglia, Somerset and the Cotswolds are unsurpassed – those at Lavenham, Batcombe in Somerset and Northleach in Gloucestershire are among the many wonders of this age. In contrast are the small, austere churches of the uplands, where congregations were sparse and funds usually in short supply. In Wales and Cornwall, many of the hamlet churches are early foundations and the medieval buildings often stand on sites associated with Dark Age missionary activities. In the north of England however, while there are some early foundations, the smaller churches of the upper dales are often quite youthful, the results of eighteenth- or nineteenth-century patronage or local growth at the dawning of the Industrial Revolution. Cornwall contains many fifteenth-century granite churches with simple towers and two or three gabled roofs covering the body of the building. Wales has many unadorned and towerless thirteenth-century buildings, while the northern English upland churches are often humble exercises in Gothic Revival styles. The Lake District contains some small churches of the seventeenth and eighteenth century, a building period poorly represented in the remainder of England, but a time when the small yeomen or 'statesmen' of this area were colonizing the fells and valleys of the former monastic estates.

In Scotland, the situation is less easily summarized. There are a number of churches on Dark Age mission-

A typical Cornish church at St Tudy. Note the slender tower, the low roofline and the way that the side aisles have separate gabled roofs.

Inside the church at St Tudy one can see how the local slate has been exploited for the creation of some exceptionally fine monuments.

ary sites, but mellowed medieval churches of the kind so common in England become rare as one proceeds northwards. Some villages and hamlets have evolved from the old 'kirktouns' – the members of the squalid ranks of farming settlements which contained churches – but most surviving rural churches are small eighteenth- or nineteenth-century buildings which were often provided by the leading estate owners of a region. In Scotland and Ireland one will, however, sometimes find late-medieval churches which display the extravagant twists and twirls of Flamboyant tracery – a continental style which England shunned in favour of the more formal Perpendicular form. The universities of Scotland have long traditions in the medical field and in the churchyards of areas all around the university centres one will often see graves protected by 'mortsafes', burials guarded by masonry or cages of different kinds which, it was hoped, would save the corpses from body-snatchers.

All questions of history apart, the country churches of Britain are a delightfully appealing and varied collection. Their stonework so often harmonizes with the local geology and they complement their settings in every respect. The mellow and prosperous lowland villages have their timeworn and imposing medieval churches, while the bleak and rugged uplands have spawned a more spartan breed of building, and throughout the islands the often inexplicable provincial fancies produced forms and trimmings which stamped each building with a sense of place.

A brief perambulation of the churchyard will end our sketch of country churches. Today, the churchyard is a rather predictable if tranquil place: either an open, yew-studded lawn with the old stones ripped up and stacked against a shady wall or else a petrified thicket of headstones. It was not always so, for while tombstones were seldom seen in a medieval churchyard and the area was often used for noisy secular activities, the hallowed ground often contained a wide variety of different structures. The excavations at Rivenhall, where a large rectangular platform marks the site of the Roman villa which preceded the church here, revealed a variety – the churchyard site of a Saxon timber church and mausoleum, a Norman priest's house and its three medieval successors, a medieval latrine, a seventeenth-century shed from which charitable distributions of herrings were made, and a chantry chapel and a sexton's house are also known to

Some timber-framed medieval buildings were associated with communal worship, like the fine guildhall at Whittlesford in Cambridge, built to serve a guild connected with the village church.

The tombstone of the village blacksmith at Houghton near Huntingdon.

have stood here. Churchyard priests' houses are known to have been common in the Middle Ages, though few survive. Attractive examples which lie outside their respective churchyards can be seen at Muchelney in Somerset and Easton-on-the-Hill in Northamptonshire.

Churchyard yews are a common and rather mysterious feature. The romantic tradition is that yews were first planted to provide bow wood for the formidable Welsh and English medieval archers yet most are relatively young. Some yews, however, are obviously very old and one in the churchyard at Wilmington in Sussex is said to have stood there for nine centuries. The earliest yews may have been planted through some hang-over from pagan beliefs, and perhaps the evergreen foliage and durable tree symbolized eternal life. Alternatively, yews could often have been planted to mark important graves or the lines of old boundaries or paths. Some of the finest old yews can be seen in the churchyard at Nevern, though most yards have a few examples. After the seventeenth century, other trees were sometimes planted for landscaping purposes. Rows of elms often border a churchyard, while there is topiary at Painsworth in Gloucestershire and some lovely old roses enhance the setting at Ewhurst in Sussex. Although we are all in favour of tree planting, it must be said that some ill-placed modern trees are spoiling the prospects of churches from Ripon Minster, Fountains Abbey and Kings Lynn down through the hierarchy, and new trees should always be sited to enhance rather than obscure the view.

The tombstones themselves are of course the most obvious historical features of the village churchyard. The most tasteful and stylish are those of the eighteenth century, but seventeenth-century examples can sometimes be found, They can give vital evidence to students of genealogy, while each churchyard contains its own carved cameos recalling episodes of devotion and tragedy. Churchyard rambles will sometimes reveal a tantalizingly interesting example, like the one in Dalham graveyard in Suffolk. How did Anthony Gibbon, born in Calcutta in 1680, come to be buried in the heart of Suffolk in 1714? Was he a native servant brought to England on an East Indiaman or perhaps the son of an adventurous early Suffolk trader?

In terms of flora and fauna, there is much more to the church and its setting than the pests which feature in so many parish appeals (with unintended humour one parish magazine recently reported that 'Death watch beetle have been confirmed in the church'). Many churches really do have bats in the belfry, while the churchyard setting can be a valuable reservoir of plant and animal life.

The natural history of the churchyard

The church and churchyard, like so many of man's creations, have been invaded by a host of plants and animals which have colonized these substitute habitats over many centuries, often developing into quite distinctive communities. If the church is ruined and the churchyard abandoned, the wildlife is all the more interesting because it has been able to develop undisturbed. Just like well-managed farms, a well-kept church with neatly cut grass, clean, regularly pointed stonework, and boundary walls cleared of weeds by spraying with herbicides provides fewer habitats for wildlife, but often has a greater aesthetic appeal – certainly to most parsons, who would maintain that a neat churchyard is synonymous with a vigorous church community. It is not necessary, however, for the church and churchyard to have an air of neglect in order to combine nature conservation with normal upkeep. Only slight modifications may make all the difference in enhancing the interesting features.

The plant life of churches and their surroundings can be divided into two types: plants growing in the grass, including the trees and bushes, and those on the stone or brickwork. Of the latter, the commonest species are lichens, which are lowly plants forming mats or rings of growth on the stones, particularly on various types of limestone. They are less common on granite and other hard acidic rocks. There are many species – nearly 1400 in Britain – and they all consist of an alga and fungus living together. Each provides some benefit to the other, an arrangement that is called a symbiotic relationship. It has been well known for a long time that churchyards can be excellent places for

*Wild plants flourishing in the churchyard at Belton in Suffolk
(Note too the early-medieval flint round tower, an architectural form
seldom seen outside East Anglia).*

lichens, the church walls and the tombstones being the favourite habitats. Many species grow particularly well on tombstones made from calcareous rocks and when people choose to erect such stones in areas which are not on limestone, they will indirectly help to spread certain species to places where they would not normally grow. In churchyards where the tombstones are of several different types of stone, the species list may be greatly extended. For example, as many as eighty-five species have been recorded at Trotten Church in Sussex, a remarkably high total when the average number is only fifty-seven in a 10 kilometre square (3.9 square miles) in the British countryside.

It is sometimes thought that lichens will damage man-made structures on which they grow. It is true that they contain various chemicals which may be mildly acidic but they grow so slowly that they have no effect on the stonework. An architectural adviser to a small church in one Midland county recently told the parochial church council that they ought to remove the lichens from the church walls because the stonework would eventually crumble away. How little he knew about lichens – he overlooked the fact that they had been growing on the walls of this church for over 800 years and there was no evidence of damage to the stonework! The subtle colours of the lichens are most attractive and the beauty of old buildings is greatly enhanced by the ancient growths of these primitive plants.

However, lichens as well as other plants are sensitive to air pollution, particularly to the sulphur dioxide component of industrial smoke – 'acid rain'. The algal component of the lichen partnership is more sensitive than the fungus, but when one is affected the whole plant dies. On calcareous stones, the acid is neutralized and the pollution effect is thus greatly reduced, but on rocks with no calcareous element there is no such defence, and only the very resistant species survive.

Mosses, small ferns and other plants will grow on church walls if they are allowed to remain – their abundance is related to the degree of maintenance. As the mortar begins to fall out between the stones or bricks, so more footholds are provided, even, in some cases, for tree and bush seedlings. The end result of this process can be seen on a ruined church abandoned to nature. The flora will depend on the nearness of seed-producing plants, but I have seen ruins that were a riot of colour of wallflowers, snapdragons, ragwort, ferns, mosses and grasses.

The degree of maintenance also affects the plant life in the grassy sward of the churchyard. In general the less frequently the grass is cut, the better it is for the insects and other small creatures which live on the vegetation or in the 'litter' layer close to the ground. Perhaps the parson may feel that he does not wish to encourage 'creepy-crawlies', but a number of butterflies feed, as caterpillars, on many common plants. Both the meadow brown and the small heath butterflies depend on grasses, while the small copper feeds on such common plants as docks and sorrels. Even the despised nettle is the foodplant of the lovely peacock, red admiral and small tortoiseshell. The comma butterfly may also feed on nettles and the little blue likes the small leguminous plants which are often common in dry grassland. A compromise between neatness and wildlife can easily be found by cutting the grass so that is is no shorter than about four inches and by leaving margins and corners where the vegetation is never cut. The frequency with which the grass is cut is also important, but if it is mown just once, in July, this will enable most insects to thrive. In fact the cost of churchyard maintenance is such that this sort of regime is often adopted more from necessity than from thoughts of conservation. In an area where the meadows of the countryside are grazed hard by cattle and sheep, the churchyard may be the only place where glow-worms can be seen on a summer's night or cowslips in the spring.

A. Chater, a churchyard botanist, has written that the unused parts of burial grounds enclosed in the nineteenth century now have a vegetation undisturbed for over a hundred years. Add to this the fact that different soil types support a different vegetation, and one has some idea of the potential richness of the churchyard flora throughout the country. In Mickleham churchyard in Surrey, 180 species of flowers and ferns have been recorded, and in many other instances churchyards of less than one acre have over a hundred species of wild plants. A small churchyard – less than one third of an acre – in Ceredigion which was enclosed in 1895 has about eighty-five species including eight ferns and four different orchids.

Churchyard trees and hedgerows are another valuable habitat for wildlife. Very often trees are allowed to grow to a great age, when natural holes and cracks in the timber provide nest holes for woodpeckers or owls (often the little owl), tree creepers, common titmice and spotted flycatchers. The yew is probably associated with churchyards more often than any other tree, and although it has a very restricted invertebrate fauna, its dense foliage and evergreen habit make it an ideal place for nesting birds and provides them with shelter in cold weather. In the winter also its berries are much sought after. Another common woody plant in churchyards is the ivy, which, if left, will festoon the walls and trees. It does no harm to the trees, and in fact preserves old

Some of the butterflies which may be found in churchyards and cottage gardens.

Red admiral (on michaelmas daisies).
One of our finest butterflies and fortunately still common.

Gatekeeper or hedge brown, a common species. The larvae feed on grasses.

Peacock, a very familiar butterfly in gardens, especially in late summer.

Orange tip, one of our early butterflies, frequently on the wing in April.

walls by binding together the loose stones. It provides cover for many creatures and is an alternative food-plant for the delicate holly blue butterfly. Sometimes it has to be controlled, but people often seem to overlook its many good qualities and regard it as a sort of parasite.

Although ivy on stone walls provides shelter and food for numerous interesting animals, many species manage quite well without it – mason bees search out the soft mortar and burrow through to a suitable cavity for their nest; and queen wasps enter by any hole they can find. Near the base of the walls woodlice, ground beetles, slugs and snails occupy any available crevice. But they do not live there unmolested; there are other creatures looking for a home, particularly spiders, perhaps the most unloved of all invertebrates – although it is probably what they look like rather than what they do that frightens people. In fact they do us a service by occupying many holes which might be taken over by less desirable species such as wasps. One spider, known as *Amaurobius ferox* (few spiders have common names), is a large and quite formidable animal which constructs a silken tube in a crevice leading to its retreat. On the outside radiating strands of silk extend in all directions from the mouth of the tube. If any insect, be it fly, wasp, bee or beetle, tries to investigate the hole and accidentally trips on a radiating thread, the vibrating signal acts like a trigger and the hidden spider leaps out and seizes its prey.

Amaurobius and its related species are common on any building where there are suitable holes and cracks. An even more formidable spider, *Segestria florentina*, occupies similar habitats. It is rare in Britain but the few places where it occurs are all in towns south of the Thames, and there are colonies, probably established for many years, in the walls of Westminster in the heart of London. This species is powerful enough to tackle any insect, and eats wasps and bees with as much gusto as it does blowflies.

The high timber church roof, unless regularly cleaned, is a favourite haunt of the large house spider, of which there are several species. You can of course see these long-legged, hairy creatures in houses, particularly during the summer and autumn when the males are searching for a mate, but the beams of the church roof are excellent places for attaching the large sheet webs which the house spider builds. It may be this habit which was remembered by the sexton in Ely Cathedral during the Middle Ages. He was accused of stealing the oil in the lamp suspended by a long chain from the roof of the nave. He protested his innocence, swearing that he had seen a giant spider crawl down the chain, drink the oil and then return to the dark recesses of the roof. In those days his explanation was no doubt believed, but no one would get away with such a story today – we are much better informed on natural history.

The cliff-like church tower also attracts house martins which nest on the outside of buildings, wherever they can glue on their mud nest; swallows, on the other hand, prefer the insides of buildings and look for perches such as high beams where they can place their nests, which, unlike the house martin's, are fully open. This is why so many churches have outer doors of wire-mesh and keep the windows closed during the spring and summer; otherwise services are likely to be disturbed by the noisy clamour of young swallows. There was an incident some years ago when a sparrow disturbed a music recital in a church with its constant 'cheep, cheep'. A church member was asked to shoot it and when the story appeared in the press, the parson received many angry letters from birdlovers.

Another hirundine, the swift, is a common inhabitant of church towers, choosing any hole or cleft which leads to a sufficiently large space for its nest. Owls also breed in church towers, the most frequent being the so-called barn, or white, owl. Forty years ago it was regularly found in the churches of the Midland counties where one of us grew up, but unfortunately it is much less common today.

In addition to these regular inhabitants, some rather unusual birds occur from time to time in church towers. A mallard duck once raised her brood in the tower of an East Anglian country church. But how the young ducklings managed to reach the ground is a mystery. Rare birds such as black redstarts prefer ruined churches, but they have been heard singing on Westminster Abbey and churches in some towns in other parts of the country. On the continent this species is a regular inhabitant of the craggy stone churches in hill regions.

Those secretive creatures, bats, of which fifteen species breed in Britain, will roost in almost any part of the church that is protected from direct sunlight. In the summer they may use a variety of roosting sites, often changing from one night to the next, but in the winter, when they hibernate, they look for sheltered places, protected against rapid temperature changes but with a high humidity. Many church roofs and towers provide just the right conditions. Although having 'bats in the belfry' used to be a common complaint – and perhaps sometimes still is – these charming furry creatures seldom cause offence, and indeed people often do not know they are there. Sometimes they fly about during services, or worse, their droppings soil the furnishings. Then something has to be done – for instance a temporary cover on the altar cloth. Up to 1975 no one thought of preserving bats, but the Protection of Wild Creatures Legislation in that year included two rare species, the greater horseshoe and the mouse-eared, and the 1981 Wildlife and Countryside Act went much further and put all species on the protected list. If bats in churches do cause annoyance, the Nature Conservancy Council is there to give advice on the best way to remedy the problem. In fact anyone with bats, whether in a church or a house, should read the Nature Conservancy Council leaflet entitled *Focus on Bats.* In it various methods are described for minimizing or eliminating the nuisance they can cause.

The Church of England has realized the value of conserving wildlife in churchyards and in 1972 published a small pamphlet called *Wildlife Conservation in the Care of Churches and Churchyards*, by E. M. A. Barker. It has many useful ideas. A survey of churchyard plants is at present being organized by the Royal Society for the Conservation of Nature, the Botanical Society of the British Isles and the British Lichen Society, aided by the many Women's Institutes around the country. Competitions are being held to find those churchyards which offer the most for wildlife.

— 5 —

THE COUNTRY COTTAGE

*Thatching in progress at Great Sampford in Essex.
Most of the ridge is still to be completed and trimming will
remove the 'shaggy' aura.*

Country cottages are loved by all and desired by most. They nestle in leafy hollows, line up enticingly on parade along the village high streets or glitter white and golden like jewels in a distant green mosaic. Whether it be neglected and engagingly rickety or tarted-up and festooned with Olde Worlde knick-knacks, one can easily be beguiled by the sheer prettiness of the country cottage. Often the blurb of the glossy village guide will take one no further than the cute façade, but to enjoy fully the heritage of rural dwellings one must discover a little more about the whys and wherefores of these humble vernacular buildings. Then it becomes apparent that the cottage is not just a dainty bauble in the rural showcase, but a real home which can often recount the social history of the countryside and which has, in the process of aging, fossilized fragments of the lifestyles and aspirations of its successive occupants.

Today, the word 'cottage' is used quite loosely to describe any small and vaguely venerable rural dwelling – sometimes even little urban dwellings and modern houses too. In the past, however, the word described the abode of a 'cottar', later a 'cottager' – a member of one of the lower and most deprived ranks in the medieval peasant hierarchy – while the occupation of a recognized cottage usually carried with it certain grazing rights on the village or township common. Although genuinely medieval cottages scarcely exist outside the pages of some guidebooks, many cottages stand on house plots which have been occupied since the early days of village formation. There are scores of place-names containing the Old English *cot* which suggest settlements that have grown from little cottage groupings – the various Cotes and Coates for example, as well as Coton, Coatham and Cotton which mean 'at the cottages'. Then there are the several Northcotes and Southcotes, names like Caldecote meaning 'cottages on cold ground', or Salcott and Glascote, settlements developed from little industrial buildings concerned, as the names suggest, with salt storage and glass making.

Other cottage sites are legacies of days of extreme poverty and rural over-population when legal settle-ment or illegal squatting took place along lanes and the edges of woods, commons and greens. Cottagers could either own or rent their cramped and shabby dwellings and, although they usually had certain grazing rights on the common and rights to cut turf and gather fuel and could sometimes tenant strips in the village ploughlands, they tended to be chiefly supported by their earnings as farm labourers. The squatter or borderer class was originally distinct from that of the cottagers, although gradually the classes tended to merge. The squatters were settlers who cleared little holdings in the poorer woodlands or wastes in the backwaters of a parish. Generally the big fish of the parish pond tolerated squatters because they could be charged rents, helped to improve the land and could work as hired hands. Sometimes such impoverished families began to pose a problem and the geographer Brian K. Roberts has quoted the description given by a seventeenth-century estate surveyor, who wrote: '. . . these cottages and inclosures doe yearly increase, yet these rents are very indifferently paid, they being a poore beggerly sort of people apt to run in Arrears from time to time'. When the arrears mounted and cottagers became a burden on the poor rates, there were plenty of hard-hearted landowners who discovered ingenious ways of removing the poorer elements and their homes. Unemployed labourers might be hired in batches to a farmer in a neighbouring parish for a year and return to find that their cottages had been pulled down and that the burden of support had been transferred from the parish.

At other times the owners of land would legitimize a squatting incident by taking a 'fine' in payment. Although the legal basis of the custom seems obscure, in Wales and in some parts of England there was a tradition that squatter rights could be won by a family which could build a dwelling on a patch of waste in a single night and the more rugged portions of many a Welsh parish display the ruins of such a little *ty unnos*, a

*Farmstead and farm cottages in limestone and red pantiles
at Newton on Rawcliffe near Pickering in Yorkshire.*

one-night house or 'morning surprise'. The barren seaboards of Ireland and Wales meanwhile are dotted with the shanties, hovels and crofts which are mainly ruined and not strictly cottages and which were the refuges of Irish Catholic peasants displaced by Protestant immigrants and destitute clansmen evicted by the Highland sheep barons of the eighteenth and nineteenth centuries.

Other cottages originated as purpose-built dwellings provided as essential accommodation in the days when any substantial farm needed a small army of carters, ploughmen and general labourers. The early stages of industrialization also saw the establishment of thousands of cottages. At first cottage-based textile manufacture could be used to buttress an otherwise unviable smallholding, while later, short blocks and then long terraced rows of working class cottages were built by factory owners and speculative landlords at the mushrooming industrial villages. In different places and at different times the cottage could play many roles. But it is one of the ironies of history that while poverty and hardship were the common denominators of cottage life, timeworn cottages are now amongst the most costly and sought-after exhibits in the estate agent's display.

Olde Worlde charm is a very commercial attribute, and although a small minority of cottages contain the fragments of medieval dwellings in their fabric, scarcely any are the genuine and complete medieval article. Larger houses of the fifteenth and sixteenth centuries are numerous, there are a good number of partly fourteenth-century survivors and a few thirteenth- or even twelfth-century houses enduring, though in much-altered forms. But these real domestic antiquities were overwhelmingly the abodes of the wealthier elements in town and village society: petty lords, yeomen, merchants and prosperous craftsmen. Peasants lived in wretched hovels which, as the Wharram

Pargetting embellishing the walls of the priest's house at Clare in Suffolk.

Timber-framing with brick infill at Breamore in Hampshire.

Percy deserted village excavations show, were so shabby and flimsy as to be derelict and in need of a total rebuilding after a generation or so of occupation. A reconstruction of one of the sturdier medieval peasant dwellings is the so-called Hangleton house, based on the plan of an excavated dwelling at the deserted village of this name, and displayed amongst a remarkable collection of saved and restored dwellings at the open air museum at Singleton near Chichester.

Some cottages consist of the dismembered portions of much grander medieval dwellings, but the oldest original cottages are legacies of the Great Rebuilding, the important house-improving movement which lapped slowly across the face of Britain, beginning in the trend-setting south-east at the close of the Middle Ages and reaching the upland provinces of the north and west during the eighteenth century. But most of the cottages which can trace their pedigrees back to the

Great Rebuilding were originally little farmsteads rather than the more lowly abodes of cottagers. Gradually, however, as the Middle Ages receded into history, the rural working class families began to acquire dwellings that were sufficiently sturdy as to survive into the modern era and, as likely as not, become converted into 'desirable period residences' for commuters, or long-dreamed-of retirement homes, weekend retreats, or the secluded abodes of authors like ourselves.

The charm of the humbler vernacular dwellings of Britain was born of poverty but rooted in diversity. Lincolnshire tempts the tourist with a strawberry and cream confection of pale limestone cottages with roofs of russet pantiles. In Dorset, the heavy swathes of thatch are like tawny teacosies enveloping walls of lime-washed cob or daub or steely flint. In the Cotswolds the stone-tiled roofs and thickets of golden gables gild an already mellow landscape, while in contrast, the flag-roofed grey stone dwellings of the Pennine dales are as gritty as the folk within. In central Wales, white walls and scarlet paint flash in the verdant landscape; walls of whitened boulders and a shaggy thatch of oat straw give many a West Ireland homestead a relaxed and jaunty aura, while dark stones and a no-nonsense façade feature in the dourer dwellings of John Knox country. There are far more regional cottage styles than there are counties in Britain, yet each one seems to encapsulate and extend the personality of its province.

Each cottage is a blend of building materials, the habits and lifestyles of the cottage community and those other less easily definable factors of tradition, fancy and craftsmanship which made up the local architectural tradition. Some of the smaller and shabbier cottages were built by their original inhabitants, but most of those which survive were provided by local landowners and built by village housewrights, carpenters, thatchers and rough masons. Cheapness was always a commanding factor, and so the use of materials which were readily to hand was either desired or else absolutely determined by the woeful shortcomings of the transport system.

Depending upon the availability of materials and on local traditions and expertise, walls could be of stone, of wattle and daub panels set in an oaken timber frame or of one of the various mud concoctions.

Top quality limestone and sandstone of grades similar to those used on mansion and great church building projects were normally only adopted when the cottage builders had easy access to a prestigious quarry, and even then the materials were normally used as coursed rubble rather than being sawn into regular blocks with smooth 'ashlar' surfaces. More usually, lower quality limestone or sandstone rubble would be hewn from the local village quarry. Away

Devon cob at Dunsford.

Few cottages built of chalk or 'clunch' have survived. This attractive row is at Newton in Cambridgeshire; the windows suggest an eighteenth century date.

from the limestone and sandstone belts an intractable stone like gneiss, a low grade slate or a perishable product like chalk 'clunch' would often be employed by the cottage builders, though shunned by the free masons who built the grander houses in the locality. Granite or 'moorstone' boulders gathered from the waste, cobbles from the beach or river bed, discarded debris from a noted quarry, flints gathered in the course of agricultural stone-picking and stones filched from derelict buildings all found their way into the cottage walls of Britain. The use of angular, craggy and lumpy materials produced the coarse textures and dappled tints which make the cottage products of the village rough masons seem so much more homely and rooted in the countryside than do the grander, smooth-faced and finely-proportioned creations of the more illustrious free masons.

The cottage-builders were seeking to create cheap

Local slate roofing and rendered rubble at Troutbeck in Cumbria.

homes rather than beauty, and sometimes the necessity for cheap materials posed problems. Often the cheap stones were too tough, too brittle or too small in size to be turned into corner stones or 'quoins', lintels or the surrounds for doors or windows. Chalk country could yield both flints and clunch for walling, but where these low-cost materials were employed then brick or stone was needed for the structural details. Similarly in the Lake District, while walls were often built of rugged slaty slabs, the corners and load-bearing details are often of blocks shaped from gritty sandstone or Shap granite. Flints, shingle and river cobbles also had to be set in thick dollops of gap-plugging mortar, while the Carboniferous Limestone blocks of the Pennine dales and the olive Lakeland slates were often bedded in clay to insulate the cottagers against

the northern winds. Sometimes the building problems or the availability of varied local materials encouraged the adoption of decorative styles. Towards the Cumbrian seaboard, lumpy granite boulders often alternate with courses of slender slates, while in Dorset one can find chequerboard walling in alternating greensand and limestone blocks or stone courses which alternate with bands of flint to create a striped effect. In Northamptonshire bands of red ironstone were sometimes coursed in walls of honey-coloured limestone. Some materials encouraged the practice of 'galleting', with the larger patches of mortar being plugged with little packing stones while occasionally 'harled' walls can be seen, with rows of pebbles being set in the mortar-filled gaps between the roughly squared building blocks. The nature of the climate also exerted an effect and in parts of Cornwall exposed cottage walls are sometimes protected by hung slates, while here and elsewhere, walls of poor rubble and mortar were often coated in a protective rendering of plaster or roughcast so that the attractive stone texture is masked. More attractive is the limewash finish used in many wet and windswept localities to protect a bedding of clay or mortar from leaching by the driving rain.

Stone was the dominant cottage-building material in Ireland and is pre-eminent in Wales, Scotland and the English uplands. In some places the tradition can be traced back into the Middle Ages and the ruins of a medieval village of stone-built dwellings can be seen on Dartmoor at Houndtor. Most commonly, however, the stone tradition superseded an older one of building in timber and mud during the seventeenth and eighteenth centuries. Cornwall is noted for its stone cottages, yet as recently as the late-sixteenth century the majority of the poorer Cornish tenants and smallholders lived in mud-walled thatched hovels. In the Yorkshire Dales hardly any dwellings survive to portray the thatch and timber-framing style of meaner dwellings which were built until the eighteenth cen-

tury. But over large areas of the English lowlands the materials which would have allowed a switch from building in timber and mud to a rebuilding in stone did not exist and in these places, as the Great Rebuilding began to wash over the lower levels of society, peasant dwellings become more substantial and durable although the basic building materials remained the same.

Various regional styles in timber-framing existed and it is very hard to see why one province would favour a particular form and shun methods that were current in other places. The most basic division was between the box-framing technique, which had been used in all the greater houses, and the cruck-framing method used only in some of the earlier of the largish medieval halls, in barns and in cottages. A number of cruck-framed cottages and small farmsteads can still be seen in the Midlands, north and west of England, although this system must have been very common in the construction of peasant hovels and small halls. It involved the use of 'A'-shaped frames to form the gables and bay divisions of a dwelling or barn, with two great curving blades of oak being linked at their upper tips to

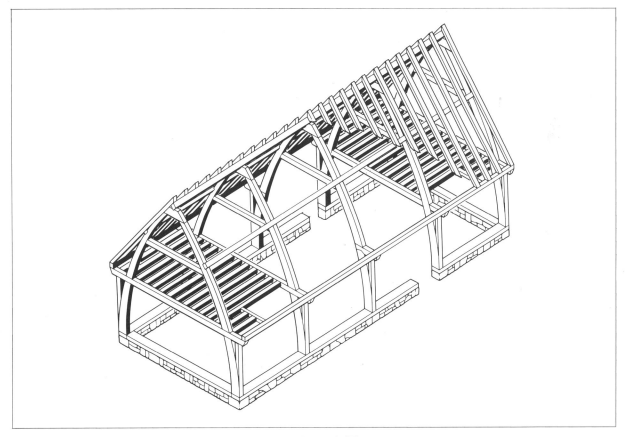

A cruck-built open-hall house

provide the basic elements in the frame. Although a cruck-framed building could be lengthened at will, its width was limited by the size of the cruck-making timbers available and so the method could not be employed in the building of larger dwellings. Thousands of little cruck-framed cottages must have been swept away as the Great Rebuilding rolled northwards and westwards.

Box-framing came in many forms, but essentially it involved the construction of a robust timber box which would support the roof and carry the walling materials used in the panels which filled the gaps between the framing timbers. By a careful study of the particular joints employed and the positioning of the vertical 'studs' and arching 'braces' it is possible to date medieval timber-framed buildings. In very general terms, the older dwellings tended to employ 'larger framing', with spacious panels of wattle and daub spanning the spaces between the very massive framing timbers. As the years rolled by, the use of lighter but more numerous timbers in 'small framing' gave rise to close but more slender framing networks. There were many regional variations, with East Anglians developing a taste for 'close studding', walls composed of rows of closely-spaced vertical timbers which contrasted with the 'square framing' favoured in Wales and the west Midlands, where the daub panels were square rather than attenuated.

The timber-framed cottages which were erected in the seventeenth, eighteenth and nineteenth centuries borrowed framing styles from the hovels which they replaced and from the grander medieval buildings of their localities. By the eighteenth century, timber-framing had become distinctly unfashionable for the homes of the wealthier classes, although in medieval times a dwelling framed in massive, costly timbers was a considerable mark of status. While the owners of the great houses tended to mask their venerable residences in coats of plaster, the timber frames of the new cottages tended to be plastered-over because of the cheap and insubstantial nature of the framing timbers. It is one of the ironies of fashion that proud cottage buyers are now exposing examples of timber-framing which were originally thought best hidden from the eyes of neighbours. Some of the seventeenth- and eighteenth-century timber-framed cottages employed the crude 'mud and stud' or 'clam, staff and daub'

A golden combination of thatch and Northamptonshire stone in this cottage at Pilton. Stone cottages are usually very difficult to date, but the design of the original chimneys (those in the gables) suggest that the cottage was built in the years around 1700.

*A delightful cruck-framed cottage with a typical 'pie-crust' Wessex roof at Ibsley in
Hampshire. The curving cruck blades can be seen forming the framework in the gable
end of the dwelling.*

building method, with the bases of the framing studs
and posts being set in earth, while the tops of the
timbers were joined to a beam or 'wall plate' and the
intervening spaces were filled with vertical staves
daubed with mud. In most cases the cottages used the
lightest and cheapest timbers available – they tended
to be built by landowners as accommodation for their
tenants and labourers and there was no great tradition
of generosity to these classes. As the old vernacular
tradition of timber-framing withered and died in the
course of the nineteenth century, cheap imported
softwoods began to supplant the traditional oak, and
cost-cutting building methods using lath and plaster
and weatherboarding were explored. And so, with very
few exceptions, the timber-framed cottages were in
every way the poor cousins of the solid oak homesteads
of the medieval era.

In some places, mud was a favoured alternative to
timber or stone. Few would boast of living in a mud
house, yet the cottages of Devon cob, Buckinghamshire

'wichert' or Essex clay lump can be sturdy, cosy and
attractive. Mud was the cheapest of all building
materials and was employed from ancient times until
well into the nineteenth century. Different mud and
clay recipes were used in different regions, either as a
daub applied to wattle and staves in the timber-framed
buildings or for the construction of entire walls.
Crushed chalk was incorporated in the wichert brew,
while a strengthening fibrous content in the form of
chopped straw or cow hair was usually added. Then
the clay mixture could be built up in thick layers, as
with cob, or shaped and dried to form building blocks
which were mortared with mud, as with the clay lump
or clay bat of the eastern counties. Thick-walled cob
dwellings are very well-insulated against the extremes
of climate, but all clay walls need a well-maintained
skim of limewash or rendering to guard against rain
and abrasions.

Brick is just a superior form of mud. There are plenty
of nineteenth-century and earlier cottages that are

built of unfired but sun-baked mud bricks. Furnace-fired bricks were used in Roman times and the apparently lost craft of brick-making was reintroduced to a few of the more prestigious building sites in the fourteenth century. In the sixteenth century, the mansions and mock-castles of brick were at least as symbolic of status as those of sawn stone and gradually – particularly in regions where timber was costly and the local stone was poor – bricks filtered down the social hierarchy. In the older building they could be used as 'brick noggin' to replace the daub panels of timber-framed dwellings and by the eighteenth century they began to appear in cottage architecture.

A rough-and-ready guide to the age of a brick cottage can be gained from a glance at the 'bonding' system adopted by the bricklayer. The oldest of the brick-built vernacular buildings often display rich russet bricks of irregular sizes that are bedded in the generous dollops of mortar that were needed to pack the gaps in uneven work. Other more sophisticated builders favoured the English style of bonding, with alternating courses of end-on 'headers' and 'stretchers' which were laid lengthways. In the eighteenth century, the Flemish bond was used in the greater houses and copied in the cottages, with each row of

bricks consisting of alternate headers and stretchers. During and after the nineteenth century, stretcher bond which consists entirely of stretchers became almost universal.

As well as being used to mask and protect a wall of lath and plaster, wattle and daub or clay, tiles could also provide an attractive or a deceptive finish. Tile hanging gives many a cottage in Kent and Sussex its warm russet aura and scaly-textured finish. In a few cases the tiles envelop a late-medieval building, but many tile-hung dwellings are built of the light, cost-cutting timber-framing that was favoured in the decades around 1800. Rather more pretentious was the mathematical tiling, which was also most frequently adopted in the south-east. These tiles simulate brickwork but escaped the taxes that were levied on brick. In the Georgian era, when timber-framing was considered gauche and backwoodsy, mathematical tiles could create the illusion of the more fashionable brick construction, although only a minority of cottagers could afford to entertain such fads. Another form of masking a cheap and lightweight structure which was favoured in the late-eighteenth and early-nineteenth century employed a weatherboarding of overlapping horizontal planks. This form of construction,

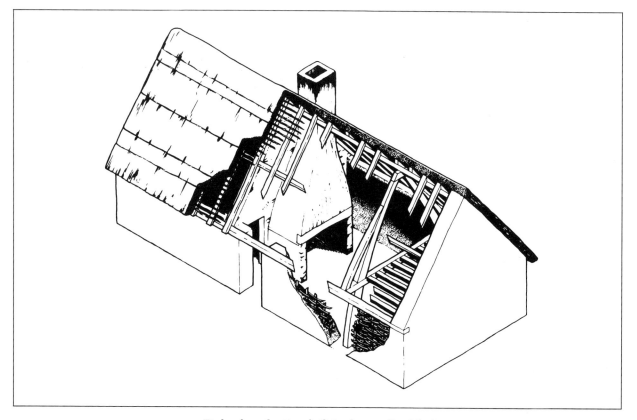

Timber-framed cottage built in clam, staff and daub

which was very popular in Essex and the south-east, originally employed boards of oak or elm which were pegged to a timber frame, although most weather-boarded dwellings seen today are younger buildings clad in cheaper planks of imported softwood which were pitched and nailed to studs and laths.

In medieval times and for many years thereafter, the roofs of cottages were almost invariably thatched using locally grown straw, reeds or, in the wilder moorland places, heather. Wheatstraw was the favoured material in the warmer, drier areas where this crop could flourish, although oatstraw was often used in the damper, wetter localities, and in fenland places where reeds were available they were often favoured for the making of darker, more durable roofs. In the Middle Ages, when peasant dwellings were flimsy and short-lived, it did not greatly matter that the life of a thatched roof ranged between fifteen and thirty years. But over the centuries the rising cost of thatching and the fall from use of the flexible long-strawed wheat in favour of less suitable short-strawed forms encouraged many cottage landlords and inmates to replace a roof of thatch with more durable materials. Hand-made plain tiles of fired clay were adopted in many late-medieval houses, and gradually, as with bricks and stone, the fashion filtered down the social scale. Plain tiles became particularly popular in the south-eastern counties, where they sometimes replaced an older tradition of roofing in tile-like shingles of oak.

Although pantiles were imported from the Low Countries in the twelfth century, it was really only in the eighteenth and nineteenth centuries that they became a popular material in cottage building. Their chinky, wavy textures and rosy hues always create an attractive and tolerably waterproof effect, yet pantiles remained strangely localized around the areas where they had arrived in Britain in medieval times: in East Anglia, Lincolnshire, Nottinghamshire, eastern Yorkshire and Durham. The trade was still strong in the seventeenth century and the pantile distributions reflect how the tiles were shipped up-river from the coastal trading ports. Later, domestic pantile industries developed in places like Barton on Humber and the western pantile outpost at Bridgwater, which had formerly imported the wares.

Many a thatched cottage was re-roofed in plain tiles or pantiles or, following the nineteenth-century railway revolution, less sympathetically, in Welsh slate. Sometimes the pitch and details of a roof can tell the story. Pantiles can give effective drainage on a roof pitch of only 30° to 40°, although both thatch and plain tiles required a steeper water-shedding pitch of around 55°. Where pantiles or slates are seen on steeply-pitched roofs, they are very likely to have replaced a roof of thatch. In areas like the Cotswolds and Yorkshire Dales there was a drift away from thatch in favour of slabby local stones. The oolitic limestone belt yielded excellent false slates which were quarried at Collyweston in Northamptonshire and Stonesfield in Oxfordshire. Swithland slates, which were quarried in the Charnwood forest, dignified many Leicestershire cottage roofs; resources of sandstone flags provided the 'thack stones' used to roof many old cottages and farmsteads in the Dales; false slates were used for roofing in the Lake District, while important slate industries developed in Cornwall and Wales. While the true slates, like those quarried at Delabole in Cornwall or around Blaenau Ffestiniog, could be split into wafer-like sheets and were exported far and wide, roofing stones like the Pennines thack stones and the Swithland slates were heavy and roofs were built with a minimal pitch of around 30° in order to reduce the burden on the rafters.

The vernacular building tradition, with its emphasis on local materials, craftsmanship and time-honoured customs, survived longest in the construction of farm buildings and cottage homes. It gradually died in the course of the nineteenth century when the railways dispersed the wares of the western slate quarries and the mass-produced products of the great new brick-works far and wide, while the drive to produce working class housing rapidly, cheaply and in unprecedented quantities resulted in the submergence of traditional fancies by standardized designs.

Plenty of older cottages still survive, displaying the local materials which endow them with both a pretty face and a sense of place. But all our talk of such materials should not lead one to forget that the cottage was much more than a tasteful confection of sticks, stones and clay. Above all, it was and is a home. All the older cottages were the abodes of impoverished peasants or industrial workers and their layouts mirrored the hardships, day-to-day needs and lifestyles of the families. Most cottages of any antiquity have been partly disembowelled, extended, prettified or effectively vandalized, remodelled again and repartitioned in order to accord with the changing circumstances and expectations of the family within. Every proud cottage owner or inquisitive traveller will want to know the age of a particular specimen. The question can be very difficult, for cottages lacked the tell-tale decorative motifs used in the greater houses, while hardly any 'authentic' examples which have escaped all later changes survive. Windows can sometimes provide the more obvious clues, with the progressive cheapening of glass during the post-medieval centuries being com-

An attractive roof in pantiles at Orford in Suffolk. Note the extension covered by the catslide roof.

bined with technical changes which allowed larger and larger panes to be manufactured, causing a shift from tiny openings with mullions of stone or timber to square-paned casements and then to large sash windows. However, since most of the older cottages have been 'refenestrated' on at least one occasion it can be very difficult to recognize the original form of the windows.

Many cottages are attractive when seen from a distance, yet the majority of the more venerable buildings have their integrity marred by recent trappings like aluminium window frames, glazed front doors, mock Georgian windows, sham shutters or even applied synthetic stonework. But this is not to say that the most interesting cottages are those which endure in the most authentic and original form. One can learn a

great deal about working class social history by mentally dismantling a cottage, so to discover how succeeding families have adapted the home according to the circumstances of their day. The clues survive most changes, so that an external chimney which is built on to a gable can mark the acquisition of a fireplace, while soot-blackened rafters in the attic can recall distant times when the focus of domestic life was an unpartitioned hall that was open to the rafters and heated by a hearth whose fumes leaked skywards through a simple smoke hole.

Although each region spawned its own distinctive version of vernacular architecture, most cottages were built to one of a few fairly standard layouts. Each one was developed to serve the needs of a particular lifestyle and the layouts would be adapted as the conditions of

Before the introduction of chimneys smoke escaped from the open hearth via a smokehole which was commonly placed at the top of the gable, as seen in this reconstructed farmhouse at the Weald and Downland Museum at Singleton in Sussex.

cottage life changed. The days of the isolated earth privy, of home brewing in the buttery and of the weekly bath by the fireside have almost disappeared and the hardships of old cottage life and the inconveniences of a once well-adjusted layout could not be tolerated by the cottagers of today.

The most common, almost ubiquitous small homestead layout of the Middle Ages was that of the long-house. Long-houses were about the size of an old-fashioned bus; long, low and narrow and built of mud, turf or crude timber-framing, although sometimes the timbers rested on a rubble base and the low walls were occasionally entirely of rubble. The long-house was essentially a one-roomed dwelling, with all the scenes of domestic life being enacted in the drab living room which was open to the rafters and heated by an open hearth. Dividing the dwelling crossways

was a crude partition which segregated the family from the adjacent byre which might house a couple of oxen. Medieval peasant long-houses were cramped, rickety buildings and they are only encountered at excavation sites or as ruins on the deserted moors. However, several more durable long-house derivatives do endure as cottages and small farmsteads. The most evocative are the deceptively 'primitive' black houses of the Western Isles. A few are still occupied, while many date only from the eighteenth century. They display the characteristic long-house layout, but with additional barns and byres often added to the long sides of the dwellings. Black houses lack sharp corners and gables and so required no dressed stones for quoins and are streamlined to withstand the Atlantic gales. Their double stone walls are packed with an insulating layer of earth and their roofs, of heather thatch which is held

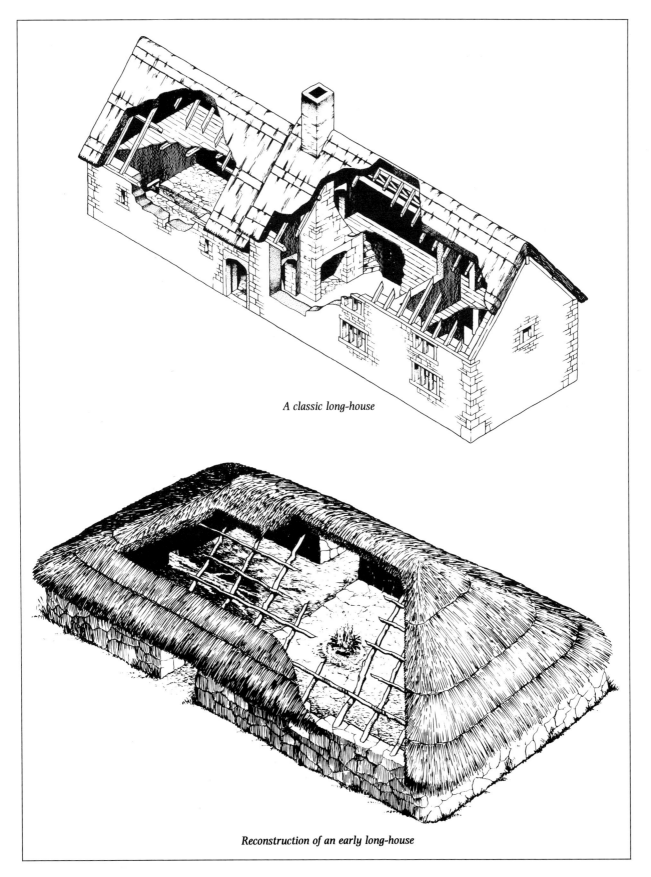

A classic long-house

Reconstruction of an early long-house

A small house in the long-house tradition at Little Langdale in Cumbria.

down by stone-weighted ropes, do not project as eaves but drain into the earthen packing.

In south-western England and some other upland localities, improved long-houses were built at the end of the Middle Ages. They were larger and more durable than their predecessors, being sometimes walled in stone, equipped with attics or sleeping lofts and with proper chimneys and fireplaces set in the cross-wall which now provided a more substantial segregation of the human and animal kingdoms. Such dwellings are often seen as ruins in Cornwall, Dartmoor and the Welsh uplands, while in the Dales, where they were known as 'coits', they sometimes remain in service as barns adjoining a later farmstead. Also in the north of England one may see the superior developments of long-houses which are known as 'laithe-houses'. Their appearance, around the start of the eighteenth century, signified rises in peasant prosperity which often resulted from the growing urban market for farm produce coupled with income from cottage textile industries. Laithe-houses were usually of two storeys,

with the dwelling house at the upslope end of the building and the byre with a hay loft above forming the laithe or barn component. Being more easily adaptable to the gradually rising expectations of domestic life, many laithe-houses remain in occupation.

An older variation on the long-house theme – and again one that was associated more with small farmsteads than with the cottage proper – was the 'cross passage' layout. This design, still prevalent in the seventeenth century, had a cross passage running through the dwelling from the front door to back door. To one side of the cross passage was the partitioning wall which contained the fireplace of the living room-cum-kitchen which sometimes had a more private sitting room or bedroom beyond it. To the other side of the passage there might be a byre – in which case the dwelling was a superior long-house – or else a service room. Many cross passage dwellings survive, although generally in a much modified form. An upper storey could be gained by inserting a ceiling over the open ground floor rooms and raising the roof, and two-

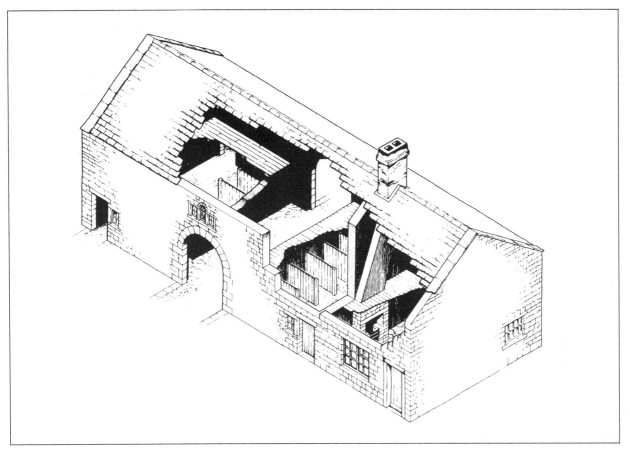

A laithe-house

storey cross passage houses were being built until the start of the Victorian era.

Cross passage houses can generally be recognized by the position of the main chimney stack, which is offset, a little to one side of the front door. Where the door and chimney are in line, the dwelling is likely to be of the 'baffle entry' type. In cross passage houses it was impossible for two rooms to be heated by back-to-back fireplaces because of the intervening passage. Entering a baffle entry house one finds not a through passage, but a small hall. Directly ahead is the baffle, a short wall which masks the two back-to-back fireplaces, while to one side is the door of a living room-cum-kitchen and to the other, the door of the parlour. Such houses were often built as two-storey dwellings, while a third room was frequently reached via the living room or the parlour.

Ideas developed in the greater houses were often adopted later in the lesser dwellings. In the seventeenth century, the double-depth or 'double-pile' layout was used in the design of more prestigious homes. Not only did the resultant boxy shape facilitate the fashionable quest for external symmetry but it also created houses that were more than one room in depth, eliminating the labyrinths of passages and access ways needed to negotiate a path amongst the long and winding ranges of end-to-end rooms. In the nineteenth century, thousands of smaller double-pile dwellings were built as new farmsteads, private dwellings and as superior accommodation for the more privileged farm

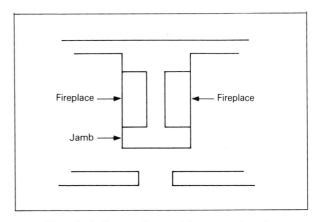

Plan of a baffle entry house with entry against the fireplace jambs

A baffle entry house showing the alignment between front door and chimney. Baffle entry designs seem to have appeared at the end of the Middle Ages and here the rather symmetrical elevation suggests a late-seventeenth or eighteenth century date, although the gabled cross-wing appears to be older. The farmstead overlooks the green at Wicken in Cambridgeshire.

employees. The front door normally leads into a living room, with the cosier parlour to one side while a kitchen and dairy formed the second component in the double-depth plan. The chimneys set above the gables

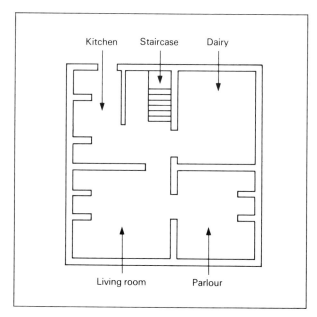

Plan of a double-pile house with four rooms on each floor

of such dwellings reflect the positions of fireplaces built in the end walls of the living room, parlour and kitchen.

Earlier attempts to obtain some of the advantages of the double-pile house, mainly dating from the eighteenth century, can be seen in the form of cottages and small farmsteads which have a long 'catslide' roof at the back, covering the projecting 'outshut' which served as the kitchen and dairy. Not all catslides are of this relatively recent date, for a few cover farmsteads which originated as medieval aisled halls, a very common farm building form in the Middle Ages, with the dwelling consisting of an open hall with side aisles that were defined by the colonnades of vertical posts which supported the roof.

Changing social conditions greatly influenced cottage building. The old feudal economy was gradually crumbling at the end of the Middle Ages and landlords depended increasingly upon hired labour rather than on feudal dues and services. At first single labourers tended to be housed in the attics and garrets of the larger farmsteads. But useful employees would marry, while as the bigger farmers became richer, more powerful and more prey to self-esteem, they were less ready to share their homes with hirelings. Large numbers of purpose-built estate and farm workers'

A superb farmstead at Fearby near Masham in Yorkshire which just predates the arrival of symmetrical double-depth houses in the area. Note how the house is just one room in depth and how the fabric shows signs of the blocking and repositioning of windows and doors.

cottages resulted. Various simple designs were employed, but the 'single fronted' form became by far the commonest. The front door, which was placed to one side of the elevation, opened directly into the living room and behind the living room was a staircase and a tiny scullery. The earlier of these cottages tended to be cramped and low, with only a ladder leading to the dormer-lit sleeping loft above the single groundfloor room. Later versions of the design were usually built as two-storey units. Single frontage cottages could be built singly, but they were commonly erected in symmetrical or 'reflected' pairs or in short terraced rows. Further enlargements and slight adjustments to the layout produced the classic 'two-up-and-two-down' terraced dwellings built in hundreds of thousands in Victorian and Edwardian times.

But not all the farm cottages of the eighteenth and nineteenth centuries were purpose-built. Particularly

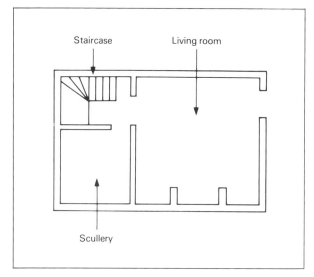

Typical single fronted cottage plan

A 'middleclass' dwelling beside the green at Nun Monkton in Yorkshire, a village which was rebuilt in brick and pantiles and incorporated the fashionable double-depth and symmetrical façade tendencies.

A Wealden house, now serving as a pub at Barrington in Cambridgeshire; note that in this design only the end bays are jettied. Wealden houses are always too grand to be considered as cottages, although they could easily be partitioned to form three humbler dwellings. Wealden houses are amongst the most delightful developments of the box-framing tradition.

after the Parliamentary Enclosure of the village open fields, when many of the more favoured and prosperous farmers migrated to stolid double-pile farmsteads erected at the hearts of their new agricultural empires, the old, village-based farmsteads were often repartitioned to provide accommodation for employees and the lesser lights of village society. Because the medieval farmsteads had tended to consist of distinct bays and ranges, a partitioning into several cramped dwelling units was easily accomplished so that the medieval

house components then became cottages.

A form of farmstead that was particularly common in the south and east of England was the 'Wealden house' (see also Chapter 8), which had an open hall as its central component with token wings at either end, with service rooms in one bay and private chambers in the other. Unlike the open central bay, the wings were of two storeys, with the upper storeys being 'jettied' or slightly projecting. By inserting a ceiling into the central bay and slotting front doors into each wing, a

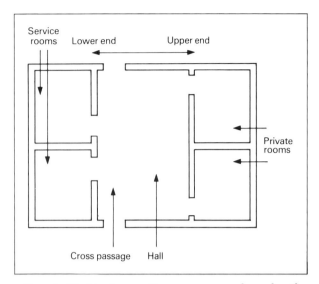

Plan of a Wealdon house with cross passage and open hearth

Wealden house could thus become three adjoining cottages. Similarly, the late-medieval 'H-plan' houses, which had a central open hall with projecting cross-wings at either end, could be converted with equal ease. Many a village street of terraced brick cottages has the repartitioned halls and cross-wings of medieval timber-framed farmsteads lurking unseen behind the brickwork façades.

No dash around the diverse realm of the cottage would be complete without a mention of that amiable eccentric of the British countryside, the cottage ornée. These dwellings represent the romantic, whimsical side of the landlord's nature and most are of the nineteenth century. Complete villages of these fairytale dwellings could be built as a by-product of the emparking and destruction of an original village, when the master decided that a landscaped confection of mock-Tudor homesteads would both house his workers and titivate the approach to his park. Other cottages, like the terraced sham-Elizabethan stone dwellings at Ripley near Ripon, result from a benevolent rebuilding of a run-down village. One of the best-known and most bizarre assemblages of cottages ornées can be seen at Blaise Hamlet near Bristol, a deliciously over-the-top manifestation of the Picturesque ideal built by the banker J. S. Harford and his architects in 1810. A few of the later and larger cottages ornées were built, not in large numbers by improving, eccentric or self-indulgent landowners, but singly, by middle-class romantics who had fallen for the whimsy but not the hardship of rustic life. Stage-set villages composed of fanciful cottages are quite numerous and they include places like Old Warden in Bedfordshire, Somerleyton and Easton in Suffolk, Radwinter in Essex, Harlaxton in Lincolnshire, Canford Magna in Dorset, Freefolk on the Isle of Wight, Eastnor in Herefordshire, Llandygai in Gwynedd, Dunmore near Stirling; and in Ireland, Adare in Co. Limerick and Tyrells Pass in Co. Westmeath. Demonstrating that romance has not entirely died in the twentieth century is Portmeirion near Porthmadog, a voluptuous wedding cake of a resort which masquerades as an Italian fishing village and was founded by Clough Williams-Ellis in the 1920s.

— 6 —

EXPLORING VILLAGES

The attractive unplanned village of Middlesmoor.

The Celtic lands entice the visitor with pageants of mountain and moor, loch or lough and the English uplands beckon with the sweeping vistas of the fells. But the charms of the English and Welsh lowlands are of a softer, more mellow and intimate kind. Here the rambler expects a detailed patchwork of fields, punctuated with patches of woodland, engraved with networks of winding lanes and with villages forming frequent islands of interest within the green mosaic. There are scores of books which describe the pretty villages and where some of them can be found, so here we attempt instead to explain the nature of villages, and how the reader may begin to understand them.

The village is rather like an ageing starlet. The long-cultivated veneer of cuteness has been described so many times. But underneath the powder and the paint and behind the myths and chit-chat peddled by the hacks there is a fascinating personality waiting to be explored, with true stories of puzzling origins, hard times and traumatic changes.

The origins of the village slip backwards into the mists of time – though not quite as deeply as we are often told. In prehistoric times, village life was a minority taste in countrysides where hamlets and scattered farmsteads were usually much more common. In some places which are too rugged and uninviting to allow the ploughing which would scour away the evidence and where village dwellings were built of durable stone rubble, the relics of really ancient settlements sometimes survive. Most famous is the late-Neolithic hut cluster of Skara Brae on Orkney, a truly remarkable survival, but there are other absorbing early village sites like the Bronze Age settlements of Riders Rings and Grimspound on Dartmoor and Rough Tor in Cornwall, and the Iron Age and Romano-British villages of Chysauster and Carn Euny in Cornwall and Din Lligwy on Anglesey. But these places were not villages as we imagine villages to be. They were not enduring settlements and could have lives which ranged from a few years or decades to a few centuries. Then, for reasons which we often do not altogether understand, the dwellings would be abandoned and the community would found another settlement.

Neither did these places have the sorts of structure or layout that we associate with villages. Usually they consisted as a rather formless scatter of dwellings and paddocks, sometimes set within a protective ditch or stockade, but without the distinct high streets, greens, churchyard and other components which we associate with living villages.

The tradition of impermanent, less frequent and somewhat formless villages persisted during much of the Dark Ages, and it was perhaps only around the reign of King Alfred the Great, or even a little later, that the age-old habits of rural settlement began to change. Gradually villages appeared which were destined to endure – or to endure as long as they escaped the fatal

A ruined dwelling at the Bronze Age village site beneath Rough Tor in Cornwall.

A ruined circular stone house at the Romano-British settlement at Din Lligwy on Anglesey showing the massive slabs of ancient limestone used in the construction of the walls and doorsteps.

accidents which were part and parcel of medieval village life. Domesday Book was compiled in 1086, two decades after the Norman Conquest, and most of the settlements which it mentions still exist as villages today. (Although it is certain that by no means all the places mentioned in Domesday Book were distinct villages; frequently up to half a dozen small villages and hamlets seem to have been condensed into a single 'village' entry.) New villages were still being created during the early-medieval centuries and we still do not know exactly why it was that, in late-Saxon times, the England of hamlets, farmsteads and fragile, shifting little villages gave birth to village England. Perhaps the change was caused by agricultural reorganization and the adoption of the open field farming described in Chapter 1, while the new field churches which were multiplying at this time could have served as magnets and anchors for settlement.

Thousands of villages in England have Saxon names and some have churches which are partly Saxon. But the villages which existed here on the eve of the Norman Conquest cannot have looked remotely like the villages which are flourishing today. Much is still to be learned about the layout and appearance of these youthful settlements, and only more archaeological excavations can provide the answers. We must imagine most of them as small settlements of thatched shacks, which nestled amongst their barns and other outbuildings in little paddocks which were sometimes loosely clustered around small, mainly timber-built churches. Most parishes would contain more than one small village, as well as a handful of hamlets, many of which were destined to perish or to become single farmsteads, for often it seems that one village would grow and suck-in settlement from the rest of the parish or manor. We do not know whether village greens were common at this time, but we do know of plenty of cases where greens were only provided during a later reorganization of an old village.

Villages did not become ubiquitous in Britain, and

even in England there were several counties where the village did not gain supremacy over the older tradition of hamlets and farmsteads. Settlements with village-sized populations could only be supported in areas which were quite generously endowed with agricultural riches, and in the Celtic lands and the English uplands the resources of good ploughland, meadow and pasture were too thinly-spread to sustain such communities. Most Scottish, Welsh and Irish villages, as well as many in the English uplands, are relatively youthful. Many are artificial feudal creations or the products of eighteenth- and nineteenth-century industrialization and estate management policy.

Anyone who takes a lead from the glossy guide books and sees the village as a timeless, ageless place can never begin to understand its true nature, for the village was vibrant, versatile and vulnerable. In the course of the Middle Ages villages turned and turned about. They could shed old streets, move, merge, shrink, collapse or gain planned additions, greens and markets. Often the traces of old layouts and alignments would be preserved within the fabric of the plan, while by the close of the Middle Ages the pace of change had slowed down, so that most villages preserve their late-medieval patterns even though they have often expanded outwards as a result of modern development around their margins. Most visitors are drawn to villages – or rather, to the prettier and more celebrated villages – because they are genuinely charming places which seem to offer contrast to and relief from the hectic, rootless modernity of the urban world. The visual and emotional charms of such villages are obvious and need no introduction, but any village visit can become far more enjoyable when one begins to explore the layout and history of the village as it is subtly recorded in the enduring landscape. Every village contains such clues, and every one has its own story, whilst often the less pretty can be one of the most interesting.

Myth and mystery converge at the village green. Myth claims that the dwellings in Saxon villages were arranged in a loop around the green so as to create a safe haven where the beasts could pass the night, secure from wolves and robbers. There is not an ounce of evidence to support the claim, and greens are not entirely understood. Often they seem to have been provided as general-purpose areas of common land, which could be venues for trading, pockets of grazing for the villagers' geese, places where drovers could pause, and as venues for local trading and for occasional games and festivities. Frequently a green where markets could be held was a later addition to a village layout, and in many places old greens have been partly or wholly engulfed by encroaching buildings. A popular and as yet largely unspoilt Cotswold village is Lower Slaughter, and here the honey-coloured seventeenth- and eighteenth-century stone cottages represent an encroachment on a former green. The dwellings, with their zig-zag profile of gables and dormers which overlook the village stream, form one of the finest compositions of village scenery, though few visitors will realize that they represent a major transformation of the old layout. Another much-visited and much-photographed village is Okeford Fitzpaine in Dorset, and here the Saxon village which huddled around the church gained a large green in medieval times and the delightful old timber-framed dwellings flanking the lane to the church are a later encroachment on this green.

While buildings have often advanced across greens, there are numerous other villages where houses were demolished to create a space for market trading, though sometimes a suitable piece of ground was available and the local lord did not have to resort to such drastic action in order to enjoy the fruits of market tolls. The situation at Culworth, as deciphered by the archaeologist Christopher Taylor, is particularly interesting. After the Norman Conquest there were two villages here: Culworth and Brime. In 1264, during a great period of market creation, the local lord bought the right to hold a market and he constructed his green or market square in the space between the two settlements. Shops and dwellings mushroomed around the periphery of this commercial area, which had now become the heart of the merged settlement and the bridge between its earlier components.

Hundreds of greens appeared as the purpose-built venues for little medieval markets, but there are others which have less obvious origins. A few, like the one at Titchmarsh in Northamptonshire, seem to have been carved from earlier gardens. The green at Swavesey in Cambridgeshire was in fact a dock until the nineteenth century, when the arrival of the railway killed off the traditional Fenland river-borne commerce. Then the decayed dock shrank to a muddy pool and a deceptive 'green' marks its place. But the deception does not end here, for the apparently uninteresting car park which links the 'green' to the village high street now covers the genuine medieval market place of Swavesey. There are other Fenland greens with interesting histories. At the Fen-edge village of Reach the situation is more complicated. Here there were originally two villages, East Reach and West Reach, sitting beside a Roman waterway or 'lode', which remained a useful little corridor for commerce right through the Middle Ages and on until the railway era. The lode terminated at the

The pond and green at Wicken in Cambridgeshire.

massive late-Roman or early-Saxon earthern frontier-work of Devil's Dyke. When a charter granting the right to hold a fair was won in the twelfth century, a fair green was created by levelling the end of this great earthwork. Now the fair and the river trading are gone, grass has covered the 'hythe' or wharf at the lode end of the green and the two villages merged long ago, yet the features of village history still linger in the landscape. At Wicken (beside the famous Fenland nature reserve), the village layout is different again. Here the green and the pond are no more than they appear to be, but two separate lodes connected different ends of the village to the network of Fenland waterways.

In any exploration of countryside history one can never overlook the might and influence of the nobles and landlords who were, and are still, the masters of the countryside. Their most obvious impact on village landscapes can be seen in the form of nearby castles, mansions and manor houses, but their control of the village scene often went far deeper. Although the signs can often be very clear-cut and obvious once one starts to look for them, the fact that so many villages are planned creations is usually overlooked by visitors – probably because the popular books present the village as an age-old and informal jumble of pretty cottages. Planned villages could be created in several different

Okeford Fitzpaine in Dorset, where few visitors will realise that the attractive dwellings represent an encroachment on a former green.

ways. They could appear when a feudal lord provided new settlements as abodes for the tenants and drudges who populated his agricultural estate. Old settlement layouts could be reshaped under the commercial stimulus of a newly-won market or fair charter, while in later times villages were often built or enlarged to accommodate mine or mill workers at a developing industrial site. Also it is clear that in the course of the Middle Ages both planned and unplanned villages often acquired planned extensions in the form of disciplined rows of cottages flanking one or other of the through-roads, reflecting local rises in population and agricultural prosperity.

Medieval village planning can announce itself in several ways. In the larger villages and those which are really failed market towns, a 'grid-iron' layout of streets which meet at right angled junctions and neat rectangular or triangular market greens often tell of planned development. New Buckenham, Castle Acre and Castle Rising in Norfolk are all neat settlements which preserve the forms chosen by their feudal masters, while New Winchelsea in Sussex is a declined medieval 'New Town' with a precisely set-out grid-iron plan. In smaller villages, particularly those of the type so common in the north-eastern lowlands of England, the peasant dwellings were often set one either side of a straight through-road which became the village high street. Often the long plots of land or 'tofts' which ran back from the dwellings were all of the same size, long ribbons of green could run between the lines of houses and the high street, while back lanes running across the ends of the tofts can neatly tie up the village package. Appleton-le-Moors near Pickering preserves its planned medieval layout as well as any of the villages of north-eastern England, but there are scores of other examples.

Precise planning of a different kind is the hallmark of most villages in the north-east of Scotland. Here, the reorganization of the aristocratic estates (described in the chapter on farms) which followed the English victory at Culloden resulted in the obliteration of hundreds of the squalid and rambling little 'fermtouns' where the peasant tenants lived, the eviction of many families and the resettling of others on improved farm holdings and in new villages. An industrial as well as an agricultural role was often intended for the new villages, with linen and fishing as the most popular choices. The new villages mushroomed in the late-eighteenth and early-nineteenth centuries and they embodied the contemporary fashions for the sorts of geometrical layout which were seen at the time to represent the triumph of the rational will over the disorder of the natural world. Tomintoul, the loftiest village in the Scottish Highlands, is the most frequently visited of these settlements. It dates from around 1776, when the Duke of Gordon advertised plots in a new village which would be furnished with a lint mill, a public house and the use of roofing stones from a nearby slate quarry. Within twenty years there were thirty-seven families established here, whose members, according to the local minister, divided their time between dancing, spinning, making whisky and drinking it. During the nineteenth century Tomintoul

gained Catholic and Presbyterian churches, though hitherto worshippers in the new village were obliged to use meeting houses and worship in an old kirk more than three miles away. Tomintoul has a very orderly layout, with the straight, house-flanked through-road forming a spine, while the dwellings and hotel in the heart of the village are set around a neat rectangular green. Today Tomintoul is spick and span for the tourist trade, although when Queen Victoria saw it in 1860 she was not amused, describing it as a tumble-down and poverty-stricken place, 'a long street with three inns and miserable dirty-looking houses and people and a sad look of wretchedness about it'.

Tomintoul is not the only village that has changed its superficial appearance. Industrialization spawned scores of purpose-built villages and, when we picture the sort of village inherited from the Industrial Revolution, we tend to think of dingy, soot-blackened terrace rows. But industrial planning could also create stylish and remarkably well-appointed settlements like Saltaire near Bingley, while in many villages which have survived the collapse of the industry which gave them birth, the original function can scarcely be recognized. Nenthead near Alston in Cumbria is a good example. It was created not by archetypal ruthless mine or mill

The planned village of Port Errol in north-east Scotland, one of the many products of the post-Culloden 'Improvements'.

owners, but by the London Lead Company, which was dominated by Quakers with their strong tradition of benevolence. The company was developing the Ramps-gill lead vein and in 1753 it created a convenient settlement for miners who had previously lived in turf shanties, lodged with local farmers or made the rough walk to work from Alston each day. Demolition and 'restoration' have masked much of the original mining settlement, which consisted of cottages in groups of four that lined a cobbled street and were stone-walled with flagstone roofs. In 1825, following a great expansion of the industry, the village was enlarged and a church, chapel, shop and bath-house were provided. As in many industrial villages, sections of planned development alternated with patches of undisciplined growth, so that the old planned four-cottage groups contrast with the seemingly random cottage scatters in the suburb of Overwater which grew on the other side of the River Nent. The decay of the lead industry, the modernization of many cottages and the conversion of the Miner's Arms pub to become the Nent Head Hotel have removed most of the clues to the real history of the village.

Planning is the key to many a village layout, but one thing which could not be planned with any certainty was the survival of a particular village. We were always taught to regard the village as a symbol of all that is durable and timeless. Consequently, post-war research has produced thousands of surprises. Aerial photography has revealed the sites of countless deserted villages which had long lain unsuspected in the countryside, and the avalanche of discovery still outstrips all attempts to list, categorize and appraise the new information. Old ideas about the durability of villages have been upended, so that the still-flourishing settlements can now be seen as the more robust and fortunate members of a much larger early-medieval flock. How did so many settlements come to perish in the quicksands of history? Researches by historians and archaeologists like M. W. Beresford and John Hurst have shown that there were a fair number of threats to village survival which were current in different places and at different times.

Firstly there were those threats which originated not in human greed and brutality, but in the unpredictable nature of the environment and climatic change. By the fourteenth century our climate was rapidly decaying and conditions became wetter, colder and more stormy. As a result of violent storms quite a number of shoreline villages were inundated by the sea or toppled from their perches on crumbling cliffs, but there were many more settlements which disintegrated more slowly. These tended to be small and youthful villages

The nineteenth-century industrial village of Saltaire near Bingley.

which had been established in the less hospitable agricultural settings as a result of the over-swollen population and encouraging climates of the earlier medieval centuries. Their fragile soils soon became exhausted and the shift towards shorter summers, greater waterlogging, cloudiness and cooler winters ensured that, around the upland margins and down in the poorly-drained clay vales, the weakened villages and hamlets perished in their hundreds.

Far worse was yet to befall, for as village England was becoming aware of the consequences of several decades of climatic deterioration, the Pestilence or Black Death arrived in 1348 and for three centuries the sporadic and unpredictable outbreaks of this terrifying disease tormented the nation. Local folklore usually reckons any deserted village site to be a victim of the Pestilence, yet proven cases of villages that are known to have been completely and permanently extinguished by the plague are quite few. In the first plague years around a third of the population seems to have perished, and while many villages must have been devastated, it seems that most were reoccupied in the years or decades which followed. But scores of communities seem to have initially escaped extinction,

These Tudor sheep clearances left a terrible legacy of eviction, desertion and homelessness, one which is hard for us to imagine, and in the 1480s a priest was able to list fifty-eight villages which had been destroyed, all just within a twelve-mile radius of Warwick.

The dust from these assaults on village England had scarcely settled when a new threat began to loom. It was becoming fashionable for members of the real or aspiring upper classes to live not in castles, but in splendid new mansions which stood isolated within expanses of empty parkland. Between the close of the Middle Ages and the early decades of the nineteenth century hundreds of suitably empty parks were created by the simple expedient of tearing down those villages which were unfortunately located within the designated areas. Sometimes, particularly in the case of the later emparkings, a new purpose-built village was provided just outside the park gates. Most readers will probably have visited several stately homes where an old church is puzzlingly stranded in the deserted parkland and where a neatly-ordered village stands, deferentially, at the gates. In each case, the fashion for emparking explains the scene. Harewood, Holkham, Houghton and Wimpole all tell the same tale.

Deserted village sites are amongst the most fascinating of places. Sometimes the pillaging of building stone and ploughing have obliterated all the obvious traces, so that the sites can only be recognized from the air. In other places, particularly where the stones employed were cheap flints or river cobbles which have not attracted stone-robbers, an isolated church provides an enduring epitaph to the village which once stood by. There are many such churches, particularly in the flint-strewn lands of Norfolk, where hundreds of little villages have perished. Egmere, Pudding Norton and Godwick are particularly attractive sites. There are many other settings where the church has completely vanished but where earthworks have endured in permanent pasture, so that by studying the patterns of bumps and hollows one can recognize the broad trough of the holloway that was once the village high street, the narrower holloways of the side streets and back lanes, the slight banks and ditches which marked property boundaries and the rectangular platforms and depressions which reveal the particular house sites. Frequently these sites are rather inaccessible or barred to ramblers, but one of the best and certainly the most informative of all deserted medieval village sites is Wharram Percy in North Yorkshire, reached from the nearby living village of Wharram le Street.

To enjoy a pretty village one needs just a pair of eyes. But to *understand* a village one needs observant eyes and a notion of the factors like planning, market

yet have been so weakened by the mortality that eventually their villages perished.

While many villages have died of natural causes, more have been the victims of human greed and vanity. A few dozen villages were wiped out in the earlier medieval centuries by Cistercian communities who depopulated their growing monastic empires to create the seclusion from lay folk which their order required. But the greatest onslaught on villages came in the years following the arrival of the Pestilence. As the great mortality made labour scarcer, so peasant tenants and labourers demanded better and better terms from their masters. At the same time, wool from English sheep was commanding very good prices, so that many landlords decided that it was more profitable to raise sheep than to take rents from peasants. From the Yorkshire Wolds to the Cotswolds and from Norfolk to Shropshire communities of villagers were evicted from their ancestral homes, ploughlands were put to pasture and the sheep grazed amongst the ruined dwellings. Small local lords might clear their estates or parts of their lands, but there were also families like the Knightleys and the Spencers which owed their rise to riches to the devastation of long chains of parishes.

The ruins of the medieval church at the deserted village of Egmere in Norfolk.

trading, shifting and shrinkage which helped to mould so many villages. Often settlements can be put in categories like 'shrunken', 'industrial' and 'planned', while there are also the hundreds of 'polyfocal' villages which have grown from the merging of formerly distinct little settlements. At the same time one can never lose sight of the fact that each village has its own particular story, so that the generalizations can only go so far. The best way to discover this is to take a number of villages within a particular locality and explore the story and layout of each. For several weeks the writing of this chapter paused at this point as the merits of different candidate areas were pondered, but then the answer arrived by accident in the course of a drive intended for the collection of photographs of field systems in the Yorkshire Dales. The villages lie on a circuit which the reader could follow, and even if the settlements should disappoint, a wealth of delightful and largely unspoilt scenery can be enjoyed.

This is a trip through the borderlands of village England, for to the east of our itinery in the Pennines foothills and upper Nidderdale there is a landscape of villages, most with histories going back at least to

The church of the deserted village survives in the park at Ickworth in Suffolk; the village itself was emparked at an uncertain date, probably in the seventeenth century.

Norman times, while to the west the high plateaux and narrow dales form environments where villages are small and few and hamlets and farmsteads are favoured. The tour begins at West Tanfield. This is the only place we shall visit which – with its medieval church, historical relics and extravagant prettiness – matches up with the outsider's view of the 'typical' English village, for West Tanfield is the stuff of which popular village guides are made. The great antiquity of human settlement in this area is underlined by the monument of the Thornborough Circles, massive henge earthworks dating back to the Neolithic period, which lie about a mile to the east of the village. West Tanfield was established by the time of Domesday Book, and although the church is in the Perpendicular style of the later Middle Ages, it has masonry of around

1200 from its predecessor in the south doorway and it contains sculpture of a Saxon date. Standing right beside the church is a fifteenth-century fortified gatehouse, all that remains of the castle of the Marmion family. Modern growth has helped to complicate the layout of this still-attractive village, but if we go back to the village as it was mapped around 1770 then things are simpler, and the historic layout seems to consist of a straight street, flanked by houses but with a broad green set neatly between a section of the roadside and the church and river-guarded castle site. So may we perhaps glimpse the traces of medieval planning amongst the less orderly patterns of later growth?

West Tanfield is a village with a double-barrelled name, and such names were almost always given to differentiate between neighbouring villages which had

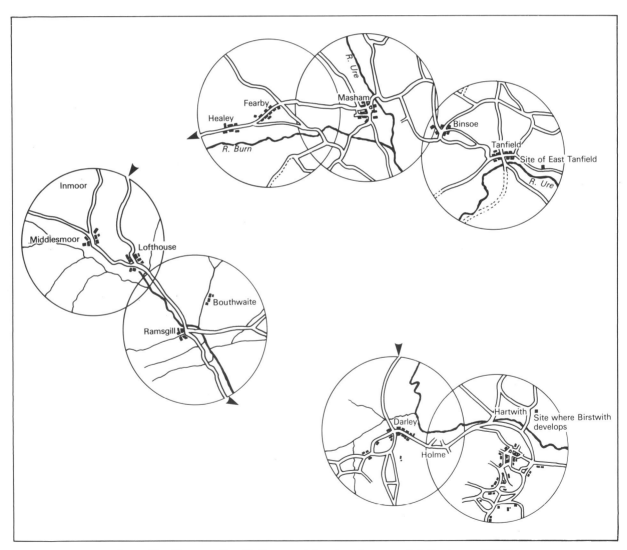

Some of the villages mentioned in the suggested route, as they appear in Jeffrey's map of 1772

a name in common. Churches, sizes and directions were all employed and there are scores of examples like Walpole St Andrew and Walpole St Clement or Great Bradley and Little Bradley. So if we have a West Tanfield, the 'West' would have been superfluous had there not been at least one other Tanfield nearby. North Tanfield is not mentioned in Domesday, and if it ever was a village, it is no more than a farmstead today. East Tanfield is certainly a goner. It was listed in Domesday Book and the name survived for centuries in the Parish of East Tanfield. We know that in 1332 there were fourteen taxable people living in the apparently quite prosperous village. But in 1517 it was reported that 400 acres of land had recently been enclosed and eight dwellings had been destroyed – so East Tanfield seems to have been a victim of the fashionable aristocratic enthusiasm for replacing peasants with sheep. But some sort of shrunken village lingered here long enough to be marked on Saxton's county map of 1577, though later East Tanfield vanished utterly. The site can still be recognized; the lane down West Tanfield to Wath still takes a little kink where it once swung to run down the former village high street, while the local name 'Town Gate', meaning 'Village Street', has survived the passage of centuries.

Villages hereabouts were clearly walloped with abandon. Sleningford lies dead in Sleningford Park, a mile to the south of West Tanfield; Howgrave and Upsland lay a couple of miles to the east, and one could probably find around a dozen deserted medieval vil-lages within a ten mile radius of West Tanfield.

From West Tanfield we take the road which passes through the townlet of Masham, a village which flourished while many nearby were perishing. The reasons for Masham's good fortune derived from a charter obtained by the lord of the manor of Masham-shire in 1250. It was probably regularizing an old customary market and it granted a Friday market and a three-day fair at the Assumption of St Mary. By 1393 Masham had gained two more weekly markets and two more fairs. Trade and prosperity flowed in along the tracks and green roads and Masham served as the outlet for a considerable area of dale, fell and vale. Cattle drovers, pack-horse traders and farmers from the nearby villages were lured from other markets by the attraction of Masham's toll-free trading. In the post-medieval period the townlet retained much of its form; it did not prosper sufficiently to become a fully fledged town, but its market still preserved some vitality, so that even in 1906 a writer described the famous September fair which was the destination of some 70,000 sheep, and dwellings still press around the old market square beside the church.

From Masham we follow one of the medieval market roads which leave the lowland world of old villages and lost villages and cross the bracing expanses of Pott Moor to the different world of rural settlement in upper Nidderdale. Just as we are about to leave the lowland world behind, our road takes us through Fearby, an interesting and challenging village. At first it seems to

The broad ribbon of green at the planned village of Fearby.

be a typical example of one of the planned 'double row' villages which are common in the northern lowlands and generally attributed to a Norman reorganization of the countryside. The through road runs between long ribbons of green, the village dwellings line the edges of the green and long tofts run back from the houses. Yet a closer inspection suggests that things may be more complicated than this and the documents contain some puzzles. In Domesday Book, Fearby or 'Federbi' is a possession of Count Alan; previously there had been two manors there, but both were now being tenanted from the Count by the old landowner, Gospatric. In 1086 nine peasant families are recorded, eight families of villeins and one family of the more lowly bordars. Interestingly, while most villages in this area were still suffering the after-affects of the recent Norman massacres in the north, Fearby had risen in value since the Conquest by some 60 per cent.

To explain the form of this village we are forced to resort to guesswork. Less than a quarter of a mile to the east of Fearby is the tiny hamlet of Fearby Cross, where a few dwellings stand at a five lane intersection where there is the stump of an ancient cross. Perhaps this is the site of unplanned Saxon Fearby? The present village of Fearby seems to consist of two linked planned villages. The western section could represent a 'Y'-shaped settlement, a form of village planning quite common in the north, with a forking road defining the 'Y' and with a small green in the sharp angle. A second planned unit in the form of a typical double-row settlement could have been added to the top of the 'Y', with its eastern end closed by a monastic and manorial group of farmsteads, still represented by Manor Farm, Fearby Grange and Park Manor Farm. This new development would have cut one arm of the 'Y', which can now be picked up a quarter of a mile to the north-east, where it reappears as Sutton Lane. Some of this speculation could be quite wrong, but it does help to show how difficult and deceptive village layouts can be. If it is correct, the complications are quite typical.

As we cross the lofty moorland watershed and enter the deep valley of upper Nidderdale we meet a very different face of village England. Here the villages are small and might be regarded as mere hamlets in the 'big village' country of the Midlands, and they are also relatively late arrivals on the settlement map. We are now well and truly in the Yorkshire Dales and, as in most other upland areas, substantial villages with old churches are somewhat uncommon.

Lower Slaughter in Gloucestershire, where the cottages have advanced across a former green.

The first village to appear as we descend steeply into the dale is Middlesmoor. It has an unusually dramatic setting, perching on a prominent hill spur which juts into the dale like the prow of a battleship. It reminds one of the defensive hilltop villages seen in some continental countries – but such settlements were not adopted in England after the hillfort era of the Iron Age. As we shall see, Middlesmoor has much in common with the other villages of the upper dale, Lofthouse and Ramsgill and the hamlet of Bouthwaite. The origin of its name cannot be traced with certainty, but it may simply mean 'a place in the middle of the moor'. The other names are, as so often, deceptive. They are Old Norse names meaning 'the house with a loft', 'the stream belonging to (someone with a name like) Ram' and 'the cottage (booth) in the meadow or clearing'. Norse settlers descended from Viking raiders had drifted into this dale from the west towards the end of the Saxon era. The names that they and their offspring gave to places still stick, and the valley is full of -thwaites, -gills and -becks. Yet despite the Norse names we can be sure that our villages did not begin as Norse settlements. Like so much of the north, this dale was ravaged by the Conqueror's Norman forces during the terrifying 'Harrying of the North' of 1069–1070. Many if not all the peasants living here were slain, while any survivors may have been winkled out and put to work on the more fertile and suddenly depopulated estates in the Vale of York. Domesday Book describes the area as 'waste'. After the Harrying it probably existed as little more than an empty hunting chase which was part of the Honour of Kirkby Malzeard, a vast estate held in the twelfth century by the de Mowbray family.

Two settlements developed from granges on adjacent monastic estates. Ramsgill is in the foreground while the roofs of the tiny hamlet of Bouthwaite peep over the trees just above the centre of the photograph.

As the dale gradually recovered, the old Norse and Saxon settlement patterns were not recreated, and in the course of the twelfth century the de Mowbrays gradually granted away their estates in upper Nidderdale to the new Cistercian Abbeys, keeping only their hunting rights. At first they favoured Byland, and only at the end of the century did they grant land to Fountains. As a result, the dale then became divided between the estates of these two great and rather distant abbeys.

The monastic estates were managed as commercial farming empires and were divided into a string of farms or 'granges' which were placed under the charge of *conversi* or lay brothers. Rather than being the foundations of Dark Age Norse settlers as their names suggest, our villages here all evolved gradually from these monastic granges. Only in the case of Middlesmoor is there a hint of an older settlement: a late-Saxon cross with an inscription to St Chad was found here, but it could mark an old Benedictine monastic cell or hermitage rather than a larger settlement. As noted in the excellent *History of Nidderdale* compiled by the local history group, the two main monastic granges were sited where the hill track which was shared by the two monasteries descended into the valley, with Ramsgill as the principal grange of Byland and Bouthwaite as the focus for the Fountains estates. Today one can climb the valley slope beside Ramsgill and look over the village and the hamlet – each developed from a monastic grange, yet each standing in a different monastic empire. Here the boundary between the empires was fixed as the 'Mere' (meaning 'boundary') Dike in 1198 after clashes between the respective interests.

We cannot know just when the granges ceased to be farms and became hamlets and villages, but we can be sure that the changes were gradual. The lay brothers were slowly superseded by independent farming families who leased the granges from their monastic owners – a practical and convenient arrangement since these farms were remote from the parent abbeys and separated from them by miles of rough country. Leases were drawn up whereby the lay farmers would tend the abbey stock, maintain the farms and deliver an annual quota of butter, cheese and livestock to the monks, while in return they would enjoy the profits from surplus stock, have use of pockets of arable land and be allowed to pasture some of their own cattle. Gradually too, some of the settlements of farmers and peasants grew, while others remained as farmsteads. At first the growth was too modest to support a church in the upper dale, though several granges had their own chapels. The one at Bouthwaite has disappeared, although a large fragment of the grange chapel of Ramsgill is incorporated into the churchyard wall of the village church of 1842. Around 1300 the market townlet of Pateley Bridge – about five miles from Ramsgill and Bouthwaite and at least seven miles from Middlesmoor – gained a parochial chapel, but outsettlements were in the parish of Kirkby Malzeard, about eight miles from Middlesmoor as the crow flies, and many more via the difficult moorland tracks. But by 1484 Middlesmoor had gained a chapel licensed for baptisms, marriages and burials, and this improvement may betoken the emergence of a village-sized settlement here.

Farming in the flood-prone meadows, steep valley-side pastures and acid, sandy ploughlands can never have been highly productive, and part-time and secondary occupations helped to foster and sustain the growing settlements. Small deposits of coal, ironstone and lead were worked during the monastic era and mining continued, sporadically, after the Dissolution of the Monasteries and until quite modern times. We know that in the nineteenth century around two dozen coal miners formed part of the population of the Lofthouse-Middlesmoor area. A few of them had small farms to buttress their poor earnings, while of the eight farmers recorded at Middlesmoor in 1851, most had other occupations too. One was a blacksmith, one a carrier, one a postman and two kept little inns. In 1900 a few miners from Swaledale moved into Lofthouse to work at the nearby Lolly lead mine.

These then are villages which took shape very slowly, several centuries after the establishment of most villages in the lowlands. In size and layout they contrast with the larger, older and often planned villages of the Vale of York to the east. They are unplanned and have grown in a piecemeal fashion as farmsteads and cottages were built beside the narrow valley-to-moorland tracks or erected on little shelves of dry, level land. Middlesmoor is the epitome of the unplanned village and a truly delightful place to visit; the view down the dale from the elevated churchyard is exceptional. With a little imagination one can still picture the lay brother from Byland standing hereabouts and peering down the dale, wondering what his counterpart from Fountains was up to at Bouthwaite.

In travelling down Nidderdale past the old market townlet of Pateley Bridge one continues for around eleven miles, through seven little villages and several hamlets, before meeting – at Hampsthwaite – a village which approaches the stereotype of the 'typical' English village with its medieval church, green, and nucleated form. Each one of these villages has its own story. Some have again evolved from granges; some are the products of the early water-powered stages of the

Industrial Revolution, and one at least, Darley, seems impossibly complex. The neighbouring villages of Dacre and Dacre Banks are interesting; around 1180 the records show that Fountains Abbey was seeking to move one of its granges and it could be that Dacre Banks marks the original monastic farm and Dacre, its successor. In any event the examples show the unreliability of place-name evidence, for 'Dacre' is probably a venerable, the older cottages still boast archaic flagstone roofs, and most visitors would not believe that just two centuries ago the site was uninhabited. As a grammar school boy this writer was taught that the Norse name and straggly layout made Birstwith an excellent example of a Viking-founded village.

Fishing villages form a distinct and particularly evocative category, although popular mythology and an abundance of contrived Olde Worlde trappings often combine to exaggerate the antiquity of these places.

Old stocks survive on one of the greens at Darley.

Fishing villages form a special category. Few had grown to any great size until after the close of the Middle Ages and most have been obliged to explore new opportunities since the modern concentration of the fishing industry in a few main ports such as Polperro (below) and Mevagissey (right), both in Cornwall.

While coastal farming communities must always have eked out their livelihoods by fishing and some of the fish carried a few miles inland for sale to neighbouring communities, it was only in the medieval period that fishing became an important element in the economies of those agricultural communities which had access to moderately sheltered and accessible coves and inlets. There hardly seems to have been a Cornish village fishing industry before about 1400, although east coast ports had long been harvesting the herring. In the Highlands and Islands and north-east of Scotland the creation of new fishing villages by more-or-less enlightened lairds and landlords was a feature of the clearances and improvements of the late-eighteenth and nineteenth centuries. After Culloden in 1746 scenes from the Tudor sheep clearances in England were re-enacted in the Scottish Highlands and sometimes attempts were made to resettle the displaced clansmen at coastal sites where, it was presumed, crofting, the gathering of seaweed or 'kelp' and fishing would provide some sort of subsistence.

The purpose-built planned fishing villages founded by the British Fishery Society were rather more hopeful places. Ullapool was built in a sheltered sea loch in 1788 to exploit the west coast herring fisheries, and Pultneytown was built to the plans of Thomas Telford as a close neighbour of Wick in 1786; in the nineteenth century up to 1000 fishing boats would use the port. Other new fishing villages appeared in the north-east of Scotland; Gardenstown was built on a cramped and unpromising site in 1720, well before the general reshaping of the landscaping began, while at Cullen an old fishing hamlet of low cottages which turned their gables towards the North Sea gales was joined by a cliff-top settlement with neatly-planned outlines which was built to house crofters ejected from the land.

Changes in the handling and processing of fish caused the industry to be centralized in a few major ports with spacious sites and good railway connections during this century. Some fishing villages – like Port Quin in Cornwall with its history of periodic desertion – have declined almost completely, while others have cashed in on their rugged and colourful history and scenic assets and now flourish as tourist resorts.

Behind the synthetic window dressings, features of the old fishing village layout have sometimes survived. Many of the bars, cafés and knick-knack shops in some Cornish fishing villages stand over the cellars where pilchards – the mainstay of the old Cornish industry – were handled. The flocks of hotels, cafés and holiday cottages which litter the cliffs like bright confetti at many of these places give a false impression of the size of the original fishing villages, many of which were no more than hamlet outposts of a nearby agricultural village. At Mevagissey in Cornwall the evidence is well-hidden. It is easy to recognize the old British word meaning 'a rivulet', and the local language must have changed from the Celtic tongue of the British folk to Anglo-Saxon, then to Norse, and it was in the process of becoming a Norse-laden English dialect by the time that the grange was founded.

Next we come to Darley, a fine example of a 'polyfocal' village made up of several merged and originally separate components. While the road along the dale now provides this village with its spine, the settlement really consists of groups of dwellings clustered around a sequence of little greens, so that the through-road forms a string and the greens are now strung along it like beads. One of the greens is particularly appealing because it still accommodates the village stocks. It seems probable that this village grew from the linking-together of a series of hamlets, some of them focussed on greens. Even so, the resultant village was not large; it did not gain its church till 1849, and this was a little building costing only £340.

Although the modern visitor will scarcely be aware of the presence of industry in this lovely dale, in fact, mining, quarrying, corn-milling, weaving, spinning and the manufacture of linen and rope all helped to mould the settlement pattern. Some of the villages like Glasshouses and Summerbridge owed their existence to the Industrial Revolution; the hamlet of Smelthouses has inherited its name and site from a lead smelting mill with water-powered bellows which was operated by Fountains Abbey as long ago as the fifteenth century, while Birstwith is another settlement that was born of industry. Here again we meet the deceptions of place-names. The name could be Norse, *Byr-stath*, meaning a farmstead, or it might be Saxon, the *staithe* or landing place of the fort or *burgh*, but while a *Beristade* is mentioned here in Domesday, the name must have related to a zone of land or a township and not to a distinct village. The village of Birstwith was, in fact, a creation of the nineteenth century and its name replaced the (untranslatable) 'Wreaks' which was linked to an old corn-milling and coal-mining site here, but not to a village. In the 1790s a cotton mill was built beside the old corn mill and by 1803 it was employing some 150 workers. In 1805 the mill was taken over by a cotton magnate from Keighley, John Greenwood, who moved into the area, built a massive neo-Gothic mansion on the hillside and set the family up as local squires and patrons.

The new village which materialized under this patronage consisted of three separate clusters of dwellings provided for estate and industrial workers, while much of the labour force must have continued to walk down to the bustling cotton mill from the surrounding flock of farmsteads. Greenwood paternalism provided the settlement with its school in 1847 and its church in 1857. The cotton famine of the American Civil War caused the mill to close, although members of the family remained in the mansion for a further century, looking over the village they had created. All relics of the cotton mill have gone and modern council and private developments have enlarged the settlement. Yet, as so often, clues to the village origin remain; visitors approaching from the east see the three great symbols of nineteenth-century establishment rule – the mansion, the church and the vicarage – as prominent hillside symbols to a past age of village-making. Even so, the core of the village seems quite fishing core of the village around the harbour, but what is not apparent is that this was a late-medieval planned village. The houses were set out around a square beside the harbour, but subsequently buildings encroached upon this planned core, creating the rows of dwellings which now press around the haven. Many other Cornish fishing villages, like the equally appealing Polperro, seem to be the unplanned products of spontaneous growth during the post-medieval emergence of the fishing industry.

— 7 —

COUNTRY PARKS
AND COTTAGE GARDENS

*At work in an attractive cottage garden at Woodbastwick
in Norfolk.*

Some of our best countryside and most of our worst has been created by the essential day-to-day business of farming the land. But there are also broad expanses and tiny nooks and crannies in the landscape which have been mainly manufactured in the pursuit of pleasure. They include the relics of medieval deer parks and the sweeping landscaped vistas embracing the great mansions of the post-medieval centuries – and also the dainty cottage garden plots which brighten so many village scenes. In the course of a country drive or ramble one may find that the urge to reshape the landscape in the quest for fashionable beauty or enjoyment has left a wealth of cameos, some of them much changed or relict and scarcely discernible, others fresh or well-conserved and quite distinctive. Each successive age has had its own ideas about the ingredients of an idyllic landscape, while the different levels of wealth and power have resulted in the pursuit of quite contrasting dreams in the lands around the rich man's castle and those beside the poor man's gate. All these efforts to recast the form of the countryside have rebounded on local ecosystems, driving out many of the plant and animal residents, but creating inviting niches for some newcomers.

We do not know how far back this urge to create landscapes for pleasure goes. The Romans certainly made orderly and sophisticated gardens beside and in the countryards of their grander villas. The Iron Age chieftains probably had their hunting estates, and some sort of royal estate or park seems to have been a part of the *oppidum* or native 'town' at *Camulodunum* near Colchester. The Iron Age peasants may have grown plots of herbs for flavourings and medicinal uses amongst their huts and paddocks, and an experimental plot of such herbs is grown at the Iron Age farm reconstruction at Butser Hill near Petersfield. Vegetables were also grown, and some overgrown banks beside the ruined stone houses at the Romano-British village of Chysauster in Cornwall outline the plots where they were cultivated.

We do know that some royal hunting forests existed in Saxon times. Occasionally the evidence still survives, as in the place-name 'Kingswood' in the Weald, while

the archaeologist Trevor Rowley mentions the record of three nobles or 'thegns' who held lands in the Forest of Dean on favourable terms in return for protecting the woodland reserve. A portion of the core of the New Forest seems to have been a royal reserve before the Norman Conquest.

The Norman kings of England earned some of their notoriety by introducing their harsh Forest Law, which removed the designated forests from the common law of the land and brought cruel punishments to bear on poachers. Earlier monarchs like Cnut and Edward the Confessor had respectively fined poachers and employed forest wardens, but by depopulating peasant lands to create or enlarge forests and by replacing the common law the Normans became widely hated. By the reign of Henry II the size and number of the royal forests had greatly increased, and he codified the Forest Law at Woodstock in 1184. Among the sixteen provisions were those which required every boy dwelling within the jurisdiction of a forest to swear an oath to keep the king's peace on reaching the age of twelve and demanded that dogs should be mutilated to prevent their pursuit of the king's game '. . . wherever his wild animals have their lairs and were wont to do so'.

The royal forests as they existed in 1189 are shown on the accompanying map. Clearly they covered a substantial portion of the realm, but it would be wrong to imagine that the areas concerned all resembled the 'Merrie Greenwood' of the Robin Hood movies. In general, only about one quarter of the area that was subject to the hated Forest Law was actually wooded. Some of the forests, like Exmoor, Dartmoor or Inglewood in Lakeland, must have carried very little woodland, while most of the forests had a wooded core that was surrounded by large areas of peasant farmland and common. There the deer could freely wander to forage, although the unfortunate peasants were forbidden to cut trees, hunt the deer or even to erect hedges or fences to prevent them from devouring the crops. The forest provided the king and his guests with hunting, although most of the beasts were slaughtered by professional huntsmen. It also yielded timber for

Key
• Reference in the Domesday Book 1086
○ Implied reference in Domesday Book
╱ Boundary where known
▨ Extent of Royal Forest by 1189
⬚ Uncertain

The Distribution of Royal Forests 1066–1200

house and castle building, fuel, materials for spears, bows and siege machines, oak for shipbuilding, oak bark for the tanning industry and charcoal for use in smelting. To meet these demands, large parts of the hunting forests must have been carefully managed as commercial woodland, while 'vaccaries' or cattle farms and horse breeding farms also existed within the forest and other parts were rented as grazing or 'pannage' for pigs.

In the course of his progress through the kingdom, the king would often move from one forest manor to another, with the reserves serving as an ever bountiful larder for the gluttonous guests. At Christmas in 1251, Henry III provided a menu comprising 250 hinds, 180 harts, 200 fallow bucks, 100 roe deer, 200 boar, 1300 hare, 395 swans and 115 cranes. More than a century later, in 1363, when the force of the Forest Law had greatly diminished, the Black Prince had 100 harts and 100 bucks slaughtered in the Wirral Forest in Cheshire, salted down and shipped in barrels to furnish a feast for the royal party in Bordeaux.

The animals upon which the medieval kings vented their bloodlust included the pony-sized red deer and diminutive roe deer, both native to Britain, although the favoured quarry was the lovely white spotted or occasionally black or white fallow deer. This now well-established species seems to have been brought to Britain as a result of Norman contacts – via Sicily – with the Muslim lands at the east of the Mediterranean and was probably introduced in the twelfth century. Of the other popular game, wild boar and hare

were native to Britain, while rabbits and pheasants are thought to be other Norman introductions. Like the deer and boar, wolves were restricted game in certain northern forests. The last English wolf probably perished amongst the marshy carrs of Holderness at the close of the Middle Ages, the Welsh wolf made its last dash for freedom in the Brecon Beacons at the start of the seventeenth century, while small packs survived in Scotland and Ireland until the eighteenth century. The fox was largely shunned by the medieval huntsmen and it was only in the post-medieval centuries, when the numbers of wild deer were much diminished and the boar had been hunted to extinction, that the aristocracy created a ritual around the tortured death of this small beast. In the eighteenth and nineteenth century the planting of spinneys and coverts provided artificial habitats to encourage fox breeding and even in modern and supposedly enlightened times foxes are still 'conserved' to provide sport – a strange word this – for those who can enjoy the painful death of a terrified creature.

In addition to the pheasants, swans and cranes mentioned above, the Norman nobles hunted and devoured a liberal assortment of wild birds. The heron was a favoured quarry in falconry, a sport which seems to have been introduced around AD 860, and the hunting birds, ranging in size from the kestrel to the eagle, were allocated according to the aristocratic rank of the huntsman. Although this medieval activity has left very little trace in the countryside today, the revival of falconry in recent times has resulted in the robbing of the nests of rare and beautiful prey birds like the threatened peregrine falcon, with some of the young birds being smuggled abroad.

In addition to the royal forests there were also many medieval chases, whose names survive in places like Cannock Chase and Cranborne Chase. These were also hunting reserves, but they were owned by nobles rather than by the Crown and so were subject to common law. Many were established on lands granted or sold from royal forests. Oliver Rackham, the biographer of the English woodlands, has identified some 142 medieval hunting forests, of which eighty-six were royal. The chases were mainly the possessions of members of the top flight of the aristocracy, people like the Bishops of Lichfield and Winchester or the Earls of Lancaster, Pembroke, Gloucester and Richmond.

Although they existed as crucial and controversial features of the medieval countryside, the forests and chases have left few obvious marks on the landscape. The hunting forests had reached their greatest extents by 1200 and then they tended gradually to surrender piecemeal to other uses. The kings were more often than not hard up and large sums could be gained by selling off woodland and surrendering the privileges that the Crown had exercised under the Forest Law. Even so, Cranborne Chase was hunted until the early nineteenth century. In some places, most notoriously in the case of the New Forest, the Norman kings extended the wooded area across peasant fields and commons. But the wooded cores of most forests had existed in pre-Conquest times because of the difficult or impoverished nature of the soils concerned. Consequently, parts of some old forests are still wooded, and clothed either in our native hardwoods or in alien commercial conifers. Woodland and some old woodland customs survive over much of the New Forest, fragments of the famous Sherwood Forest endure, while the heaths of Cannock Chase now carry a black blanket of conifers. Only very rarely were the boundaries of the great game reserves marked by earthworks which could endure as monuments to the age, although this was the case with a part of the Bishop of Lichfield's Cannock Chase, which was delimited by a boundary bank in the vicinity of Huntington – a place-name which could well mean 'huntsman's hill' or 'huntsman's farm'.

Deer parks on the other hand were generally defined by earthen banks and ditches, so that, although very few examples still endure as deer parks, their extents can often be recognized. While sporting analogies may be inappropriate to the gory rituals of hunting, it might be said that the deer parks stood to the vast open forests and chases as putting greens do to golf courses. They were far smaller than the forests, covering areas variously comparable to very large fields or small parishes. The animals contained were not free to wander, but confined by lofty banks topped by sturdy palings; ditches guarded the inner faces of the banks but the confines of the deer parks were periodically breached by deer leaps, allowing wild beasts to enter but not leave the park.

'Hayes' or deer parks existed in Saxon times in England and the Welsh border counties and many were created in Scotland during the Norman period. While the chases were reserved for the top people of medieval society, the owners of deer parks included hundreds of lesser lords. The greater aristocrats often controlled large numbers of these parks and at various times the Earls of Lancaster held forty-five, the Dukes of Cornwall twenty-nine, the Bishops of Winchester twenty-three, while the most splendid example was the royal park at Woodstock in Oxfordshire, created around 1100 from

A deer park at Place House near Titchfield in Hampshire as portrayed in an early-seventeenth-century map. The rectangular park is shown to the left of the house.

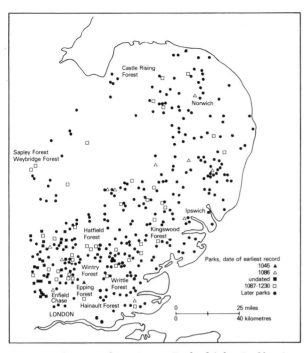

Medieval Deer Parks in Eastern England (after Rackham)

a probable Saxon predecessor and surrounded by a walled circuit of seven miles.

Several hundred deer parks were created in the course of the thirteenth century and the medieval realm contained at least 2000 examples. In Charnwood Forest (never, apparently, a royal forest), four deer parks could be found in a zone just four miles long, at least five other examples existed elsewhere in the

Forest, while the county of Leicestershire contained at least forty-two deer parks. The heyday of the deer park was in the years around 1300, and it has been estimated that by 1330 there was one park for every four English parishes, but following the labour shortages and and economic difficulties which followed the arrival of the Pestilence in 1348, scores of deer parks fell into neglect and many were later converted to other uses. Madeley Great Park in Staffordshire which was created in 1204 was still being hunted at the end of the seventeenth century and a handful of old deer parks, like the one beside Ripley Castle in Yorkshire or Bradgate Park in Charnwood Forest, still contain deer. The boundaries of Bradgate Park have been enlarged since medieval times, but the old records tell how the park was created in 1241 by surrounding an area with walls, ditches, hedges and palings. Poachers seem to have posed a serious threat in the area and Whitwick Park nearby is known to have been raided on many occasions; that the local communities regarded poaching as a respectable if risky undertaking is evidenced by the fact that the nine raiders who entered this park armed with swords, sticks, bows and arrows in 1289 and took fifteen deer to the value of forty pounds, numbered three local clergymen among their ranks.

Although most deer parks have gone, many still existed in one form or another at the end of the Middle Ages, when printed county maps like those by Saxton began to appear. Reproductions of the county map can usually be seen in public libraries and readers may well be surprised to discover how numerous such parks

Fallow deer in the medieval deer park at Ripley near Harrogate in Yorkshire.

were in a chosen district. Many parks can still be traced in the countryside. Often their bounds are traced by hedge banks or lanes, as with the park at Ongar in Essex, founded in Saxon times and set astride a Roman road. In many places their massive enclosing earthworks are still prominent features, as at Frome St Quintin or Wimborne St Giles in Dorset, while in other places they may be reduced but discernible relics, as above Wadenhoe church in Northamptonshire. Often the parks were of an oval form, with the manor house or castle of the owner set at the more pointed end of the oval, as at Devizes, where the oval park ran south-westwards for almost a mile from the castle and castle town.

At Laxton in Nottinghamshire, a deer park existed in the twelfth century, but a far more obvious survival from the period is the earthwork complex of the Norman motte and bailey castle. This castle was the venue of the Forest Courts of Sherwood Forest and the hereditary keepership of the Forest was vested in the powerful de Caux family who had Laxton as the baronial seat. Between the reigns of Henry II and Edward I, the kings of England were regular visitors to Laxton and the deer park will have stocked the menu for many a royal blow-out. Fish ponds were often constructed in or close to deer parks and here the ponds which existed along Radbeck will have contributed to the feasts. Other lavish entertainments may also have been staged, for one of the fields near the castle ruins is still known as Justing Field Close, suggesting a place for jousting. In many other places, one of the common 'Park' place-names may be the only obvious clue to the existence of a park though the numerous 'Hay' names often denote other kinds of enclosures.

In the medieval period, the West Riding of Yorkshire contained more than seventy parks. At least three clustered around Knaresborough in the royal forest of that name and they included one of the largest examples, the 2250 acre Haverah Park, which seems to have been created out of peasant commons seized in the late-twelfth century. Haverah also contained a fortified hunting lodge, which survives as a ruin known as John of Gaunt's Castle. A few more of these hunting lodges survive, including the Barden Tower in Wharfe-dale, one of an original six lodges housing the keepers of the Forest of Barden, while just beyond the outskirts of Thetford the lonely stone-edged flint tower which lurks on the forest margins was the Prior of Thetford's warren lodge, one of many fortified lodges built in medieval times to protect the valuable rabbit warrens

The Barden Tower in Wharfedale, a fortified medieval hunting lodge in an area which had extensive medieval forests.

of Breckland.

Although the deer parks were in decline at the end of the Middle Ages, a new age of parks was slowly dawning. The old deer parks had not been landscaped, but, to repeat Leonard Cantor's quotation of the Elizabethan bloodsports enthusiast John Manwood, they were '. . . stored with great woods or coverts for the secret abode of wild beasts and also with fruitful pastures for the communal feed'. But gradually the nobility were gravitating from their stark castles to softer but opulent mansions, and the idea that a great country house should be set amidst a swirl of country-side that was reorganized to provide tasteful vistas took root in the post-medieval centuries.

When we create new landscape, whether it be a great park or a tiny flowerbed, we not only express our own personalities and tastes, but we also tend to articulate the fads and fancies of the contemporary world. The age of humanism which arose from the ashes of the Middle Ages, contained several currents of thought which were to impact like thunderbolts upon the British scene. Intoxicated by the erosion of religious restraints and triumphing in the technological ability to reshape townscapes and countryside on the grand scale, the victory of human will over the 'disorderly' natural world was proclaimed in the creation of new and aggressively man-made vistas which were mar-shalled according to geometrical principles. The fash-ions of France and Italy were very influential in seventeenth-century England, where the property-orientated political climate and the incredible wealth of the landed and merchant families fostered a profusion of great houses and gardens which were set at the hearts of the majestic rural estates. Medieval gardens had tended to exist as compact enclosed boxes, with the small and neatly set-out plots of herbs and flowers being sited in courtyards or hemmed in by walls or trellises. As the new fashions were adopted, ornamen-tal gardens were often placed on terraces overlooked by the magnificent new mansion, while the beds, which could be square, circular, semicircular or polygonal, were divided into intricate symmetrical geometrical patterns by networks of pathways and low hedges.

The insistence on formality continued, if abruptly, from the terrace to the enveloping park setting, for the continental fashion demanded avenues of trees, charg-ing arrow-straight to the distant horizon or converging on focal points where items of fashionably classical

A typical expanse of landscaped English parkland near Up Cerne in Dorset. Note the artificial lake and the carefully-positioned native and exotic trees.

Chestnuts and statuary in the avenues at Anglesey Abbey in Cambridgeshire, National Trust.

sculpture might be displayed. Many avenues would culminate in a Greek or Roman temple, while broad canals and geometrical display of topiary also had their place in the scheme. Elm and lime were often favoured in the planting of avenues, while imported shrubs like the cherry laurel and bay combined in ornamental groves with native species like the dogwood, spindle tree and elder. Elsewhere, strangers to the British landscape like the cypress, horse chestnut and larch were used.

At Hall Barn near Beaconsfield the elements of a seventeenth-century park landscape survive, with linked avenues radiating from vantage points and a straight ribbon of lake. The only genuine survival of a formal Elizabethan garden is at Kirby Hall in Northamptonshire, where the garden plan has been reconstructed following the rediscovery of the stones used to edge the beds, while at Lyveden New Bield quite nearby there is a magnificent Elizabethan summer house-cum-banqueting hall. Formal gardens fell from favour in the eighteenth century and the only garden designed by George London and Henry Wise, who had also worked together at Chatsworth, Blenheim, Hampton Court and Windsor, and still surviving in substantial detail is at Melbourne Hall in Derbyshire, where one can see long avenues, fountains and paths, which burrow through the overhanging yews. Inkpen Old Rectory in Berkshire is a small garden designed according to French principles at the end of the seventeenth century.

It is hard to estimate just how great an area of England and Wales was affected by the rampant emparking movement, but a survey of 1696 suggested that about one tenth of the landscape was occupied by forests, parks and commons, with woods and coppices covering a similar proportion. In some well-parked areas like Buckinghamshire, large and small parks could often be encountered at intervals of around two miles and in the south of the county it was very difficult to travel for five miles without meeting an example. Much peasant farmland and many entire village communities were sacrificed to emparking, while scores of roads had to be diverted as they approached the hallowed precincts of the new parks.

In the eighteenth century, an English school of landscape design developed. The poet Alexander Pope harangued against the over-stylized vistas which had been created according to the French, Dutch and Italian models, and while Classical symmetry and

formality were perpetuated in the architecture of the century, the English love of the more natural countryside reasserted itself. Parks and gardens were no longer a negation of Nature, but gradually and increasingly they became celebrations of the diversity of the natural world, marrying human ingenuity to the themes suggested by the living landscape. In such ways the new parks were more closely in harmony with English conditions, and as the geographer Hugh Prince has pointed out, 'The English did not dine or entertain or parade outdoors; they did not want to stride up and down interminable avenues on a gusty afternoon'. The new ideas found an early and powerful expression in the grounds at Castle Howard in Yorkshire, where the house by Vanburgh was begun in 1701. Here, the park was a great island of greenery quite separate from the bustle of the workaday peasant world outside; the Arcadian vistas were contrived from the innate characteristics of the rolling countryside – but the scenes were only achieved at the expense of the living village of Hinderskelfe, torn down to make way for the house.

By 1720, uncompromising geometry was 'out' and the great landscape architects of the eighteenth century sought to recreate in England the sorts of scenery which provided backdrops for the paintings of the seventeenth-century French painters Claude Lorrain and Nicolas Poussin. Such goals could only partially be achieved, since few park settings could offer very much in the way of plummeting slopes or foaming streams. The attempt to marry the Classical mansion to a setting of vibrant and seemingly natural parkland was developed by William Kent (1685–1748). He sought to emphasize the inherent qualities of terrain, often building a distant monument as an eyecatcher which would provide a counterpoint to the informal landscape, deforesting a valley bottom to emphasize the depth of the cleft, while planting hilltop groves and thickets to elevate the crestline. One of his most typical creations was Rousham in Oxfordshire. With its edge scalloped by the meanders of the River Cherwell, the sloping park contained ponds, woodland, an elm-flanked walk, tree-studded lawns and follies: a Gothick mill and an eyecatcher in the form of a distant trio of buttressed arches set in a gable and supposedly resembling the gateway of a ruined castle. Here he captured Pope's ideal of 'Spontaneous beauties all around advance'.

In the second half of the century, Lancelot 'Capability' Brown (1716–1783) emerged as the foremost tweaker of the English scene. He designed more than 200 parks and gardens and his work can be seen at Blenheim, Longleat, Chatsworth, Warwick Castle and many other noble seats. He was one of several

*Landscaped woodland with avenues focussing on a 'temple' at Blickling in Norfolk,
a National Trust property.*

*A magnificent specimen of the London plane in the park at Mottisfont Abbey,
Hampshire, a National Trust property.*

eighteenth-century designers who destroyed the landscape creations of the previous centuries – and particularly vulnerable were the terrace gardens and other
formal flowerbeds, since the new vogue demanded that
the parkland should lap like a green tide against a
mansion's walls. Brown sought, in essence, to encom-
pass a great house in an uninterrupted sweep of
delicately reorganized countryside, removing uncompromising and unharmonious features like old
avenues; keeping the immediate setting of the mansion
free of rival attractions; producing broad idyllic vistas of
deer pasture, while gently diversifying the oceans of
grassland with stipples and clumpings of trees which
yielded to heavier belts of woodland. As a focus for his
creations, Brown was seldom able to resist a limpid
expanse of water, often created by damming a natural
stream to provide lobes of lake fed by a languid,

serpentine river. But while the natural contours of the
scene were orchestrated by the curving lines of lake,
stream and woodland margins, the totality of the
composition always predominated over the details. He
planned in the long term as well as on the grand scale.
His new creations were often criticized when the
straggly saplings seemed dwarfed by their setting, and
the singer was long dead before his songs could sound
with the fullness of maturity.

Brown had worked on a broad canvas and was
exposed to criticism that the great vistas he created
lacked the humanity and romance that details could
endow. Many of his ideals were perpetuated and
developed by Humphry Repton (1752–1818), a land-

The landscaped lake and parkland at Holkham Hall in Norfolk.

scape manipulator who is particularly interesting to historians of the English scene because of the record of changes preserved in some of his famous Red Books, with their 'before and after' drawings. Thus at Bayham Abbey in Kent we can see how the hedges of pastures were removed, the edges of woodland scalloped and thinned and new trees planted to create an expanse of open grassland which was dotted with trees and gently melded into the surviving wooded country. Meanwhile, the ruins of the medieval abbey were titivated and romanticized without any great concern for the archaeological issues.

Repton's designs revealed the increasing concern with detail and whimsy. In the course of his career, the competing Classical, Oriental and to some extent even the Picturesque modes in landscape design became overtaken by the vogue for Romanticism, with its heavier underlining of the importance of things natural. Much of the parkland which endures today was created in the decades around 1800 by thinning out the woods and tree clumps planted during earlier phases of landscape creation. As the years rolled by, changing social and economic conditions greatly reduced the numbers of new parks which were created, but at the same time the resourceful and often courageous plant collectors were scouring the furthest corners of the world for new plants which could be developed by the mushrooming nurseries and offered to the masters of the countryside. Men like David Douglas, Robert Fortune and J. D. Hooker were amongst the dozens of collectors who unleashed a galaxy of new trees, shrubs and flowering plants upon the parks and gardens of Britain. At places like Tresco Abbey gardens on Scilly, Chatsworth in Derbyshire or Mottisfont Abbey in Hampshire one can begin to glimpse the multitude of introductions.

Romanticism and a robust and sometimes quirky individualism merged in the Victorian parks and gardens, with the magpie mentality of the age producing Indian, Persian, Chinese and Tudor themes and many others too, while the arrangements were stocked with the new exotic species. Amongst the many fashions in circulation was that of parkland with specimen trees – bizarre and expensive plants which were now presented as the foci rather than the trappings of the scene. While various types of parkland survive from the different ages of landscape creation, the commonest seem to be those which combine tree-dotted pastures à la Repton and Victorian specimen plantings.

Further changes in the social and economic fabric of Britain have resulted in scores of hitherto private park domains being opened to the public. Some of these places still dance to the tune of a particular phase and fashion in the manipulation of the countryside, although most reveal several layers of adaptation to match the changing tastes and vogues. Very rarely a park may still preserve old features inherited from the peasant countryside and many of the trees and shrubs in the park at Ickworth in Suffolk seem to be descended from medieval hedgerow plantings. A few parks are the almost pristine creations of a single giant of the landscaping fraternity while a handful, like John Aislabie's Studley Royal, beside Fountains Abbey, strongly reflect the taste and choices of a particular owner. Parkland is seen in many forms, and although the expanses of grassland that are stippled and blotched by loose scatters and bolder clumps of trees create a landscape that is reminiscent of an urban infant's painting of the countryside, the scene produced is quite synthetic. It is not natural countryside nor one created by peasant toil, but an artificial product made for pleasure and for the status that a fashionable park endowed upon its owner. Each lake, canal, avenue, grove, temple, folly, obelisc, ride and viewpoint reminds us of the incredible wealth and privileges of the old masters of the countryside, and also of the changing ideas about the ingredients needed to compose an ideal landscape.

From the seventeenth to the nineteenth centuries, the emparking movement removed hundreds of innocent villages, obliterated countless historical features and transformed hundreds of thousands of acres of peasant ploughland, hedged pastures, open commons and heaths. At the same time, it created canals, rivers and lakes where there where none before, sprinkled the countryside with eyecatchers, follies, grottoes, cascades and temples and planted millions of trees, many of them still living today. It has been estimated that between them, Brown and Repton planted some twenty million trees and it was often the case that commercial forestry made parkland a profitable as well as a fashionable form of countryside.

In addition, the movement caused the introduction of hundreds of types of exotic trees to the countrysides of Britain. Among the native species which were favoured for their landscaping capabilities were the elm, oak, lime, hornbeam, beech, holly, elder, dogwood, spindle tree and Scots pine, but the almost endless list of introductions include the sycamore – a late-medieval introduction from France which was a surprisingly favoured tree in some earlier parks – the horse chestnut, the plane, larch, various types of cypress, redwood, Chile pine or 'monkey puzzle', Douglas fir and various other firs, spruces and cedars.

Today, a landscaped park is a luxury which, beyond

Strixton in Northamptonshire where sheep graze on the earthworks which mark the terraces of a sixteenth-century garden which was abandoned in the seventeenth century. The church of the shrunken village is seen in the background.

the confines of the more profitable stately homes, only the members of a tiny millionaire minority can afford or support. Consequently one can often detect the signs of a relict park within a working countryside. We know of one park where, through the eccentricities of owners past and present, longhorn cattle ramble through a neglected jungle composed of hundreds of different types of exotic tree, all a century old, while peacocks scuttle through collapsing ornamental arches to crouch in the tangled brushwood that was once a walled garden. Occasionally, as at Foellalt on the outskirts of Llanddewi Brefi in central Wales, one may see the incongruous sight of exotic conifers dotting an

otherwise workaday pasture. Elsewhere, a grove of mature trees with an underwood of rhododendrons imported from the Caucasus mountains may survive the changes as pheasant cover. Imposing walls and gateways often signal the approaches to a park; the road will still divert in deference, picking its way around walls which now contain just working farm-land. The lawns at Castle Ashby which were land-scaped by Brown preserved the undulating contours of a remarkable display of old ridge and furrow plough-land, sadly recently destroyed by the ploughing of the grassland. Wherever one sees the common sight of pasture or ploughland dotted by loose clusters of

Chestnut blossom on a specimen parkland tree. The chestnut was highly favoured by the designers of landscaped parks.

tastefully placed chestnuts, elms or oaks and wherever a lane is hemmed and screened by ranks of beech, hornbeam, elm or lime, then a lost park is strongly suspected.

Lost gardens may also be seen, as at Harrington in Northamptonshire, where the scarps and hollows in the pasture outline the terraces, beds and the site of the mansion which they accompanied. Perhaps the most interesting lost garden site and certainly one of the most accessible is at the hamlet of Strixton in Northamptonshire, where the earthworks are clearly visible from the A509 between Bozeat and Wollaston. From the churchyard one can look down on the platforms in the pasture which were once imposing terraces, while the garden remains lie amongst the earthworks of the deserted village of Strixton. Similarly at Godwick in Norfolk there are the earthworks of a garden that was extended across the site of a decaying village.

Water gardens and temple in the landscaped park at Fountains Abbey in Yorkshire, a National Trust property.

The natural history of wood pasture

The wildlife of parkland, or wood pasture, as ecologists prefer to describe it, is a blend of historical survivals from the past and more common plants and animals which come in when man disturbs the natural balance by using the land in different ways. The blend will vary depending on the degree of change and whether it has been a rapid progress or has taken place gradually over a long period of time. But in many wood pastures the thread of history is strong, and some special habitats have survived despite the many changes taking place around them. Old trees, for example, may have a direct link with primeval conditions because whatever else has happened to the land, there have always been some which have grown to old age with much decayed wood, so preserving with them their own characteristic flora and fauna of tiny animals and plants.

In the post-war period some commercial forests and private parks – relics of old royal forests, chases or deer parks – became public open spaces or statutory Country Parks, and quite a number are owned by the National Trust. A few have fallen on hard times, with their natural history interest abandoned or neglected, and in others greatly increased public recreational use will gradually overwhelm the surviving old trees, their loose bark torn off and the hollow trunks stuffed with litter or burnt out by fires.

The truth is that conservationists did not recognize the value of wood pastures until it was almost too late. The splended two-volume *Nature Conservation Review*, by the Nature Conservancy Council (1977), lists all places known at that time to be of some importance for wildlife, but includes only a few of the better-known

White park cattle, a very old breed of uncertain origin which survived in a few parks and is now being introduced to others.

Young fallow deer with developing antlers in velvet, a non-native species introduced for the chase.

wood pastures. In the following years, however, an effective review of the surviving wood pastures throughout the country was made by the Nature Conservancy Council, and at the same time other exciting studies on the historical background to the natural history interest of woodlands were being made by Oliver Rackham at Cambridge and George Peterken of the Nature Conservancy Council. These helped us to understand more clearly how wood pastures have developed through the centuries. In addition Francis Rose of King's College London discovered that the ancient trees characteristic of so much parkland had a rich lichen flora and was able to develop a theory which linked them with primeval conditions.

What has survived today?

The name 'wood pasture' was proposed by ecologists because it emphasizes its two main features – trees and grassland – although both of these vary considerably according to the situation, soil, and so on. Quite a number of the oldest form of wood pasture, the ancient deer parks, still have deer today, although of course they are no longer kept as a source of venison – their use in the past – but because their owners and the visiting public enjoy seeing deer as part of the country scene. Herds of fallow and red deer still roam Bradgate Park in Charnwood Forest, and also Moccas Park in Herefordshire, Windsor Park and quite a number of others.

When some were converted to landscape parks around our magnificent country houses, the great landscape gardeners often incorporated the surviving old trees in the new design. There are many beautiful examples of these formal parklands, many of which are opened to the public for at least part of the year.

Another type of wood pasture is the wooded common. These are areas of land with common grazing rights which may have overlapped with royal forests or even deer parks in some instances. Wooded commons include some well-known areas, like the beautiful Burnham Beeches in Buckinghamshire, which is managed by the City of London as a nature reserve and public open space, and two others in Sussex which have become nature reserves of the County Naturalists' Trust. One of these, Ebernoe Common, is an ancient oak-beech high forest, and the other, The Mens, is a lowland deciduous wood, thought to be similar to the ancient Wealden forest. However, few genuine wooded commons survive outside the area of the Weald and the Chilterns in Dorset and Wiltshire. Elsewhere in the country many commons which were traditionally grass- or heather-covered have become wooded since the 1950s because myxomatosis wiped out the rabbit population. Although in some places the numbers of rabbits have recovered they are still not as numerous as they were and trees and scrub have been able to grow unhindered by the rabbits' nibbling.

But this recent type of wooded common does not have such an interesting bark flora nor the rich invertebrate life found in the ancient trees of parkland or on the true old wooded commons. Like the formal parkland, most of the latter are now public open spaces and the common rights of grazing and cutting wood are no longer used. This is in the best interests of the fauna and flora – plants are able to flower and set seed and the dead wood is left lying on the ground to encourage the insects which live in this type of habitat. In times past the trees on wooded commons were frequently pollarded, with the fresh growth cut off every few years to be used as firewood or winter fodder for animals. Today pollarding is often neglected except where riverside willows are concerned, although one can still see it in parts of Normandy. The regular cutting of fresh branches tended to retard the growth of the trees so they probably lived to a greater age.

The Sika deek introduced to parks and zoological gardens but some escaped and established wild herds in many parts of Britain and Ireland, including the New Forest and Bowland Forest.

The third type of wood pasture, winter-grazed woodland, is rather specialized, and is found in lowland valleys which traditionally were used as winter grazing for sheep or deer, and adjacent to the upland summer grazings. In the West Highlands of Scotland seasonal migrations from upland to lowland are still part of the sheep farming economy but few woodlands of this type now survive, because most of the lowland pastures have been greatly improved agriculturally, to provide better grazing for the animals in winter. The few winter-grazed woodlands which still exist are in Devon, Somerset and Wales. The best example, the Warner Comb Valley Woods in Exmoor, is one of the main wintering grounds of the deer from the moorlands of the Exmoor National Park. Scientists have listed sixty-eight wood pastures of all types in Great Britain, fifty-six of which are in England and six each in Wales and Scotland. Although over three-quarters of these are known to have a conservation interest, not many are actually protected by being made into nature reserves.

The ancient tree and its inhabitants

There is no doubt on this evidence that wood pastures are an important wildlife habitat in the British country-side. But what are the particular animals and plants

A number of ornamental birds like peacock and various types of pheasant were introduced in parkland. A silver pheasant displaying in the grounds of Anglesey Abbey.

that make them so interesting to naturalists? The fauna and flora of healthy trees consist of species that live on the external parts, particularly the leaves, flowers, fruit and bark. Sooner or later, however, other creatures begin to make use of the tree. Beetles burrow into the bark or the wood, a broken branch allows fungi to attack the living wood through the wound, rot holes form, and the bark becomes loose. If branches are broken or diseased in some way so that rot can enter the centre or heartwood of the tree, in time the whole of the trunk may become hollow. Usually this is a slow process extending over many years, but in some cases, for example with Dutch elm disease, the fungus, which is carried into the tree by a burrowing beetle, can spread very rapidly and within a year or two a very large tree can be dead.

While this process of ageing and decay is taking place, many new habitats are formed. Loose bark, for

instance, attracts a multitude of new inhabitants – spiders, beetles, harvestmen, pseudoscorpions, and so on. There is a considerable difference between the fauna of dry dead wood, such as a dying branch in the tree canopy, and the fauna of wet dead wood, for example fallen timber which is in contact with the ground vegetation. Dry wood rots only slowly and if it is part of the canopy it very often acquires a fauna dominated by several species of mites. A small spider, *Thyreosthenius parasiticus*, is also frequently found in considerable numbers under the loose bark of dead branches in the canopy of trees, yet elsewhere it only occurs in mines, sewers and similar dark, damp places.

The rotten heartwood of a tree is usually damp because the rain can penetrate through rot-holes in the trunk, enabling fungi to live in it and grow rapidly. Many beetles also prefer this type of habitat, and their larvae either feed on the wood or else on the fungi

[199]

responsible for the rotting process. As the beetle larvae penetrate throughout the decaying wood they create galleries and crevices, so that an army of invertebrate animals always on the lookout for a new home – wood-lice, snails, centipedes, millipedes, spiders, collembola – immediately take over the abandoned galleries. They feed either by scavenging, eating the fungal threads, or else preying on the other inhabitants.

Gradually, perhaps over a very long period, a complex community of species occupies every micro-habitat, each having its own particular function and utilizing different parts of the dead wood system. To the naturalist, therefore, a half-dead tree, with a far greater range of habitats and therefore more wildlife, is much more exciting than a mature healthy tree. If our decayed tree is also surrounded by fallen branches, damp from ground moisture and perhaps covered by mosses, then even more animals will come to live and feed in the rich harvest of rotting wood. This entomological paradise is now quite rare, and yet in primevel woodlands it must have been a very common sight. The reason is that over-mature trees have no place in the modern forest – they take up valuable space which could be growing healthy timber. There are still rare examples in a few parts of Europe of virgin forest, scarcely touched by man. In one part of northern Greece where there are no roads or villages there is a magnificent natural forest where the fallen dead wood is so abundant that it makes walking quite difficult. It has been estimated that about a quarter of the timber there is dead, either standing trees or fallen trunks and branches. Consequently the dead wood fauna is extraordinarily rich, recalling the words of Charles Elton, who said that in a natural forest dead and dying wood provides one of the greatest animal resources, and that if all this wood were removed the total fauna of the forest would lose about a fifth of its species of invertebrate animals.

The flora of tiny plants, lichens and mosses which grow on decayed wood can be examined without any damage to the tree. But it is quite different when an entomologist wishes to study the insects living within a tree or a fallen branch. Some part of the wood must be destroyed while he excavates for the species living there, and tears off the loose bark in order to take the animals living beneath it. The unscrupulous entomologist who thinks only of enriching his collection can cause great damage and a fallen tree which has perhaps been gradually rotting for twenty years or more can be destroyed in a couple of hours. This danger is known to naturalists and most exercise great care to take only a small part of the decayed timber for examination, and similarly large pieces of loose bark which are taken off can be fixed back on the tree by knocking in a couple of nails.

In Britain scientists have found a great many invertebrate species, mainly beetles and flies but also a few spiders and pseudoscorpions, which live in dead wood. Others, no longer found, were part of our fauna in the past because remains have been recovered in fossil wood. A particularly splendid longhorn beetle, *Cerambyx cerdo*, so called because of its long graceful antennae which curve back like horns, has been found more than once in 3000-year-old bog oaks in the fenland peat. Two specimens were discovered a few years ago beautifully preserved in large galleries in a bog oak dug out of a field by a farmer. For some reason they had died before they could emerge and take wing in the primeval Neolithic forest. This longhorn is still found in continental Europe, where forests with dead trees survive, but has not been seen alive in Britain. Other species which would have been characteristic insects of dead wood in Neolithic forests have now become adapted to houses and other buildings. The best known is probably the common woodworm – the scourge of timbered houses and old furniture – but even today it is also an inhabitant of dead hedgerow trees, fence posts, and similar situations. The even more dreaded death watch beetle is much more choosy because it usually occurs only in the timber of very old buildings and in nature it also is confined to the very old trees associated, for instance, with wood pastures.

The lesser stag beetle prefers dead ash wood and although widespread in the southern half of England, in the north it too seems to live mainly in the ancient trees of such places as wood pastures. The magnificent greater stag beetle, the largest of the European beetles, prefers oak, and for some strange reason it is mainly found in Britain in the woodlands of the Home Counties and occurs not infrequently in London's parks and gardens. The larvae live in the timber for three to five years before pupating and becoming adult. Those absurdly large mandibles of the male beetle, which make it such an impressive beast, are thought by some entomologists to be used for fighting and competing for females, but others regard them simply as ornaments with no real function. Certainly it is not able to bite – yet the female with much smaller jaws can inflict quite a painful nip. Although some beetles living in dead wood appear to show a preference for certain kinds of trees, entomologists generally think that the type of tree is not so important as the state of the rotting wood itself, and there is, in fact, a remarkable succession of species from those which attack hard dry wood to those which do not appear until it is soft and rotten.

Trees attract many different species of spiders, some

of which live in the bark crevices, on the exterior of the trunk or in the foliage. When part of the tree dies and the bark becomes loose, other common spiders move in and sometimes virtually take over the spaces which are created. Others, mostly rather small spiders, enter the galleries and crevices in the soft rotten wood and feed on any soft-bodied creatures they come across. One of these species, called *Tetrilus*, is more or less confined to this habitat, although it also occurs in ant nests adjacent to old trees. It is a pale, rather fragile spider, only 3mm or 4mm in length, and spins a small, delicate web. In rotten wood it is difficult to see because it merges so well into the background. Why the large ants whose nests it shares are prepared to tolerate it is a mystery. Like all spiders it is a carnivore and if not feeding on the ants themselves, or their larvae, which perhaps seems rather unlikely because of its small size, it may be stealing the food brought in by the worker ants.

A related species called *Tuberta* is very occasionally found on tree trunks, although it is not specially associated with those which are in an advanced state of decay. *Lepthyphantes carri*, another spider about 3mm in length, is mostly associated with decayed ancient trees. In Britain *L. carri* is very rare and has only been found in a handful of places, but it has some very common relatives which occur all over the country. It lives inside hollow trees or beneath the loose bark and has been taken under fallen branches on the ground. Another of its habitats is the twiggy nest made by jackdaws, which of course is itself usually placed inside hollow trees. The rareness of this species has always puzzled arachnologists. For example, it was discovered in a decayed hollow tree in Donington Park, Leicestershire, and although about forty other trees in the Park which were of the same age and also decayed were repeatedly examined, the spider was not seen again. Similarly a large number of trees were carefully examined in Sherwood Forest, which still has some ancient oak trees. The spider was again found in one place only and seemed to be completely absent from the rest of the parkland even though the trees would appear to provide very suitable habitats.

Some beetles are also known to behave in this way. There is a well-known example of a rare beetle of rotten timber which was found in only one tree in the New Forest and when this was felled and the wood taken away the beetle apparently disappeared. Some of our few species of pseudoscorpions are likewise associated with ancient trees. These small creatures are predatory and the largest, *Dendrocernes cyrneus*, is rather rare. It likes roughly the same type of conditions as *L. carri*, hiding under loose bark, and is mostly to be found in

wood pastures – although it also inhabits a small wood for which there is no evidence of an ancient origin.

The plant life of wood pastures is not usually very rich, probably because grazing eliminates the taller woodland plants and grasses tend to dominate. We might be tempted to believe that the New Forest, which is perhaps the finest example of wood pasture in Britain, or even Europe, is an exception to this because its rich flora is well known. However, most of the rare plants recorded occur in the wet boggy areas or protected woodland and not in the open grazed areas. Because the number of ponies in the Forest has been steadily increasing, and the area they have to graze in is less, the rich flora has greatly diminished. We have the same problem in other wood pastures which are now important recreation areas. The herds of fallow and red deer in Bradgate Park, a square mile of ancient deer park in Leicestershire, are kept in considerably greater numbers than the park vegetation can support because the public like to see them grazing among the trees. The heathy grassland is overgrazed, preventing the regeneration of the magnificent old oak trees, and as these die, they are not succeeded by younger trees.

However, the botanist who visits wood pastures is interested primarily in the tiny plants such as lichens and mosses which grow on the old trees rather than the vegetation on the ground. As a tree gets older the 'chemistry' of its bark seems to change and favours those lichens which do not grow, or else are very scarce, on younger trees. Only the continuity of ancient bark enables them to survive. But of course this is not the only factor which determines whether rare lichens will grow. If the trees are in a region where there is atmospheric pollution, they will die even though the host trees are not affected. Again in some parts the land between the trees is cultivated or else the park itself is surrounded by cultivated fields. There is now evidence that the dust from artificial fertilizers and the drift from herbicide sprays may kill off some of the bark flora. Lichens and mosses grow best in clean air with a high humidity so that in general they are richest in the west and the north, and wood pastures in industrial areas or the drier parts of eastern England generally have fewer species.

The two native British oaks, the pedunculate, which is the more common, and the sessile, are usually the dominant trees in wood pastures, and it is on them that the largest number of lichens have been recorded. Francis Rose of London University recorded 324 different species of lichens on oaks, the richest bark flora of any native tree in Britain. It seems that oak trees that have existed for thousands of years in our countryside have enabled more species of lichens and mosses to colonize them and become adapted to their bark conditions than other trees which, although also common, have perhaps not had the wide distribution of oaks. The ash tree, with 255 species, and the beech, with 205, come next on Rose's list, but there are eight other common trees and shrubs which recorded well over 100 lichens each. Nevertheless very few species of lichen are restricted to only one kind of tree. The same is true for invertebrate animals, although in both cases preference is shown for one particular tree or group of related trees.

Wood pastures in the modern world face a rather uncertain future. The succession of trees of all ages is very important in their management, but the right conditions often do not exist because of recreational pressures, overgrazing, and even such activities as cultivation. Where they have a full degree of protection, such as the Wychwood National Nature Reserve, the New Forest, Windsor Forest, Sherwood Forest and Epping Forest, or properties held by the National Trust, they will survive for many more years to come. In too many cases, however, when trees that are in fragile old age die, there will be no others to follow in the cycle of decay, maintaining the continuity of habitat which the special fauna and flora require, and extinction will not be far away.

Cottage gardens

Some parks sit more easily in the countrysides of Britain than others, but all seem to some extent interlopers and somewhat contrived. Another form of rural vista that has been created for pleasure is the poor man's park: the cottage garden. The scale may be miniature and the designs diverse, but the cottage garden always seems quite at home in its village setting and seldom fails to gladden the eye. There must be almost as many definitions of the craft as there are cottage gardens – and each authority offers a different diagnosis. Yet none would doubt that the cottage garden is a distinctive horticultural form and this

Cottage gardens often contain a blend of native and introduced plants. In this corner of one of the authors' cottage gardens orange Crocismia *from Africa and pink* Monarda *from North America are mixed with the native purple loosestrife.*

undisciplined, colourful and evocative tradition has influenced the design of countless modern suburban plots.

The essence of cottage gardening involves the informal arrangements of traditional garden plants – mainly perennials – to produce groupings of plants which flower in sequence and complement each other in foliage, form and hue without ever seeming to result from a carefully co-ordinated campaign of planting. Often the path from gate to door provides the main feature and axis of the cottage garden, while in the past, though much less so today, vegetables were combined with flowering plants to bolster the economics of the plot.

Though redolent of Olde Worlde things, the cottage garden is a relative youngster in the countryside mosaic. Cottage gardens as we know them today certainly did not exist in medieval times. Then the typical village dwelling occupied a sizeable plot of land, a ribbon-like 'toft' running back from the house or a more rectangular 'close'. Sometimes these plots were ploughed to raise a crop of grain or legumes, sometimes they must have been used to pasture a milk cow, goat or geese, but some space must also have been used for growing vegetables for the peasant household. Useful herbs may also have been grown there, although many will have been gathered in glades and hedgerows. But with land scarce and famine a frequent visitor, it is unlikely that toft and close land could have been spared for floral displays. A garland of woodbine or ivy growing round a cottage door may have been the only decoration of the domestic setting, although the old folk ballads contain many reminders of the peasants' sensitivity to the beauties of the countryside.

When we look at medieval village layouts, which may be fossilized in living villages or marked out by the earthworks at deserted sites, we find scant evidence of front gardens. The dwellings mainly lined the high street and side roads, fringed the green or were scattered amongst the patchwork patterns of closes. After the Middle Ages, front gardens gradually appeared. They could be obtained by encroachments which nibbled into the margins of the green or high street or could be gained during a rebuilding by positioning the new dwelling a little further back in its toft or close. It was really only in the nineteenth century, and often under the influence of Picturesque and Romantic movements, that front gardens became a standard component in most new building works.

As the young tradition became established, the countryman or woman was able to express both the love of Nature and a personal sense of colour and design. Being generally as poor as church mice, the cottage gardeners could seldom afford the exotic plants which the nurseries and seedsmen offered, yet the range of potential garden inmates was enormous. There were plants like honesty and foxgloves which grew in the wild and also cultivars of native, continental and eastern species which had grown in the gardens of the gentry for centuries, like roses, irises and pinks. Then there were the plants raised from seeds, cuttings and seedlings which were donated or filched from the gardens of the local mansions and others which circulated by swop, favour and natural seeding amongst the village gardens.

Then, as fashions in gardening changed and the disciplined municipal flowerbeds of gaudy exotic annuals enjoyed a vogue and influenced most suburban planting schemes, the cottage gardens which so often endured in the villages became a preserve for many fine old flowers that were temporarily out of favour and which would, in many cases, have otherwise been lost. This writer acquired a wilderness which years before had been the cottage garden of gardeners working at a nearby mansion. As the undergrowth was cleared, some delightful old flowers resurfaced: venerable rarities like the lace-edged polyanthus, an old strain of blue and grey delphinium as well as peonies and old roses which had doubtless found their way here from the master's garden. Now, as fashions have turned again, the cottage garden repertoire of plants is being explored and exploited as nostalgic townsfolk introduce a breath of the old countryside into their urban plots. Auriculas, old roses, violas, old fashioned pinks and herbaceous perennials like delphiniums, aquilegias, phlox, bergamot, globe flowers and day lilies are all winning back niches in the modern garden.

Most of the cottage garden plants have pedigrees of cultivation which extend back for many centuries beyond the days of cottage gardening. Pinks were used to weave garlands and coronets by the ancient Athenians, who called the plant the 'flower of Jove'. It is possible that the 'gillyflowers' of medieval England arrived as seeds attached to building stone brought by the Normans from France. Pinks and carnations have been cultivated here since at least the fourteenth century and one variety dating from this time, Fenbow's Nutmeg Clove, is still in cultivation. Cottage gardening was not just the preserve of rural village folk, for it had a powerful appeal to nineteenth-century workers in the new industrial townlets. The weavers of Paisley had an unbounded enthusiasm for the breeding of pinks and created many new varieties. Meanwhile, the Lancashire cotton workers developed show auriculas from stock introduced to Britain in the sixteenth century, and the miners of Yorkshire and Derbyshire specialized in the new pansies, distant cousins of Shakespeare's 'Love in Idleness', *Viola tricolor* or heartsease, a resident of many medieval gardens.

Primroses were also grown in medieval gardens and a cross between the primrose and the cowslip around the end of the medieval period produced the hybrid oxlip, which may have been crossed with a Caucasian primrose to produce a red polyanthus in the seventeenth century. In the eighteenth century, varieties with beautiful gold or silver lacings to the petals appeared and in the 1860s several hundred varieties of these lovely plants were on offer. But then they fell from favour, so that in the 1950s the resurrection of the lace-edged polyanthus depended on stock preserved and surviving in a few cottage gardens.

Old roses should have a place in every cottage garden. The range is vast. It includes the many *Rosa alba* hybrids and the venerable *Rosa alba semiplana* – the old white rose of York. There are the Bourbon roses, born of a cross between the China and the Damask roses on the French island of Réunion and including old favourites like 'Queen Victoria' and 'Madame Isaac Periere'. The Damask rose is said to have been brought back from Damascus by Crusaders (although it could have been introduced to England by the Romans), and the Damask group includes the York and Lancaster rose, whose pink and white blooms were seen as a symbol of reconciliation after the Wars of the Roses. Members of the *Rosa gallica* group have been cultivated since the Middle Ages and the red rose of Lancaster was an early import from the rose growing and perfumery district of Provins near Fontainebleau. The musk rose is one of several types of rose mentioned by Shakespeare and popular cottage garden forms include 'Buff Beauty' and 'Felicia'. In 1799 Miss May Lawrence illustrated *A Collection of Roses from Nature* with etchings of ninety different types, but it was in the following century that the garden hybrids really proliferated, with new species roses from China being used to produce a multitude of hybrids. Many old roses have been lost or have lost their vigour and earlier this century it may have seemed that the whole genre might be displaced by the bright new hybrid tea and floribunda forms. But now the pastel tones, arching foliage and sweet perfume of the old rose is back in favour and many a cottage garden contains an old rose which has lived right through the fall from grace.

The art of cottage gardening involves careful systems of planting to produce the illusion of a spontaneous and unmarshalled explosion of colour. But the village garden is much more than the exclusive abode for the selected members of the garden community – as all gardeners will know. It includes unwelcome intruders in the form of weeds and pests, useful visitors and residents like hedgehogs and toads and a variety of birds, animals and insects which are attracted by the largesse of the cottager or the scraps of sustenance which are spin-offs of the gardening habit.

Nature in the garden

Most of us like to encourage birds and butterflies in our gardens, even if we resent insect pests and do all we can to eliminate them. Many insects are useful predators and others are parasitic on garden pests, so that the control of undesirable species should be carefully balanced in order to preserve those which do good. This is best done by local application of a pesticide with a small handspray, avoiding wholesale spraying of all the vegetation. In a very large garden this may be too time-consuming but by arranging it so that plants which need regular applications of insecticides are all in a relatively confined area, most of the rest is uncontaminated.

The value of a garden for wildlife depends as much on variety of habitats as it does on size. Some very large gardens are so formalized that they have little value to wildlife, while much smaller urban gardens have a remarkable wealth of bird and insect life because their owners do all they can to encourage them. Important wildlife habitats range from large trees to stone walls with many small crevices, a well-formed rockery, ivy allowed to grow on walls or trees, a compost heap, a pond, or an area of uncut grassland. Birds and other animals have three basic needs in order to thrive: sufficient food, shelter for roosting, resting and avoiding predators and somewhere to breed. Food for birds can be easily provided in the winter if one follows the advice in the numerous publications of the Royal

*Some birds which are common visitors to the garden,
especially when winter food is provided.*

Blue tit.

Robin.

Goldfinch.

Greenfinch.

Society for the Protection of Birds. In the summer, any small leaf warblers which might nest require many shrubs and trees of native species to provide them with adequate food, ground vegetation and, of course, freedom from pesticide sprays. In general there is no need to put out nuts and seeds when the warmer weather arrives in the spring as there will be plenty of natural food. Nest boxes may be essential for tits, some finches and other birds such as the spotted flycatcher and common redstart if there are no natural holes, ivy-covered trees, shrubberies or banks of honeysuckle.

Most gardens have a lawn. It is the place in which to play, to sunbathe or just to sit and enjoy the fresh air. Keen gardeners pride themselves on maintaining the traditional English lawn, envied and copied by many other countries – an even, very short, totally green sward made up only of fine grasses. A great deal of effort is needed to produce this sort of 'green baize' – herbicides, fertilizers, lawn sand, rolling, spiking and regular cutting. To lawn fanatics this is well worth the time and expense, but if the lawn is a large one, it is economic *and* a help to wildlife if the part furthest from the house is left alone, except for cutting once a year in the late autumn. A very varied vegetation soon develops depending on the nature of the soil. In this writer's garden of calcareous clay where part of the grass is treated in this way, there are cowslips, ladies smock, thistles, cow parsley, a few docks and field mallows. On the cut part of the lawn, dandelions, clovers, small *Trifolium* species, and daisies are common. When all these flowers set seed in the late summer we are seldom without goldfinches, linnets and greenfinches.

The well-known naturalist and broadcaster Ted Ellis describes how part of his garden was ploughed and levelled and then allowed to develop naturally. At first it was only a weed patch but by occasional cutting it became an attractive meadow with many spotted orchids, ladies smock, marsh thistles, and knapweeds, which attracted goldfinches and other seed-eating birds. The abundant sorrel plants in his grassland provide food for a population of small copper butterflies. Grasses are the foodplants of several common butterflies – the speckled wood, meadow brown and ringlet – and gardeners who are really keen on encouraging butterflies will tolerate a nettle patch. Even the Royal Horticultural Society one year allowed the Nature Conservancy Council to include nettles in a display on wildlife in gardens at their Annual Show. We are more aware of butterflies in high summer when they seek out nectar-bearing flowers in herbaceous borders. The common buddleia is exceptional in this respect, and in particular, from this writer's experience, the mauve-

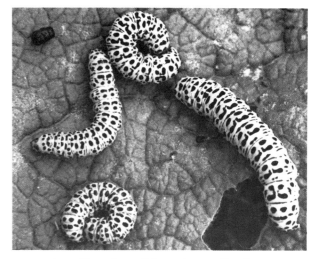

Caterpillars of a mullein moth on mullein leaves in one of the authors' gardens.

flowered variety. The common houseleek, and almost any type of daisy and aster, are much sought after by butterflies. In this writer's garden there are giant tobacco plants and large banks of honeysuckle which both attract night-flying moths and also the humming-bird hawk moth, which we see almost every year.

Honeysuckle berries are a useful food for birds in the late autumn and the nature reserve garden should have other berried shrubs and trees. Cotoneaster, ivy, holly, hawthorn, elder, wild rose, brambles, ornamental cherries and crabapples are all easily obtained and will grow almost anywhere. The songthrush, blackbird, redwing and fieldfare are likely to be the most frequent berry-eating birds in the garden but less common species may occasionally appear. I have seen waxwings eating cotoneaster berries and ornamental cherries. The nutritious nuts of the beech tree or even hornbeams in larger gardens attract the brambling, a winter-visiting finch from Scandinavia, and our own resident, but rarely seen, hawfinch. Oak trees are even more useful because they have more insects living on them than any other tree species in Britain. Even a single small oak is an object lesson is ecology for the discerning naturalist prepared to examine and observe the seasonal change of wildlife on leaf, branch and trunk. It is also an example of native trees (or plants) being preferred to exotic species. Plants from distant parts of the world are usually unattractive to our native fauna, which is not adapted to the 'chemistry' of the unfamiliar plant.

A garden habitat of special interest is the pond. However small it may be, standing water seems to attract a multitude of creatures, particularly if there are no fish. Goldfish are notoriously greedy and will go on eating as long as there is food. They provide endless interest in ornamental ponds but if the aim is to have a variety of water beetles, water bugs, dragonfly and damselfly larvae as well as frog spawn, the pond is better without fish. Most insects depend in some way on vegetation so it is important to have both aquatic and marginal plants. These aerate the water with oxygen and provide dead vegetation for snails and other creatures as well as returning nutrients to the plants. A pond should not be sited under trees because the accumulation of leaf fall may be excessive. Rotting leaves use up too much oxygen and produce toxic chemicals so that other life, particularly fish, may die. They also need to have a section one-and-a-half to two feet deep, where there will always be water in hard winters. Marginal or shallow-water vegetation greatly enhances the variety of wildlife and can be grown in pots or specially prepared ledges where the water is only an inch or so deep. An intermediate section where the water is about six inches deep is also useful because frogs prefer to spawn in this depth of water. A fountain or waterfall helps to aerate the water and the latter may encourage thick banks of mosses if water is allowed to trickle down the rock face.

Of the more unusual minor habitats in gardens, the compost heap is often of considerable interest, although it must be made up mostly of dead leaves and grass clippings, not just domestic and garden waste. A compost heap of leaves and clippings is like the dead vegetation that is found in woodland, but on a grand scale. Grass and leaves rot down slowly and usually have many air spaces between the pieces of vegetation. Hedgehogs burrow in to hibernate for the winter, grass

Two frequent visitors to the garden, the wood mouse and the hedgehog. The hedgehog is just about to uncurl; note how its spines provide an all-round protection.

snakes incubate their eggs in the additional warmth of the compost, and many invertebrate animals thrive, particularly small beetles, flies and springtails. Attracted to this abundance of food are numerous predators from shrews to beetles, but especially small spiders. In some cases money spiders may be so abundant that the silk they spin covers the heap with a shining sheet like polythene. At the bottom of the heap the leaves become fragmented by invertebrate larvae and fungi and the same sort of animals that live in soil move into this thick layer of organic material.

Drystone walls and rockeries provide an 'arid' habitat in the garden. The crevices accumulate dust and debris which form a soil suitable for small plants such as the ivy-leaved toadflax or even tall plants such as *Verbascum* species. Several ferns grow in wall crevices, and the rock face, particularly if it is calcareous, will gradually become covered with lichens – provided atmospheric pollution is low. Several spiders live in the crevices and catch their prey on webs spun along the rock surface and radiating out from their retreats. Jumping spiders, which do not spin webs but hunt by sight, are usually common and will also be found on the walls of houses. The most frequent species is the common zebra spider, easily identified by the black and white pattern on its back.

Gardens in the middle of towns are generally not so rich in wildlife as those in suburban areas, and the latter less so than gardens in the countryside. The Chelsea Physic Garden was started in the seventeenth century to grow herbs useful in medicine. At that time the garden must have been on the edge of the countryside, but today its fauna is mainly limited to hardy species, having suffered the Industrial Revolution and atmospheric pollution which scarcely improved until after the last war.

Another famous garden in London, at Buckingham Palace, was intensively studied by the London Natural History Society in 1961–1962. There has been a garden on this site since the sixteenth century but it was much later that it became part of a Royal Palace. The garden has been altered and redesigned many times so it has suffered considerable disturbance. When the survey was made, air pollution was still quite bad in London and the gardens were maintained in an orderly and neat state, as they, of course, are today. An enormous number of plants have been introduced over the years, including a black mulberry which is said to have been planted in 1609. There is a lake of three-and-a-half acres in the total area of thirty-nine, but not much wildlife is associated with it and there are also two-and-a-quarter miles of gravel paths. In 1961–1962 a total of 260 species of wild plants were recorded compared with 475 in all the central London parks. Three hundred and two species of Lepidoptera were seen but these included only three butterflies, the small and holly blues and the red admiral. The holly blue is the only butterfly which breeds there. The birdlife was poor, recording only twenty-one species, but this does compare favourably with the seventeen species in the 105 acres of St James and Green Parks, twenty-three in the 635 acres of Hyde Park and Kensington Gardens, and twenty-eight in the 574 acres of Regents Park and Primrose Hill. Perhaps a survey today, when atmospheric pollution in London is not such a serious problem, would record more species of birds and other animals, but it shows very clearly the poor state of wildlife over large areas of urban parks. The garden nature reserve must be carefully planned and managed if it is to fulfil its potential, and ornamental or public amenity gardens are not adequate substitutes.

— 8 —

THE CHANGING WORLD
OF THE FARM

*Bridge Street Farm near Long Melford in Suffolk,
a timber-framed building with old brick chimneys and roofing
in plain tiles, built in the style of the Elizabethan era.*

Most countrysides in Britain are working landscapes, and each is partitioned amongst a flock of land-holdings and tenancies, most of which contain a farmstead. The farmstead, with its farmhouse and its little complex of farm buildings, serves as the headquarters and supply base for agricultural operations on the lands around. For many generations the farming lifestyle has had a very special appeal, and the numbers of children who have aspired to become farmers must rival those of the intending engine drivers. Often the crowning joy of a Christmas or birthday was the gift of a model farmyard, complete with a quota of cattle, sheep, pigs, chickens and geese, with a turkey, a heavy horse and also 'Farmer Giles' decked out in boots, britches and weskit.

In the real world, however, such delightful 'mixed farms' are being rapidly replaced by specialized production units. Lovely, well-tended countrysides are being devastated by the onslaughts of prairie farming, and a new word, 'agri-business', has entered the language. The romantic world of the rumbling harvest wagons and heavy horses seems to have gone for ever. But some lovely and fascinating traditional farm buildings still remain, while in many rugged places the hardy hill farmers are still heroic and often impoverished figures, whose labour maintains the landscapes that we love. In this chapter we emphasize the old rather than the new worlds of farming, for the country-lover will find no pleasure or interest amongst the cavernous abodes of battery chickens or the concrete veal and pork factories.

We began the chapter on churches by exploring the question of why these buildings are where they are – and the same question can be asked of farms. The discerning rambler will soon realize that a high proportion of farmsteads in England and Wales are between around 130 and 250 years old. This is easily explained, and where such eighteenth- and nineteenth-century buildings are seen to be surrounded by straight walls and hedgerows outlining rectangular fields, then one can be fairly sure that the scene is a product of the Parliamentary Enclosure movement described in Chapter 1. Previously, most farmhouses in the lowland areas stood within villages and the majority of our surviving medieval and seventeenth-century village dwellings were originally the homes of farming families. But when Enclosure repartitioned the village fields, the favoured families would frequently migrate from the village to settle in a new farmstead that was built in a convenient spot close to the core of the newly consolidated land-holding.

But not all our dispersed and solitary farmsteads belong to the aftermath of Parliamentary Enclosure. It is true that in many counties, particularly those of the English Midlands, the medieval rural landscape was dominated by nucleated villages mainly composed of clustered peasant farmsteads. Yet there were other counties, like Essex, Kent and Devon, where the village never gained such an ascendancy, while Cornwall was traditionally a land of hamlets composed of just two, three or four farmsteads. In such places the habit of scattered and solitary settlement can have a very long history.

This point was underlined by Warwick Rodwell's fascinating excavations in the area around the church at Rivenhall in Essex. The decaying church served a parish with no old village but instead a scatter of farmsteads; the parish itself could represent a very ancient estate, while the core of farming operations in the area lay close to the church. Beside the church were found the traces of an Iron Age farmstead, a Roman villa and a succession of Saxon halls and medieval manor houses. The other scattered farms in the parish also stand on very old sites, for documents show that farmsteads have stood in these places since at least early-medieval times. In the same county the archaeologist Tom Williamson has studied the evidence of lost settlements as it is revealed by pot fragments of different ages which are exposed at the old dwelling places by ploughing. His 'field walking' surveys have produced many little sites which show a succession of Iron Age, Romano-British, Saxon and medieval farmsteads. Such methods can only really be used at deserted sites, but we can be sure that there are scores of living farms which stand on a patch of ground that has been home to a farming family since Roman or prehistoric times.

A Lakeland farmstead near Pike O'Stickle. It is located on level, sheltered ground above the reach of flooding. Note how in this part of Britain the farmhouses are limewashed and sometimes rendered, while the adjoining byres are in drystone walling.

Sometimes the antiquity of a farm site can be revealed by a study of old maps and older documents, but although the surviving buildings usually reflect the age of a Parliamentary Enclosure farmstead, many old farm sites are far older than the standing buildings. Sometimes a clue is preserved in the name of a farm, and in the north of England many farms have Old Norse and Old Danish names, given in the centuries which bracket the Norman conquest when Scandinavian dialects were spoken in the north, with -by and -thorpe endings denoting farmsteads or small settlements, while -scale, -ergh and -sett endings all derive from words describing seasonal settlements on summer pastures. Further south, other clues are found in the traces of moats which can be seen around many larger farmsteads, with Suffolk alone containing hundreds of examples. Rectangular moats were commonly dug around medieval manors and around the more substantial farmsteads. Sometimes they helped to drain the site and to give a small measure of protection against roaming vagabonds, but the homestead moat seems to

have been primarily a status symbol which aped the splendour of the moated castles of the aristocracy. Usually these moats are partly infilled or scarcely visible, but many more complete examples can still be seen, as at Otley Hall in Suffolk, Eltisley in Cambridgeshire or Foxearth in Essex.

Moated manor and farmstead sites can be found beside villages or in isolated situations, while a number of other solitary farm sites were established in the course of the Middle Ages. A few of these farmsteads were created to play special commercial roles within great feudal estates, like the horse studs and cattle farms established in some woods and forests. Far more numerous were the medieval farms that were founded in the course of colonizing outlying areas of woodland, moorland or marsh. Such places were often named 'Newham' or 'New Farm' or they could take their names from their owners or from noteworthy current events – and the old Antioch Farm in Dorset could have a name inspired by accounts of the Crusades. Scores of other farms originated as medieval 'gran-

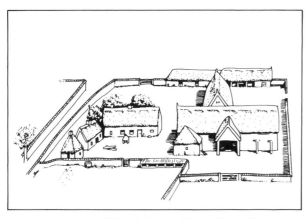

Reconstruction of Prior's Manor House, North Elmham

ges' – farming centres established within the great monastic agricultural empires – and 'Grange' farm names are very common. In the area around Fountains Abbey in Yorkshire we can still find Sutton Grange, Thornton Grange, Cayton Grange, Hutton Grange and several other examples. There are other solitary farmsteads which stand in places which were once bustling villages, for frequently a single farm would survive the destruction of the community. This was the case at Malton in Cambridgeshire, where the village, which had been in decline, was cleared by eviction in 1517. Landowners who had torn down a village to create sheep runs across the deserted fields would need a base for their shepherd; monks who had removed a peasant settlement could replace it with a grange, while farmers who had bought out their village neighbours would gain sole command of the settlement site. In ways such as these, an isolated farm often became heir to a deserted village.

It is often interesting to speculate on why the founders of a particular farmstead chose their site. In the lowland areas one site might be no better than many other possibilities, provided that the ground was free from flooding and a source of water was available. But in the more difficult upland areas it is plain that great care was taken to choose the best situation. Streams and springs provided water supplies in areas too rocky to permit the digging of wells, while light, warmth and shelter were important considerations. In such places the majority of farmsteads have their frontages facing southwards and are built on south-facing slopes. They avoid the bottoms of the deeper valleys where the sunset comes earliest, and they also shun other clefts and pockets which act as frost hollows when the chilled, dense masses of air come rolling down the hillslopes. Where possible they also avoid the most exposed hilltops and plateaux, taking advantage of any slight dips or shelter which the terrain provides,

and the farmsteads are often screened by short shelter belts that are planted on their windward sides.

Every farmstead has its own story and its own reason for being just where it is, although often the origin will be lost in the mists of time. Standing farm buildings can usually be dated with more precision, although an old farm house will usually show the evidence of many stages of adaptation. (In the Middle Ages farms were known as 'messuages' and the word 'farm' then referred to the feudal practice of farming-out portions of estate land for a fixed payment.) In looking at old rural dwellings it is not always easy to draw firm lines between manor houses and farmsteads and farmsteads and cottages. Many farmsteads were manor houses, many farmsteads were converted to become cottages or attractive 'period' dwellings, while occasionally cottages could be knocked together to become farmhouses. Several of the house types (like the laithe-houses) which are introduced in the chapter on cottages were originally built as farmsteads. One widely adopted form of manor house and farmstead that was built in the earlier medieval centuries was the aisled hall. A number of older timber-framed farmsteads still have an aisled hall at their core, although this layout is usually hard to recognize following the insertion of a ceiling to create two storeys and the removal of the aisle posts which supported the roof or their inclusion within later partitioning walls. To see an aisled hall in a form that is close to its original fourteenth-century condition one can visit Edgar's House at the museum of East Anglian Life at Stowmarket in Suffolk, while aisled structures can be seen in grand and uncluttered forms in a number of surviving medieval aisled barns.

A little later in the medieval period the 'hall and cross-wing' form of timber-framed farmstead became very popular. The traditional open hall, which served as a general-purpose venue for all social and business activities, provided the core of the house, and the living and service space was often increased by the addition of cross-wings at one or both ends of the hall. Such extensions to the house could produce 'L', 'T' or 'H'-shaped house plans. Medieval farmhouses closely resembled the dwellings occupied by other relatively prosperous members of the community like merchants and craftsmen, while any surviving medieval farmstead is likely to have experienced many modifications. One particularly attractive example is Markings Farm at Whittlesford in Cambridgeshire. At first it appears to be a medieval hall and cross-wing house, but while the

A moated farmstead at Foxearth in Essex.

main range, with the clear traces of a former smoke hole in the gable, is a genuine late-medieval farmstead, the cross-wing dates only from the nineteenth century. Once built it became the main farmhouse, while the medieval range was partitioned to form two subordinate cottages.

One especially noble fifteenth- and sixteenth-century development of the hall and cross-wings concept was the form of timber-framed farmstead known as a 'Wealden house' (see Chapter 5). Here the hall, which was originally open to the rafters, provides the central unit and is flanked at either end by vestigial cross-wings. These were built as two storey units, with their upper storeys being 'jettied' or projecting slightly, while a single straight roof covers all three components.

Both stone and brick were adopted in the houses of the wealthier farmers long before they became standard materials for the building of more lowly cottages. Towards the close of the medieval period stone farmsteads appeared in northern, western and Midlands areas which had suitable building stones, while shortly afterwards farmsteads of brick began to be built in southern and eastern areas lying outside the stone country.

*Markings Farm at Whittlesford in Cambridgeshire;
late-medieval farmstead with a nineteenth-century cross wing.*

In the Lake District the Dissolution of the Monasteries, which marked the end of the Middle Ages, released vast acreages of monastic land. Ownership passed to the local farming families who had previously been tenants of the monasteries. Gradually they began to prosper as yeomen and lesser gentry and were known as 'statesmen'. Some of the stone farmsteads built by the statesmen families still endure, and the best is Townend at Troutbeck, a National Trust property which is open to the public. The Great Rebuilding, which has resulted in the construction of thousands of superb timber-framed hall and cross-wing farmsteads in the south and Midlands, was slow to penetrate the Lake District. It arrived during the seventeenth century, although another century was to pass before it had made its full impact on the dwellings of the lower orders of Lakeland society. In the homes of the statesmen, cruck frames and walls of wattle and daub were superseded by superior constructions in stone. Townend was built to replace the old Browne family house in 1623–1626 and this new house still survives as the core of the present building. According to the traditional practice it was divided into two parts by a cross passage or 'hallan'. The original entrance doorway opened into the hallan and to the right was the working part of the house, the kitchen or 'down house'. To the left, via a short passage or 'mell', was the heated living room, known as the 'fire house' or, more simply, 'the house'. Perhaps a little later, special sleeping accommodation for the master and mistress was provided by the addition of a 'bower' to the back of the fire house, while children and servants slept upstairs in the loft which was divided by 'clam, staff and daub' partitions. The chambers in the loft were probably open to the rafters and thus very chilly.

Superior farmsteads like Townend were not the first stone farm buildings to appear in the far north of England. The small rises in prosperity which had allowed the Great Rebuilding to enter the area were partly the result of the greater security from border raids across the disputed Anglo-Scottish boundary following the union of English and Scottish crowns in 1603. Hitherto, the larger farmers and lesser gentry had sought the protection of stone walls. Although they could not afford to build true castles, they frequently erected square towers or 'peles' beside or as part of their homesteads. Many, like Kentmere Hall near Windermere, a fourteenth-century pele tower with an attached farm building of the sixteenth century, and the much grander Sizergh 'Castle' near Kendal, still survive. Border farming families of a humbler standing sought security in 'bastles'. These medieval defensive farmsteads had some feature in common with the older Norman stone manor houses like Boothby Pagnell manor near Grantham. They were solid rectangular buildings designed for upper-floor living. This level was reached by a stone staircase built against an outside wall, while the more vulnerable ground floor served as a cow house or stable.

When a measure of security and prosperity came to the north most farming families could still not aspire to

An eighteenth century laithe-house at Darley in Nidderdale, showing the arrival of the fashion for a symmetrical façade and double-depth construction.

the relative grandeur of a home like Townend. Celia Fiennes visited the north-west in 1698 and described 'villages of sad little hutts made up of drye walls, only stones piled together and the roofs of the same slatt (slate) . . . for the most part I took them at first sight for a sort of houses and barns to fodder cattle in, not thinking them to be dwelling houses . . . '. Her first impressions were partly correct, for she must have been seeing long-houses and early laithe-houses of the kinds described in Chapter 5. As these dwellings were improved the full partition between the family and the byre was adopted and the houses were built with two distinct storeys, although they were still just one room in depth and extra accommodation at ground floor level was gained by extending the roof downwards to cover an 'outshut' extension. In the Lake District the typical late-seventeenth- and early-eighteenth-century farmstead was built with local stones gathered from the fields or stream bed; the walls of the house were mortared or insulated with mud and coated in limewash, while the adjoining byre was of natural drystone walling. Many of these attractive half grey and half white buildings can still be seen. As national fashions in building penetrated the area so there was the familiar switch to symmetrical façades and the adoption of the double-depth plans described in Chapter 5 which eliminated the need for outshuts and other extensions. However, the spacious symmetrical farmhouses of the Georgian and Victorian eras were too expensive for most fell farmers, so that scores of the older laithe-houses were not replaced.

In other parts of upland Britain the development of the farmhouse followed a different course. Discerning travellers in the north-east of Scotland may be amazed by the stereotyped nature of the granite farmsteads there. The explanation is found in the history of the region. This was an area of vast estates owned by the traditional lairds and clan chieftains. 'Improvements' began on a few progressive estates like Monymusk before the final English victory at Culloden in 1746. After Culloden the ancient warlike lifestyle, which judged a landlord and leader according to the number of armed clansmen and tenants that he could muster, broke down. Warlords became commercial estate owners and so the lairds set about rationalizing their properties. Countless poor tenants were evicted and the estates were re-divided into fewer, more viable tenancies. The old 'fermtouns' of clusters of peasant hovels were swept away and the favoured few were housed in

new dwellings. These late-eighteenth- and early-nineteenth-century farmsteads which appeared in their hundreds throughout the countryside of the north-east might almost all have been taken from a single plan. They are two-up-and-two-down buildings, symmetrical according to the fashion of the day, with a centrally placed entrance, bedrooms lit by the dormer windows or roof lights and with chimneys set at either gable, allowing a fireplace in each room. Here the lairds were so powerful that the slate of rural settlement could be wiped bare. Uniformity became the hallmark of the architecture of the area, and one can still tour all day

and hardly see a farmstead which deviates from the standard.

In Ireland, as in Scotland, there were not the numerous social grades of farmers that existed in England. Consequently these countries did not acquire the broad spectrum of different farmhouse types which echoed the subtle but important differences in status. Both countries were sharply divided between lords and tenants, although the Protestant settlers of the Ulster plantations added a third element in the north of Ireland. Until the eighteenth century Ireland, like Scotland, was prey to war and raiding, so that the

estate-owning classes sought protection in defensive tower houses. The farmsteads of their tenants had several features in common with the farmsteads of the British uplands. Many which date from the eighteenth and nineteenth centuries survive to demonstrate the old vernacular methods of building. Although stone roofing flags were used in a few areas such as the south of Co. Clare, most peasant farmhouses are thatched in oat, wheat straw or reed. The timber-framing tradition which was so deeply rooted in England seems to have been rejected in Ireland. Timber may have been scarce and perhaps the moist climate discouraged the use of

*A nineteenth-century farmstead at Clint in Nidderdale.
The façade is dour and symmetrical, but note the contrasts
with the farmstead in the previous photograph. The windows are
vertical sliding sashes, the roof is in imported slate rather
than local flags and the vernacular feature of projecting stone
'kneelers' at the junction of the gable and eaves has
been abandoned.*

structural timbers. In any event, roofs were carried by walls of stone rubble or mud rather than being supported by framing timbers. These Irish roofs are steeply pitched to shed the heavy rainfall, while thick walls and small window openings give some protection from the fierce Atlantic gales. The small rectangular farmsteads reflect both the climate of Ireland and the poverty of their original occupants. They are of just a single storey, with the floor space partitioned to provide a living room and one or two smaller sleeping or working rooms.

Within Ireland there are some regional variations on this small and stone-built theme. In Ulster a form of the Scottish 'but and ben' peasant farmstead reflects the close contacts between the two countries. Here the chimneys built into each gable heat the living and the sleeping room. In contrast, in the south-east the roofs are hipped rather than gabled and the plan is of the baffle entry type (see p 151), with the centrally-placed hearth and chimney serving only the living room. In the west the dwellings are still of a single storey, but here the groundplans are sectioned to provide a central kitchen-cum-living room with bedrooms at either end. One of these bedrooms often superseded the adjoining byre which featured in the original form of this long-house plan. Here the chimney is placed in the partitioning wall separating the kitchen and a bedroom. Chimneys only arrived in the peasant dwellings of western Ireland during the nineteenth century and previously there was an open hearth and the doors placed at either side of the kitchen could be opened to produce the through-draught needed to waft away the peat smoke. Humble, archaic and perishable peasant farmsteads were still being built until relatively modern times in western Scotland and Ireland and most of the seemingly medieval 'black houses' of the Hebrides are only nineteenth-century buildings, while in the west of Ireland the apparently prehistoric blister-shaped 'clochans' with rubble walls and thatched roofs were being built until the middle of the eighteenth century. The geographer F. Aalen has described how the three-

New House Farm in Bishopdale (the name implies that an older farmstead stood on this site), a superb laithe-house in the style of the early-seventeenth century.

roomed farmsteads of western Ireland could have evolved from such clochans as the groundplan became rectangular, the chimney replaced the open hearth and the byre became a store room or extra bedroom. In parts of north-west Ireland another variation developed in houses which display a small rectangular projection in the side wall of the central kitchen; this is a 'bed out-shut', which provided a little extra sleeping accommodation. A fine selection of Irish peasant farmsteads reconstructed from the traditional designs favoured in the different regions of the country can be explored at the excellent Bunratty folk museum near Shannon airport.

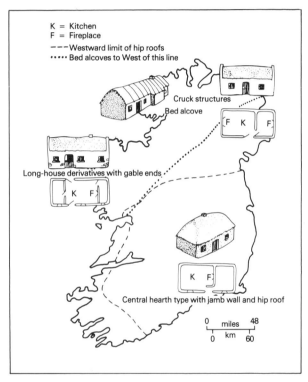

Regional Farmhouse Styles in Ireland

The Great Rebuilding was a late arrival in Scotland and Wales, but when, in the eighteenth century, it did arrive it tended to sweep away most of the older dwellings so that neither country has a heritage of medieval and seventeenth-century farmsteads to compare with the English legacy. The majority of farmsteads seen in Wales today embody Georgian and early-Victorian symmetry and many were built as double-pile dwellings. In some places, however, the survivors of the previous generation of farm buildings can still be seen. They are derivatives of the ancient long-house tradition, consisting of a long range of buildings, just one room in depth, with the bedroom at the higher end of the range and then the living room, which was originally separated from the byre by a cross passage. As in the Pennines and some other rugged districts of England, the original long-house may survive as a barn, with its domestic replacement, a symmetrical two-up-and-two-down or double-pile house, standing nearby. Like the other Celtic lands, Wales is essentially a country of stone farmsteads, although timber-framing in styles similar to those of the English West Midlands can be seen in the borders and occasionally elsewhere and there are a few cob buildings in the north of Dyfed.

The vernacular farmhouses of Britain and Ireland reflected the local building materials, climate, traditions and prosperity of the different regions, while the nature of the local farming lifestyle also determined the sorts of farm buildings which were needed. In the moist areas where livestock farming then predominated, byres and sturdy hay barns were essential, while in the affluent grainlands, threshing barns and stables for the heavy horses which pulled the ploughs and harvest wagons were required. But the farm buildings which a farmer or husbandman owned were determined by his wealth and the scale of his farming operations, so that at a number of deserted medieval village sites one can distinguish between the earthworks which trace the mean little peasant long-houses and the much larger 'courtyard farms' which were owned by a few more affluent neighbours. In the courtyard type of layout a central rectangular courtyard was flanked on three or four sides by ranges of farm buildings. The enthusiasm for this simple form of farmstead plan was remarkably durable, for it was used at least from medieval times and often still featured in the model farms built on great estates under the progressive influences of the eighteenth- and nineteenth-century Agricultural Revolution.

Most old farms were mixed farms, growing various crops and raising different types of livestock, although naturally the balance would vary from one sort of environment to another. Different farm buildings had different roles to play and in addition to the farmhouse which housed the farming family and some of their servants, many farmsteads included a covered barn for threshing and grain storage; accommodation for cattle, horses and pigs; and the farmyard itself, which served as a place where stock could exercise and where straw and muck from the stables, sty and cow-house could be stored until it was spread across the ploughland. The great barn was usually placed at the northern end of the yard, where its bulk provided some shelter against cold north winds. The yard itself would then face southwards to catch the sun which would warm and

The medieval abbey barn at Lacock in Wiltshire, a National Trust property.

dry its flags or cobbles. Often facing the barn across the yard were the sheds where carts and machines were stored, with their open entrances looking northwards to avoid both the sunlight and the driving rain carried on the south-westerlies which might warp or rot the timbers of the vehicles. The stables were generally set on the western side of the yard, facing eastwards towards the rising sun so that at dawn the ploughmen and carters would have some light as they began their chores. The farmhouse could form part of the ranges around the yard, but is was often sited just to the south of these buildings, while the stackyard where the unthreshed grain that could not be accommodated in the great threshing barn was often conveniently sited just to the north of the barn.

These barns, the most noble of all farm buildings, are a legacy of the pre-Victorian centuries when threshing was accomplished by hand by beating the ears of grain with a hinged stick or 'flail'. Most have a central cross passage which is closed at either end by great double doors. At harvest time the wagons would enter by one set of doors, discharge their cargo of sheaves into the cavernous bays which flanked the passage and then leave via the other set of doors, and the next wagon would enter. During the autumn and winter the grain was threshed on the hard floor of the barn passage and

the doors were opened to create a draught. The threshed grain was winnowed by being tossed in the air so that the wind could carry away the chaff.

The threshing barns were generally more imposing than the farmhouse itself, and in the cathedral-like interiors of the older barns one can gain the most vivid appreciations of the medieval craft of timber-framing. Some barns that date from the times of the Crusades survive, and the oldest surviving timber-framing endures not in a house, but in the aisle posts of a private barn at Belchamp St Paul in Essex; it is of a late-Saxon date. The great aisled barns of the medieval period have an incomparable grandeur and a particularly fine example, formerly an Abbot's barn and dating in parts to the thirteenth century, can be explored at the Museum of East Anglian Life at Stowmarket in Suffolk. The cruck-framing technique of the northern and western counties did not permit the erection of such gigantic structures, but in these regions the emphasis was generally placed on livestock farming rather than the cultivation of cereal crops, so that small threshing barns were usually adequate. A delightful cruck-framed threshing barn from Herefordshire, which has cruck blades of black poplar and walls of woven split oak pales and which may date from the sixteenth century, is displayed at the Avoncroft Museum of

Magnificent timber-framing in a massive threshing barn at Bassingbourn in Cambridgeshire.

Buildings near Bromsgrove. Extra height could be gained if the cruck blades were carried on walls, and the Abbey barn at Glastonbury is a superb example of this technique and seems to date mainly from the fourteenth century. Many but by no means all of the surviving medieval threshing barns were tithe barns, where the church stored its tenth of the local farming surplus. A number of such tithe barns have survived and there are other excellent examples at Bradford-on-Avon in Wiltshire and Great Coxwell in Oxfordshire.

At the start of the nineteenth century horse-powered threshing machines enjoyed a brief burst of popularity before they were in turn superseded by steam-powered machines. The horse was walked in a circle, turning a wheel which transferred the power to a shaft driving the threshing machine, which was housed nearby in the old barn. The horse and wheel were often provided with a shelter known as a 'gin-gang' and some of these circular early-nineteenth-century buildings can still be seen abutting against an older barn.

Once threshed, grain needed to be stored in a dry, weather-proof place that was secure from rodents. Often this space was found within the threshing barn or above the cartshed, and the farmer relied upon the rag-tag collection of working cats to keep the rats and mice in check. But in some places a purpose-built granary was preferred. These were generally square, boxy buildings of timber-framing and brick noggin with pyramidal roofs of thatch or plain tiles, and they were set above the reach of vermin on brick legs or mushroom-shaped 'staddle stones'. Several post-medieval granaries are on public display; there is a typical early-eighteenth-century example at the Weald and Downland Museum at Singleton in West Sussex; the Avoncroft museum has a late-eighteenth-century granary built over an open cartshed, and an attractive example in brick has recently been re-erected inside the ramparts of the Iron Age hillfort at Wandlebury near Cambridge.

Many old barns have survived in reasonable conditions because they remained useful as store houses after the arrival of mechanized threshing. The stables built for plough beasts and cart horses have often been less fortunate, and have usually been demolished or gutted to serve as machinery stores. In medieval times oxen were much more numerous than heavy horses and in a few places ploughing was still being accomplished by oxteams until the start of this century. A few ox stables are said to endure in Wales, being distinguished by the wider doors needed for these animals with their spreading horns. Really old cattle sheds are much less common than old barns and in the Middle Ages cattle were usually wintered in open 'crew yards'. Straw was provided as litter to give a dry footing, and the enormous accumulation of manure from these yards was then carted to the ploughlands. Cattle sheds or 'hovels' were usually simple buildings, with a gabled roof that was often of plain tiles being carried on widely-spaced upright posts. These sheds were normally part of the farmyard range of buildings and were built next to and often at right angles to the threshing barn. Several mid-eighteenth- to mid-nineteenth-century examples are displayed at the Weald and Downland museum.

Until the arrival of the railways the dairying industry was held in check by the problem of transporting the products rapidly to markets. Each peasant family aspired to own a milk cow, butter and cheese for local sale were produced in the larger farmsteads, while fresh milk for the townsfolk tended to come from squalid urban cowhouses, and large cities could have dozens of these establishments. Model dairies producing cheese and butter featured in many late-eighteenth- and nineteenth-century estate improvement schemes and excellently preserved examples of such dairies can be seen at Easton Park in Suffolk and Lanhydrock House in Cornwall. On the smaller farms of the period a room or annex of the farmhouse was used as a dairy and the manufacture of butter and cheese was the preserve of the farmer's wife and daughters. Improvements in the transport system allowed milk to be moved rapidly to centralized dairies and the commercial production of cheese and butter in farmhouses was undermined, while mechanized milking and strict hygiene regulations have transformed the older milking parlours.

Dovecotes are amongst the most attractive of the old agricultural buildings. Because of the devastation which the domesticated rock doves could cause in the surrounding grain fields, in medieval times the right to keep these birds was monopolized by the lords of manors. Near Bruton in Somerset there is a splendid medieval stone dovecote, a towering building with niches for hundreds of birds, which was formerly the property of the local abbey and another monastic dovecote survives at Perimon Priory on Anglesey. The most impressive surviving manorial dovecote was built at the end of the Middle Ages at Willington in Bedfordshire and is now preserved by the National Trust. The keeping of 'doos' was avidly followed in parts of Scotland where there are heavy concentrations of dovecotes, one of the older examples being built in the angle of the garden wall at Crathes Castle on Deeside. After the Middle Ages lesser landowners began to keep doves and many small seventeenth- and eighteenth-century dovecotes survive. In areas with good building stone, cylindrical designs were favoured and good examples can be seen at Wadenhoe in Northamptonshire and Avebury in Wiltshire. In the north the birds were often accommodated in lofts above farm buildings which can be recognized by the rows of little entrance holes, and nesting niches were sometimes provided above hay barns or cart sheds. In the southern and eastern counties brick and weather-boarded buildings resembling granaries were built as dovecotes. The birds entered via a louvre at the peak of the roof and one example at Great Yeldham in Essex still houses doves. By the end of the nineteenth century most dovecotes had become redundant although in previous centuries the fledglings had provided a valuable if sometimes costly source of meat. Several of the square dovecotes were converted into cottages and there are examples at Grantchester and Comberton in Cambridgeshire.

Another feature of the medieval manorial and monastic economy, but one which was not later adopted by smaller landowners, was the fishpond. These ponds provided a source of fresh meat which could be harvested in large quantities and which could be eaten on days when Catholic practice frowned on the consumption of fresh meat. They were abandoned in the post-medieval period, perhaps because of the changing character of religious observance, the in-

A small dovecote in weatherboarding and plain tiles at Great Yeldham in Essex.

crease in the coastal fishing trade and the shortage of skills or labour for fish-keeping. The ponds varied in form, ranging from the great gouges near Fountains Abbey to the remarkably disciplined lines of canals at Anglesey Abbey in Cambridgeshire. Most typically, a large trapezoidal or rectangular pond would be created by surrounding an area of flat meadow land with low earthen embankments. The pond could be filled by diverting a stream and the flow of water was regulated by sluices. Smaller ponds were normally constructed beside the main pond as 'stew tanks' for the raising of

fry. Very few manorial fishponds still contain water, but in unploughed land medieval fishponds can often be recognized as prominent earthwork features. There are good examples beside the villages of Ludborough in Lincolnshire, Harrington in Northamptonshire and Landbeach in Cambridgeshire.

Two types of farm building which are much more localized than those previously described are spinning galleries and oast houses. In the Yorkshire Dales and the north-west of England many small farms were not viable and before the Industrial Revolution gathered momentum and sucked manufacturing into the new mills, cottage-based textiles industries supplemented the farming incomes. Some farm buildings contain 'spinning galleries'. These open-sided galleries could have been used for spinning as they received more daylight than the interiors of the farm buildings, although they may have been used mainly for the drying of fleeces. A few can still be seen in the Lake District and there is one in the wool barn beside Townend in Troutbeck.

The cultivation of hops was introduced to the south-east of England in late-medieval times, though specialized oast houses for storing and drying the crop did not appear until much later. Oast houses are still a hallmark of the Wealden landscape and were used for storing the long canvas bags, known as 'pokes' or 'pockets', which contained the gathered hops. These were dried by a kiln burning charcoal or coke and the oast house kilns were equipped with moving timber

cowls with projecting flyboards to catch the breeze and keep the back of the cowl to windward, an invention of the 1790s. At first the kilns were rectangular with pyramidal roofs and a number of these buildings can still be seen, although in the nineteenth century the more commonplace cylindrical kilns were constructed, before the quest for cheaper buildings brought a reversion to rectangular designs. Oast houses are no longer an essential feature of the brewing industry; oil or electricity is now used to dry the hops and the kilns and cowls are redundant, although the new machinery is often housed in an old oast.

Not all farm buildings were grouped together beside the farmhouse, and if the oast house is the hallmark of the Wealden landscape, the scattered hay barns are an equally distinctive feature of the Pennines scene. Dating mainly from the Enclosure years of the eighteenth and nineteenth centuries, these barns were dispersed throughout the fields in order to minimize the

The spinning gallery at Townend, Troutbeck, Cumbria.

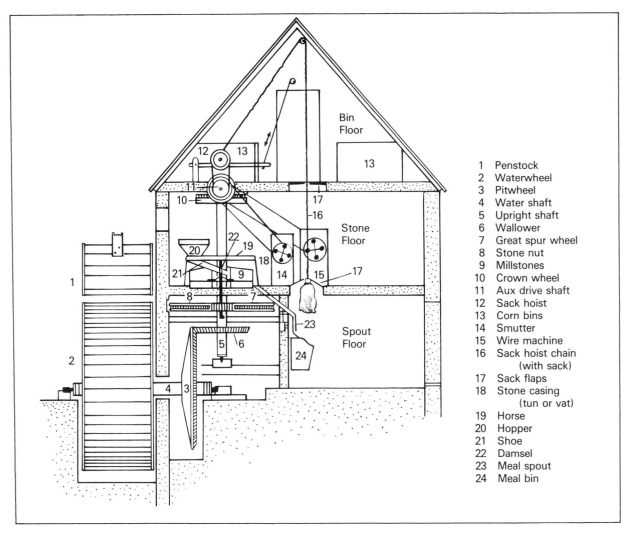

Bin
Floor

Stone
Floor

Spout
Floor

1   Penstock
2   Waterwheel
3   Pitwheel
4   Water shaft
5   Upright shaft
6   Wallower
7   Great spur wheel
8   Stone nut
9   Millstones
10 Crown wheel
11 Aux drive shaft
12 Sack hoist
13 Corn bins
14 Smutter
15 Wire machine
16 Sack hoist chain
      (with sack)
17 Sack flaps
18 Stone casing
      (tun or vat)
19 Horse
20 Hopper
21 Shoe
22 Damsel
23 Meal spout
24 Meal bin

Lurgashall Mill, Museum of East Anglian Life

distance travelled by hay coming in and manure going out to the fields. Cowhouses occupy a part or the whole of the lower floor and the hay fodder is stored in the loft above.

As well as having his own private farm buildings, the farmer depended upon other buildings which were used by many members of the farming community and he also gave his custom to the village smithy and wheelwright and needed access to a market where his surplus production could be sold and new stock and essential supplies could be purchased. Mills were needed to grind the grain. In prehistoric times grain was ground in a 'quern', which consisted of two stones that were rubbed together or revolved upon each other. Rotary querns were still used furtively by medieval peasants seeking to avoid the tolls levied at their lord's mill, although watermills were built in Britain from Roman times. Perhaps the most archaic type of

surviving mill is the 'click mill', with its small waterwheel set horizontally in a stream. Such simple little mills were once common in the upland areas where grain production was very modest, although just one example survives in working order, on the moors near Dounby on Orkney. Illustrations of timber-framed mills with vertical wheels appear in several medieval documents and in the seventeenth and eighteenth century many lofty weatherboarded watermills with their distinctive projecting sack hoists were built in the main grain-producing areas. Scores of these buildings survive as private houses, although few still have their waterwheels and milling gear in place. A fine seventeenth-century example has been re-erected at the

A well-preserved watermill in brick and weatherboarding at Houghton near Huntingdon. Note the projecting sack hoist.

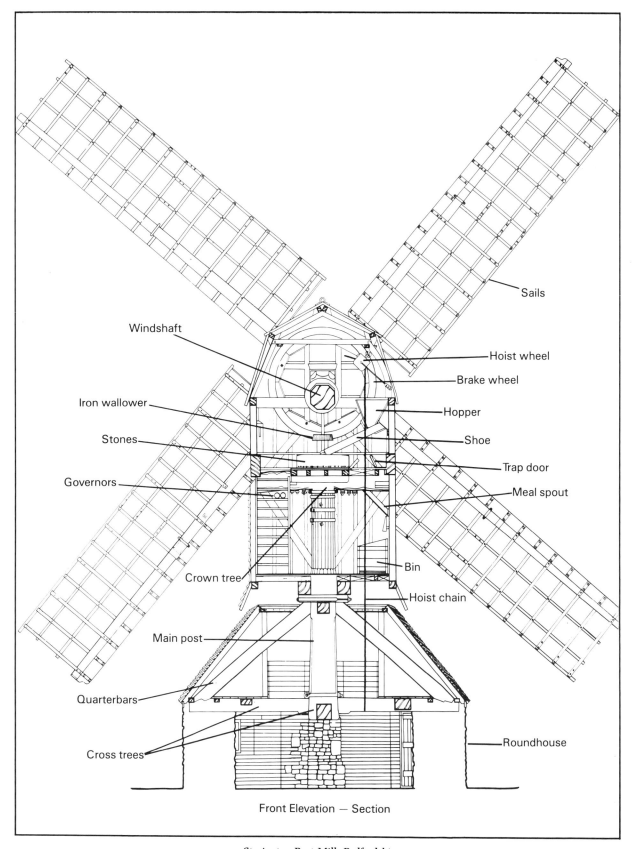

Windshaft

Iron wallower

Stones

Governors

Crown tree

Main post

Quarterbars

Cross trees

Sails

Hoist wheel

Brake wheel

Hopper

Shoe

Trap door

Meal spout

Bin

Hoist chain

Roundhouse

Front Elevation — Section

Stevington Post Mill, Bedfordshire

Stowmarket museum and there is another seventeenth-century example with stone walls at the Weald and Downland museum. The Domesday survey of 1086 mentions hundreds of watermills and Sussex alone contained 157 of them. These will have been small and relatively flimsy buildings, for surviving watermills date from the seventeenth and later centuries, although many of them stand on the sites of Saxon mills.

Whether a manor or farming community opted for a watermill, a windmill or both depended upon the local topography and levels of grain production, and many parishes had a watermill in a sheltered cleft and a windmill or two in exposed and elevated positions. Windmills were introduced at some time during the Middle Ages, perhaps as a result of overseas contacts forged in the course of the Crusades. Like the watermills, they harnessed a free and renewable natural energy source to turn a shaft and this power was transmitted via various cogs and gear wheels and was used to revolve great circular millstones of grit or French burr stone. The medieval windmills were small timber structures and no examples have survived, although their positions can often be recognized in field

A post mill at Saxtead Green in Suffolk.

names, other common place-names like 'Windmill Hill' and also from the remains of the little earthen mounds which carried the cross trees and post which supported the mill. Traditional features of windmill design can be recognized in the oldest surviving mills which are of the 'post mill' type, like the very recently restored seventeenth-century example at Bourn in Cambridgeshire, believed by some to be the oldest remaining example. The light, weatherboarded body of the mill could be turned to allow the sails to catch a wind coming from any quarter and it was mounted on a solid upright post which was anchored by cross trees at its base. Later post mills were sometimes equipped with fantails and turning gear which assisted the directing process, as at Friston in Suffolk. During the seventeenth century new designs were introduced in which the sails were mounted on a revolving cap while the body of the supporting tower remained rigid. In the 'smock' type of tower mill the body was weatherboarded and the oldest surviving smock mill, dating from about 1650, has been restored and stands at Lacey Green in Buckinghamshire. The wooden towers were vulnerable to the elements and since windmills were, of necessity, built in exposed places, the later mills tended to be built with cylindrical towers of brick. A small number of stone-towered mills were also built and examples can be seen at New Bradwell in Buckinghamshire and another, known to date from 1822, is at High Ham near Langport in Somerset and is maintained by the National Trust.

Not all windmills were in fact mills. Most of those seen in the Norfolk Broads were drainage pumps, and before the introduction of steam and diesel engines the drainage of the East Anglian Fens depended upon little wind pumps driving scoop wheels which lifted surplus water from one drainage level to another. Just one of these little Fenland wind pumps survives, at the National Trust Wicken Fen nature reserve.

Before the development of speedy and efficient long-distance transport systems which could disperse agricultural produce far and wide, farmers used local markets for their trading. Medieval lords were eager to obtain market charters because they could gain lucrative tolls from market users. Many ancient customary markets conducted trading for centuries before a formal charter was obtained, although the authorities attempted to prevent debilitating competition between markets that were too closely spaced and efforts were also made to punish forestallers who traded before they reached the lawful market. The weekly village markets were usually modest little gatherings and scores of them had lapsed before the close of the Middle Ages. But if a lord was lucky he might obtain the right to hold one or more annual fairs, which were much more exciting occasions and would be visited by bands of itinerant merchants bringing goods from far afield. Village crosses and market squares or greens are legacies of the old fair and market network, while sometimes a green still accommodates a market house or a guildhall. Many guildhalls were court and trading centres associated with a particular local craft guild, although others were not linked with the economic life of a community but with guilds associated with the nearby church. Most market houses which have survived have experienced a succession of different uses following the eclipse of the old village market, but they were originally intended as a venue for the courts which regulated market trading and as places where the gear for temporary market stalls was stored.

After the close of the Middle Ages the gradual improvements in the transport system slowly transformed the marketing of agricultural produce, while the growing towns sucked in more and more farm production. Local subsistence was outstripped by commercial production and markets became fewer and more centralized, as did the food processing industries like milling and dairying. These changes spawned new generations of industrial buildings, like the great maltings established beside the road and water routeways to the capital. Some, like those at Snape in Suffolk, are as impressive and fascinating as almost any of the older agricultural buildings.

Many of the traditional features and structures of farming life which are the foci of so much nostalgia are now redundant and decaying. Venerable aisled barns begin to topple after the modern vehicles collide with their aisle posts or their timbers rot following the neglect of their roofs. Meanwhile the agri-business movement has given rise to new firms which specialize in buying-up and 'modernizing' old family farms. This 'modernization' often sadly involves the destruction of most of the older buildings, which are costly to maintain or too small to accommodate the juggernauts of modern farming.

In previous centuries peasants, husbandmen and yeomen were primarily concerned with family subsistence and the profits from the sale of surplus produce were a welcome bonus once the needs of the household had been met. The goal of self-sufficiency demanded a mixed form of farming so that most families and communities would seek to produce their own grain, fodder, seed, meat, eggs, milk and butter, and the quest to achieve a good measure of balanced sufficiency

A tower mill at Denver in Norfolk.

*Remarkable industrial buildings at the Maltings at Snape in Suffolk,
with overhanging sack hoists.*

Without working dogs the work of the hill farmer would be almost impossible. This puppy is a border collie/old English sheepdog cross.

The Soay sheep, thought to resemble the breeds introduced by farmers around 7000 years ago.

endured until modern times on many small family farms. The traditional mixed farm, with its rickyard, pastures and meadows, its beef and dairy cattle, sheep and pigs, its duckpond and its chickens pecking in the yard, still features strongly in the popular perception of farming, but it has become a rarity in most parts of the British countryside. The old mixed farmer did not gamble on a single crop because prices could be unpredictable, but the support prices now offered give firm guarantees so farmers can specialize in particular crops.

Victims of a more gradual form of 'modernization' on the farm have been the old breeds of livestock which had been developed to suit the particular preferences and environmental conditions in the distinctive provinces of Britain. The Welsh borders had Hereford and 'smoky-faced Montgomery' cattle, the damp pastures of the west of Ireland were grazed by Kerry cattle, the English Midlands and the Craven district of Yorkshire supported longhorns, while Galloway, Ayrshire, Aberdeenshire, Guernsey, Jersey, Gloucestershire and Devon all had their local breeds to enhance the strong regional character of these places. The provincial

breeds of sheep, pigs and ponies were equally redolent of place and the nation drew strength and pleasure from the strongly developed character of its different components.

A few of the old breeds were truly ancient, like the Soay sheep of the St Kilda islands which resembled sheep introduced to Britain by the first farmers around 7000 years ago, while Orkney and Manx Longhtan sheep are said to have been brought by Viking settlers. But most old breeds were refined in much more recent times and were brought to perfection by selective breeding to reinforce the best characteristics of a region's stock as part of the Agricultural Revolution. As breeding eliminated the more motley strains, shows

Longhorn cow and calf.

were organized where breeders could compete and spread the gospel of selective breeding and careful records and stud books began to be kept. As John Vince has described, the improvement of the longhorn stock dates from 1775, that of Ayrshire cattle to the early years of the nineteenth century; the Shire horse stud book goes back to 1770, while registered Suffolk heavy horses can be traced to 1768.

In the course of this century most of the old British livestock breeds have fallen from favour. This is partly because housewives have demanded different, leaner cuts of meat and partly because farmers have sought new breeds to produce more meat more rapidly. In the post-war period foreign breeds of cattle like the Charolais, Chianina and Simmental have gradually displaced the native breeds from the British pastures as the techniques of animal husbandry have become standardized.

But recent research has shown that the imported breeds which swept all before them are not as economic and productive as was claimed. They may gain weight rapidly, but to do so they often require high inputs of costly foodstuffs. Meanwhile some of the old breeds have been lost for ever; twenty types of livestock died out in the course of this century, while even breeds like Cotswold sheep, which were very popular in the first half of the century, became scarce and threatened. Other breeds were preserved by individual enthusiasts or lingered on small farms in the rural backwaters until the Rare Breeds Survival Trust was formed in 1973 to organize a campaign of survival for the old livestock.

The Trust has enjoyed many successes and at the same time it has been realized that more than sentiment and conservational issues are at stake. The old breeds, developed to suit particular regional environmental conditions, preserve invaluable genes and they can be used to produce new crosses as the currently fashionable imported stock lose their vigour and become inbred and prone to disease. In addition, the old breeds are often excellent livestock in their own right. This was demonstrated in 1983, when an event which would have been unimaginable a few years earlier took place and a Large Black pig won a major championship at the East of England Show, with a British Saddleback in second place.

The Trust has grown rapidly since its formation and now has more than 4000 members and is assisting the survival of more than forty breeds of livestock. There are now a number of centres which are approved by the RBST where members of the public can see a broad selection of old breeds displayed (see Appendices).

A British white calf, a long-established hornless breed of cattle.

Jacob sheep have become quite popular as livestock which are decorative as well as useful.

— 9 —

MOUNTAINS

A spectacular expanse of limestone pavement above Malham Cove in Yorkshire.

So many people are now familiar with the superb scenery and wildlife of the Alps and Pyrenees, that the British mountains might seem rather dull and uninteresting. Even the highest peaks reach only a modest height by alpine standards and there are no glaciers or permanent snows. Nor are the mountain valleys enriched with those wonderful meadows, full of wild flowers, so characteristic of the Alps in early summer. Yet British mountains have a character of their own and their own special features in the scenery and valley flora. They are our only true wilderness areas and every year attract thousands of people who like to get away into the wide open spaces, breathe the mountain air, and climb up to where they have magnificent views over the countryside. Although the flora and fauna are not rich, they are a constant source of pleasure and interest to naturalists and there is always the possibility of the chance discovery of some new plant or animal, as has, in fact, happened several times during the last thirty years.

England has two mountain systems, the Pennines and the Lake District. The former is a range of plateaux, uplifted in blocks to give the landscape a stepped appearance, extending to the Cheviots in the north and the Derbyshire Peak District in the south. The highest point is Cross Fell, at 2930 feet, and there are several others over 2000 feet, including The Peak in the Peak District National Park. The Pennines are often called the backbone of England and certainly form an important watershed, with the main rivers in the north flowing either south-west or south-east. The principal rocks are Carboniferous Limestone and Millstone Grit, the latter being slightly younger once lay over limestone, but much has been eroded, though it caps the edges of the uplands in many places. Sometimes the grit forms dramatic features resembling the granite tors of the moors of Devon and Cornwall, as at Brimham Rocks near Ripon. Most of the mountain moorland of the Pennines carries a rather uniform vegetation – dwarf shrubs, mostly heather, and a good deal of coarse grassland with sedges and rushes. In early times, when the first people colonized these hills, they would have seen a continuous forest perhaps extending as high as

2000 feet or even more in places. Pollen which has been preserved in the peat is evidence that it was almost entirely deciduous, with hazel, birch, elm, alder, oak, and still a little pine, which had been more common before man penetrated these wildernesses. In the thousands of years which followed the settlements in the valleys he needed timber for fuel and domestic purposes and the farmers cleared areas by burning to provide grazing for their sheep, goats and cattle. The earliest clearances in the Pennines may have been made by Mesolithic hunters, seeking to open up hunting ranges and to extend the pasture. The pasture was poor, so young trees were a welcome addition to the diet of the stock. Today few places remain which show even a trace of original forest.

The most interesting part of the Pennine chain in botanical terms, Upper Teesdale, has already been described in the section on uplands but there are other places of interest which have fortunately been protected, either as National Nature Reserves or by the Yorkshire and Lancashire Trusts for Nature Conservation. Colt Park Wood and Ling Gill in Yorkshire, both National Nature Reserves, are fragments of a once extensive subalpine ash wood which covered much of the lower parts of the Craven Pennines. Colt Park Wood is situated on rough limestone pavement, so fissured by erosion that it has no agricultural use, apart from intermittent grazing. At times when grazing pressure was low, trees managed to take root in the crevices, and a woodland developed. Ling Gill, also on Carboniferous Limestone, is a steep-sided ravine with a moist and shady environment. The trees are mostly ash with some hazel, hawthorn, bird cherry, rowan, wych elm and birch. Both of these reserves are no longer grazed, being regarded as too dangerous for sheep, and have a remarkably rich flora – globe flower, wood cranesbill, the baneberry, the giant bellflower, herb paris, the northern bedstraw and a subalpine species, the alpine cinquefoil. The Colt Park grikes (see below) and the Ling Gill ravine are both rich in bryophytes which thrive where there is high humidity.

Limestone pavement is scarce in Britain, the finest examples being Gait Barrows in Silverdale, Cumbria,

Limestone forms some fine mountain scenery in Ireland. This is Knocknarea near Sligo.

and Scar Close, Yorkshire. It is formed on a limestone plateau where acidic rain has eroded deep crevices, usually called grikes, while the smooth rock between is the clint. Limestone country with pavements and other typical features such as sink-holes, caves, dry valleys, underground streams and caverns is generally known as karst, a name derived from Yugoslavia, where this landscape is best developed. The best-known British karst regions are Ingleborough Fell on the western side of the central Pennines, reaching 2350 feet and with all the classic features, and Malham Cove and the gorge of Gordale Scar in the Yorkshire Dales National Park, both with spectacular limestone cliffs, and very popular tourist sites. The Burren in Co. Clare, western Ireland, is a much more extensive landscape of karst but here there are no gorges or cliffs; instead a rolling country-side of bare, rounded limestone hills.

The Peak District, at the southern edge of the Pennine Chain and lying mostly in north Derbyshire, is probably the best-known hill region, apart from the Lake District, and was Britain's first National Park. It has a landscape of peat-covered hills, dissected by deep ravines, limestone dales and gorges cut into the surrounding plateau, and swift-running streams with dippers and grey wagtails. As elsewhere in the Pennines, there are two main rock types, a coarse gritstone and a hard limestone, both from the carboniferous period. The poor soils on the gritstone form the 'Dark Peak', mainly because of the rather sombre colouring of the heather-clad moors and the brown peaty soils. On the other hand the limestone country is generally known as the 'White Peak', the rocks and walls being pale grey and the vegetation greener, more varied and attractive. Several million people visit the Peak District every year to walk the moors and climb the gritstone crags, and here the Pennine Way, one of Britain's long-distance footpaths, begins its journey to the north.

The Lake District is the most picturesque region of

Raven Crag in Cumbria.

the English highlands, a blend of mountain and water. There are thirteen principal lakes which are mostly orientated in a series of radial valleys from the centre, while the mountains between achieve heights well above those in the Pennine Chain. Scafell Pike is the highest point at 3210 feet, and not far below are Helvellyn, at 3118, and Skiddaw at 3053 feet. The core of the district is formed of rocks which are around 500 million years old: the ancient sedimentary rocks of the Skiddaw Slates and the volcanic rocks of the Borrowdale Volcanic Series to their south. Once, the whole area was levelled by erosion and formed a shallow sea in which Carboniferous Limestone was deposited. Then the area was uplifted to form a great dome and the limestone was eroded away from the crown of the dome so that it is now encountered at the approaches to the Lake District.

The Lake District is a land of extraordinary variety, dark crags, scree slopes and rocky cliffs, and yet below in the valleys are green fields, woodlands and sparkling waters. Although wild and impressive, it is a friendly landscape, moulded by man for more than a thousand years and thankfully now preserved by the National Trust and National Park from the excesses of industry and destructive exploitation. Even in the early-nineteenth century when it must have been remote and perhaps even largely unknown, it was much loved by the people who had discovered its charm. The poet William Wordsworth wrote his guide to the Lake District in 1835 and much later the delightful books of W. G. Collingwood have some of the finest descriptions of Lakeland and its people.

The true alpine vegetation occurs on the oldest and poorest rocks and also on softer, volcanic intrusions, limestone being absent at the highest altitudes. Among the steep and crumbling gulleys of the Wastwater screes, there are deep ravines of a reddish volcanic

The barren, waterlogged grazings above Eel Crag near Rosthwaite in the Lake District.

The Scafell range includes Scafell Pike, the highest of the English mountains.

rock, where shrubby cinquefoil grows, a rare plant also found in Teesdale. Another mountain rarity is the red-flowered alpine catchfly, which lives at 8 500 feet in the Alps and is found in the Skiddaw mountains where quartz veins of rock, which are unusually rich in pyrites, run through slate. These localities are generally in inaccessible areas safe from collectors and also from grazing sheep.

Many interesting mountain plants in the Lake District are found in marshy places (flushes) below springs and on the sides of small water courses, or on rock surfaces wet with running water. These often have thick banks of mosses in which other plants grow such as the mossy and starry saxifrages, and the opposite-leaved golden saxifrage may cover the ground, itself rather like a large moss.

The moist rock ledges where some debris has collected are good places for the plant-hunter. Fortunately they are often almost impossible to reach and form a refuge for the yellow mountain saxifrage, roseroot,

mountain sorrel and the sea campion, which is not infrequent at these high altitudes. The crags of the Helvellyn ridge are known as one of the localities for other very local plants. By careful exploration and using field-glasses to examine inaccessible corners, the naturalist should see the mountain avens, purple saxifrage, moss campion, possibly the alpine saxifrage, which is now very rare, the hoary whitlow grass and mountain everlasting.

The mountain slopes may look bare and lifeless but they are important habitats for specialized plants and animals. Screes are the home of the mountain fern, parsley fern, and the most typical of Lakeland plants, the alpine ladies mantle. The botanist naturally looks for the best plant localities in order to see the less common species and frequently these are very small patches of ground, perhaps only a few square yards. The rest of the high mountain tops are windswept with few plants of interest; a few grasses, bilberry and cowberry, and of course the curious mountain moss

The glaciated slopes of Pike of Blisco in the Lake District.

Rhacomitrium, which is more abundant on the higher mountains of Scotland. This moss and a few sedges seem to be able to grow in the most exposed and inhospitable mountain regions wherever there is a small sheltered spot on the lee side of a stone or hummock.

The mountain flora of Lakeland is not rich compared with the Scottish mountains and the same can be said for the invertebrate fauna which includes a few beetles, bugs and hymenoptera. The freshwater invertebrate fauna of the lakes is rich but most species also occur at lower altitudes. The well-known mountain ringlet butterfly, the only alpine species in Britain, is not uncommon and generally lives above 1800 feet. The caterpillar feeds on grasses and is occasionally locally abundant on mountain pastures. Mountain spiders in Britain have been well studied and there are many species more or less confined to this habitat. In general they are found on all mountains but a few of the less common species are known only from Wales or

Scotland, and Lakeland also has its own montane fauna. It consists of only two or three species of spiders which have so far not been found on other British mountains. Most of the widespread mountain species are small money spiders which live in the vegetation close to the ground. An exception is a large, dark wolf spider whose chosen habitat is mountain screes. It occurs in the Lakes and North Wales but is more widespread in Scotland. It even lives on the isolated island of St Kilda, where there are some fine scree slopes, though at a lower altitude than on the mainland. For many years this fine spider was only known from mountain screes in Britain but it has recently been found in Scandinavia.

Lakeland has most of the typical montane birds in Britain: curlews and golden plovers are widespread on the moorlands, and the rare dotterel, which seldom ventures below 2000 feet, breeds in small numbers in one or two closely guarded localities. The peregrine falcon has long been a familiar bird of the rocky cliffs above the Lakes valleys and although it declined very considerably during the period of widespread use of pesticides, it is now beginning to return to most of its old haunts. The little merlin is the typical hawk of the upland moors but there are no breeding hen harriers or ospreys, in spite of the amount of water and fish available. Nevertheless Lakeland has enticed back the golden eagle, which last nested towards the end of the eighteenth century. Two hundred years ago it was hated by the sheep farmer and destroyed at every opportunity. There are now two, possibly three, pairs which breed in the Lakes and which have not in any way made a nuisance of themselves to the sheep farmers. The raven breeds in many mountain areas, usually on crags between 1250 and 2000 feet, in fact in situations often chosen by the peregrine falcon. Formerly the raven was more abundant and widespread, but today perhaps not more than about forty pairs breed.

In Wales there are many beautiful upland areas: among them the popular Brecon Beacons National Park and the valley oakwoods of central Wales, the home of the rare red kite. But the highest mountains are in the Snowdonia massif, Caernarvonshire, and Cader Idris in Merioneth. Snowdonia is a complex of three peaks dominated by Snowdon itself at 3560 feet, the highest point in Wales or England. Separating these summits are the wild glaciated passes of Llanberis and Nant Ffrancon. Snowdon has the only mountain railway in Britain, the old coaches and cogwheel engine carrying thousands of tourists every year. The rock faces of the Snowdonia valleys are a great favourite with rock climbers as they offer slopes of varying difficulty on which to try out their skills, and there are numerous footpaths for those who prefer to walk.

The interesting mountain plants of Snowdonia are mostly associated with the presence of a certain limestone of Ordovician age, which either caps some of the mountains or more often outcrops in certain places. The long ridge of the Glyder, so well known to tourists, is one such locality. Much of it is composed of lavas producing acid soils with *Rhacomitrium* heath as the typical vegetation but on the west side of Big Glyder an outcrop of dolerite, a basic igneous rock, supports a mountain grassland. Calcareous soils above Llyn Idwal not far from the lake, have a number of plants of special interest for Wales; the scarce mountain avens, moss campion and purple saxifrage. On Snowdon and Cwm Idwal a highly calcareous volcanic rock outcrops on some of the cliffs. The flora is one of the most distinguished on the Welsh mountains, including four saxifrages, mountain avens, moss campion and the

striking Welsh lily not known anywhere else in Britain.

The extensive area of acidic soils is generally poor grassland heavily grazed by sheep. The highest regions receive an annual rainfall of over 170 inches, which makes it one of the wettest places in Britain, although this falls off sharply at lower altitudes. Cader Idris is a fine mountain on the south side of the Mawddach estuary with an immense escarpment facing north. Its highest summit, Pen y Gadair, is just over 2900 feet and is distinguished by having one of the finest corries in Britain, whose cliffs fall 975 feet. Acidic soils cover most of the mountain, producing a poor grassland with dwarf shrubs of bilberry, cowberry and heather. Calcareous soils are local but where they occur the same mountain plants grow as found on the Snowdon range – globe flower, Welsh poppy, mountain sorrel, mossy and purple saxifrages. Snowdonia has no eagles, although the buzzard is common and the red kite does not range as far as the northern Welsh mountains to breed. The old slate quarries of Snowdonia, long abandoned by man, have been colonized by the chough, which nests in rock crevices. Its call is a welcome sound to the walker on the sombre mountain slopes.

In early times there is little doubt that the mountains of Snowdonia were forested, as elsewhere in Britain. Records dating from the middle of the sixteenth century mention scrub but no trees, so that the same process of clearance for sheep pasture must have already taken place. The Cistercian abbeys are known to have had huge flocks roaming the hills – the most effective method of preventing tree growth. The continental visitor used to extensive mountain forests will comment on the bareness of the landscape in Snowdonia, the same impression created by the Scottish mountains, where a Polish professor once said to me that he had never seen so much devastated landscape.

In Wales the wolf is thought to have become extinct by the end of the sixteenth century, partly due to forest clearance, some of which may have been done purposely to hunt out the packs. At that time the Central Highlands of Scotland were in a more primitive state, with wild moorland and some original forest in which roamed wolves and red deer. Contemporary historians have described the abundance of wolves north of the Highland line in the sixteenth century, and how travellers were afraid to go through the great pine forests of Rannoch and Loch Aber without protection. The forest was burned in order to drive out the wolves; local documents record this happening around Loch Aber and Loch Awe through to Rannoch and Atholl. The last wolf for which there is clear evidence was killed in 1680, although persistent tradition claims

Only the hardiest lichens and mosses can survive on the summit of Snowdon.

that small numbers survived until 1743. With the large predators exterminated it was possible for cattle farming to expand, the animals wandering at will over the mountain pastures and sometimes becoming quite wild. During this period, when better prices for beef could be obtained south of the border, large herds were driven along drove roads leading to English markets. As on the cattle trails in America, local people found it profitable to slip out under cover of darkness and steal a few cattle for themselves. Rustling was a problem, but it was another factor that eventually stopped the annual cattle trek. Towards the beginning of the nineteenth century the wool trade became profitable and the big landowners turned from cattle ranching to sheep grazing; in the process they dispossessed the clansmen in order to create more grazing land, and thus deprived them of their livelihood.

In the late-nineteenth century shooting of game became very popular as a country sport, sometimes because the Industrial Revolution brought the wealth

with which to buy grouse moors and deer forests. Gradually sheep gave way to the establishment of sporting estates, and large areas in the Pennines and especially in Scotland were turned over for the purpose of raising as many grouse as possible for sportsmen willing to pay large sums for a few days' shooting. In 1940 it was estimated that one-fifth of Scotland, covering approximately three and a half million acres, was devoted to the rearing of game, either red grouse or deer. Sheep were tolerated outside the shooting season but nothing was allowed to interfere with game-bird rearing. The expansion of game farming led to the employment of gamekeepers, whose job it was to ensure that no predators on the hills killed the valuable grouse. The wild cat, pine marten, polecat, eagle, osprey and sea eagle were all rigorously persecuted both by the gamekeepers and elsewhere by sheep-farmers. The polecat disappeared from England and Scotland but survived in Wales, where it is now widespread; under protection it is beginning to spread eastward into the border counties of England. The pine marten is more widespread, with small colonies in parts of Wales including Snowdonia, the Lake District and a few other places in upland England, but it is in Scotland where it is most common. It is protected by law but can be shot where it causes damage to game or other interests. The golden eagle has also responded to protection and expanded its range, making Scotland one of the best places in Europe in which to see this bird. The osprey was less able to stand the onslaught of gamekeepers and collectors and became extinct as a British breeding bird in the late-nineteenth century. Then in the early 1950s a pair nested at Loch Garten and made headline news. In succeeding years, thanks to the fine work of the Royal Society for the Protection of Birds, the osprey has nested successfully by several Scottish lochs. The public can still visit the Loch Garten hide and as many as 30,000 bird-watchers have done so in one year.

Northern Scotland, Orkney and Shetland are the haunts of birds which do not breed anywhere else in the British Isles. These are not all montane species but in the high north the distinction between lowland and montane habitats is sometimes blurred. The arctic and great skuas nest at fairly low altitudes on coastal moors and are more widespread in Orkney and Shetland than in the north of Scotland itself. The whimbrel is best known as a nesting bird in the Shetlands but a few pairs breed from time to time in Orkney and on the northern Scottish mainland; its main breeding range is in Iceland and Scandinavia.

In the 1950s a new species was added to the list of birds which breed regularly in Britain – the wood sandpiper, another typical Scandinavian bird. It is still very rare; never more than five pairs have been recorded in any one year. It likes to nest in boggy places close to the reedy lochs where it feeds. The most characteristic wader of the wet mountain valleys in northern Scotland is the greenshank, a bird of truly wild places, sometimes nesting at over 2000 feet. Its trilling song and conspicuous display flight make it easy to find, but the nest is fortunately extremely well camouflaged. On the open moors the hen harrier is a familiar bird of prey, hiding its nest in the tall heather. It is common in Scotland and Ireland but only a few pairs have colonized the moorlands of England and Wales. It was previously kept down by gamekeepers but has been increasing in recent years, again as a result of protection. It is interesting to note that it has always been common in Orkney, where there are no large sporting estates and hence no reason for farmers and landowners to shoot it.

In addition to the ring ouzel, which is the typical

The rowan or mountain ash is a tree of rocky places. This one is growing on the strange Millstone Grit outcrops at Brimham Rocks on the flanks of the Pennines near Ripon.

thrush of hill country in Britain, the redwing and fieldfare are common winter visitors everywhere. They have nested in many places in recent years, the redwing only in central and northern Scotland, in woods, gardens, and even on open hillsides, frequently near water. The fieldfare is not confined to Scotland and after the first breeding record in Orkney in 1967, a few pairs are now scattered from Shetland to Stafford-shire and Derbyshire. For over a hundred years the fieldfare has been expanding its range westwards and now even breeds in the Netherlands and Belgium as

polders. The snow bunting first nested in the Cairngorms in 1909 but the small group of five pairs lasted only three years. For the next thirty-three years breeding was not recorded but since 1945 a few pairs have raised young most years, although not more than three nests have been known in any one year. It is the most northerly breeding passerine bird and has a very tenuous hold in the Scottish mountains. A few pairs have been recorded nesting elsewhere in Scotland and further north in the arctic it commonly breeds at sea level, like the dotterel.

The numerous small lochs at modest altitudes in Scotland are the home of the red-throated diver. Although it likes to build its nest on the edge of a loch or on an island, it feeds either at sea or on the large coastal sea lochs. Its preference for breeding on the smaller lochs enables it to range widely in Orkney and Shetland as well as in Scotland. On the other hand the larger black-throated diver selects the larger lochs for its nests and is only known in Scotland and the Western Isles. Both are delightful to watch, being quite unlike any other aquatic bird in Britain.

On the high plateaux of the Cairngorms at about 3000 feet the invertebrate life is very specialized. It includes several species of sawflies which live on the dwarf willows found at that altitude. One species of sawfly is only known on Mount Braeriach in the Cairngorms. There are also flightless weevils and ground beetles living among the stones and at least four small moths which feed on crowberry. It is known from recent research that there is also a constant rain of small invertebrates which are transported from the lower levels by the wind and deposited on the mountain tops, but few are able to survive. Nevertheless there are several species of money spiders that are so well adapted to mountain conditions they are only found on the tops of the Cairngorms. It is an odd experience to climb to the top of Cairngorm itself and find in that barren, almost vegetation-free stony terrain several species of spiders living deep amongst the stones which are not known elsewhere in Britain. One of the most widespread species is named after the famous mountaineer Edward Whymper, who was the first to climb the Matterhorn and other mountains in the Alps.

Snow seldom remains throughout the year in the Cairngorms but it is not unusual for snow patches to last for quite a long time into the summer. Small flies, beetles and spiders are often found on these summer snow beds, having been deposited with aerial plankton. The snow keeps them fresh and refrigerated so they provide snow buntings and even carnivorous ground beetles with an ample food supply. This is a similar situation to that in the arctic, and this writer has seen

well as in Britain.

The mountain tops of the central massif of Scotland, the wildest and most desolate region in Britain, are the habitat of the dotterel. It is a true montane zone where there is only grassland, moss and lichen heath, and occasionally dwarf heather. Here the snow lasts longer than elsewhere and the cold wind sweeps over the plateau, even in summer. Although the dotterel chooses such places in Scotland, in the arctic tundra of Scandinavia it breeds at sea level and even stranger still, it has nested for several years on the Dutch

snow buntings on Bear Island in the White Sea foraging on a still day when midges were common. As the air cooled in the afternoon hundreds of these tiny flies landed on the snow patches to remain in cold storage until needed by the buntings.

In recent years several new plant and animal discoveries have been made in the Scottish mountains of species previously unrecorded in Britain but well-known in the Alps or Scandinavia. Most of the plants are rather insignificant and would not be noticed except by a specialist, but *Diapensia* is rather a remarkable exception. A low evergreen perennial which grows in dense cushions and has narrow shiny leaves, it is certainly not inconspicuous with its mass of short-stalked white flowers, each of which is at least half an inch across the corolla. It was first found on a bare rocky hilltop in Inverness-shire by an amateur ornithologist, probably in a place which most botanists would not think worth exploring. Although other new plants will no doubt be discovered, it is more likely that new invertebrate species will be found. There are far more species than there are of plants and we know less about our mountain fauna.

In the 1940s when the Nature Conservancy and the Countryside Commission (then called the National Parks Commission) were established by the 1947 Act of Parliament, Scotland chose not to have National Parks, partly because it was felt that so much of Scotland was wild country that giving National Park status to some areas and not others would be ill-conceived. Nevertheless scientifically important areas could be defined, and the Scottish branch of the Nature Conservancy created fifty-nine National Nature Reserves and 955 Sites of Special Scientific Interest, many of which are in the mountains. Other areas are protected by the Scottish Wildlife Trust and the National Trust for Scotland. The finest of all is the Cairngorm National Nature Reserve. It includes the most extensive area of land above 3000 feet anywhere in Britain. The edges of the high plateau have been sculptured by glaciers into huge corries which probably excel in grandeur any others in Scotland. There are also long, moderately steep slopes where skiing is a popular leisure pursuit in winter when there has been a good snowfall. The sports activities, based on Aviemore, have developed rapidly since the war and as it all takes place within the National Nature Reserve there is a clash of interests between the commercial concerns who promote skiing holidays and nature conservation. The former want to build more ski lifts, roads and buildings, and the nature conservationists want to keep the area as natural as possible. It is a familiar controversy, to be found in many areas in the Alps.

In 1978 the Countryside Commission for Scotland published a list of 'National Scenic Areas'. Although they do not have formal status they follow the National Park concept and are in fact nearer to the continental type of National Park, which is situated in wild country with no significant commercial interests and where human settlements are scarce or absent.

National Nature Reserves preserve the best of the Pennines, and the Lake District National Park has the added safeguard that the largest landowner within its boundaries is the National Trust. Snowdonia is also a National Park and has several National Nature Reserves. Although it has no problem of ski runs, it is a favourite with climbers and outdoor centres for hill-trekking. In this way it fulfils a valuable educational role for young people and at the same time preserves the natural environment.

— 10 —

WETLANDS

Reed beds at the Wicken Fen Nature Reserve in Cambridgeshire, where reeds are still grown for thatching.

There is only one term which adequately describes the great variety of habitats formed by fresh or brackish water – 'wetlands' – places where land is either water-logged or with standing water, or is part of a larger area where water is the dominant feature of the landscape. It includes peat bogs, river marshes, fens, reservoirs, village ponds, and flooded gravel pits. It also covers some coastal marsh and estuaries, which are described in the chapter on coasts.

To our early forefathers, the extensive marshes that formed part of our primeval landscape must have seemed as permanent as the mountains and rivers; but the ingenuity of man has no limits and even in Roman times there is evidence of land drainage on the siltlands adjacent to the Wash. Succeeding generations followed their example and gradually the marshy land and open water were drained away, first by the once familiar windmills, and then in the nineteenth and twentieth

The lakeshore of Buttermere in the Lake District.

The village pond at Nun Monkton in Yorkshire.

A fenland type of landscape around old watercress meadows at Fowlmere in Cambridgeshire

An old canal at Skipton in Yorkshire.

centuries by steam, diesel and finally powerful electric pumps, until all our best watery ground had gone. With it went a wildlife of plants, birds and animals whose richness we can only guess at from the few fragmentary records which remain. Throughout the greater part of this history the drainers, who were groups of men able to invest large sums of money, regarded themselves as pioneers creating new land and doing great service to the community by turning pestilential marshes into productive agricultural land. The complaints came only from poor people who lived in the marshlands and were deprived of their fish, wildfowl and reed harvest, the only products available to them to maintain their homes and earn a living. At that time they were an underprivileged community with no one of influence to support them, and were soon forgotten. Today we are much more aware of the scientific interest of wetlands and the pleasure they give to tens of thousands of naturalists and bird-watchers. We also know that marshland can disappear almost overnight because modern pumps are highly efficient, draglines and bulldozers can build banks and drainage ditches in a few days and the farmers plough and sow their seed immediately the water table falls.

Most of the main surviving wetland areas in England and Wales are under threat of change or reclamation; it is only a question of cost and public opposition, because there is no drainage problem that modern technology cannot solve. East Anglia has the largest number of important British wetlands including the marshes in

The River Test in Hampshire, a swift-flowing trout river on chalk.

A wind pump at Thurne in the Norfolk Broads.

the valleys of the Rivers Bure, Yare and Waveney in Norfolk, and the coastal broads in Suffolk, while the coastal marshes at Minsmere and Walberswick are famous bird haunts. The Fenland 'Washes' (uncultivated land which takes flood water) of the Rivers Nene and Ouse, much of which is now in the hands of conservation societies, have become of international renown for wildlife. In Somerset, the levels and moors in the flood plain of the River Parrett and its tributaries are very important historically as well as for wildlife. The Amberley Wild Brooks along the River Arun in West Sussex has recently survived an attempt to drain it for agriculture but the threat remains. The Derwent Ings in Yorkshire (Ing is an Old Norse word, more common in the north of England, meaning a marshy meadow liable to flooding) are important as refuges for winter wildfowl, as are some of the land subsidence areas now permanently filled with water.

Wetlands are being reclaimed all over continental Europe, and the effect on wildlife is clearly demonstrated by the Red Data Books of Endangered Plants (International Union for the Conservation of Nature and Natural Resources). The greatest number of species becoming rare or extinct in recent years, or now in a vulnerable state, are those typically associated with wetlands. The international scale of the problem was recognized when a series of meetings were held by conservationists beginning in 1962 and leading to the signing of the International Wetlands Convention at Ramsar in 1971. This requires contracting nations to designate and conserve internationally important wetlands and also to maintain a policy of wise use for all such land within their territories. The two British wetlands on the Ramsar list are Minsmere and the Ouse Washes.

Water is one of man's most valuable commodities and it is not surprising that he must try to regulate it to meet his needs – which are considerable. On average

The River Bure near Stokesby in the Norfolk Broads.

each person uses between thirty and forty gallons a day for domestic purposes, while industry takes an enormous amount of water for processing its products. To make one ton of steel 400 tons of water are required, and ten gallons are needed to refine one gallon of petrol. The farmer needs it for irrigation but does not want it to flood his land. Open water is in great demand for recreation, so that new reservoirs must be managed with this in mind.

Most of the water which is used for domestic purposes, for irrigation and by industry is eventually returned to the permanent waterways, but not in the same state as when it was pumped out. Less than a hundred years ago the greater part of the rural population disposed of their domestic waste into cess-pits or septic tanks. Nowadays most rural communities have main drains so that all the material which was formerly trapped in the ground is now released via sewage works into the waterways.

A dramatic recent instance of this is the change which has taken place in the Norfolk Broads. In the 1950s the naturalist crossing the larger Broads could look through the transparent waters and clearly see the vegetation on the bottom. This writer remember's doing this when shown the rare bottom-living plant *Najas marina* on Hickling Broad which was known from no other locality in Britain. About that time many rural areas in the region of the Broads were being connected to main drains and the sewage works piped the effluent, rich in organic nutrients, into the rivers and thus to the Broads. These chemicals activated the growth of small algae, tiny unicellular plants which thrive in this sort of environment, and in the course of a few years the clear waters turned to a green 'soup'. As light could no longer reach the plants living on the bottom, they died.

In the 1950s the Broads were known as one of the best pike fishing waterways in the country, but twenty years later these fish had become scarce. Some of the breeding birds also declined, particularly the bittern, the pride of Broads birdlife. One wonders why this change was not predicted: the effects of adding a rich nutrient supply to waterways have long been well known, but neither local biologists nor the Water Authority in the Broads seem to have realized what would happen. A phosphate-stripping plant has now been installed at one of the sewage works as an experiment to see how far the changes can be reversed.

River valleys as we see them today are one of the most beautiful features of our landscape. Each valley was fashioned thousands of years ago by natural processes; in some areas by run-off from melting ice, the scouring of glaciers creating typical 'U'-shaped valleys, and in others by natural erosion when in flood, when the river's course often changed as deposited material blocked its route. A waterway that follows a sinuous route may be a nuisance to water authorities, who find maintenance easier where the course is straight. In the flat lands of the Fenland basin it has been easy to canalize the rivers so that they simply follow the shortest route to the sea, for example the Nene and Ouse when they enter the Fens.

The prevention of flooding is also another great problem which faces the water authorities in Britain, costing considerable sums of money each year. In the flat lands of the Fenland basin flood control is essential to protect the homes and farms of the local people, and as we know from flooding in the past, the damage caused can be enormous. Many Fenland residents remember the floods of 1947 when heavy rainfall burst the banks of some of the dykes and vast areas of farmland were flooded.

Open-water wetlands in Britain can be divided into two main groups – standing, and running, waters. They tend to have quite distinct faunas and floras, although in flat land the drains could be regarded almost as standing water because the flow is so slow, and along the edges of lakes where there is constant water movement by wave action the fauna has certain features which are similar to that found in running water. Flowing streams carry many small pieces of debris and organic matter in suspension which are utilized by filter-feeding invertebrate animals, most of which are absent from standing waters. In general, running water has a fairly constant temperature and is well aerated, that is, rich in oxygen for fish and other aquatic life. Standing waters range from the village pond with its semi-tame ducks and the dew pond on the Downs to large natural lakes, of which there are some fine examples in the Lake District and Scotland, although they are rare in lowland Britain and Wales. The scarcity of large areas of natural open water in the lowland is more than made up by artificial lakes, large reservoirs and many water-filled gravel-pits. In fact there is more man-made open water now than there was natural water two hundred years ago.

Even the Broads, a popular centre for water-borne recreation in Britain, are not natural. Their fascinating history was not explained until the 1950s when the botanist Dr Joyce Lambert began to study the marsh-land vegetation and its history by taking a large number of peat cores along transects which cross both marsh and open water. She found that the vegetation

The River Ure at sunset.

often showed abrupt changes and that the boundaries followed straight lines. By greatly increasing the number of bores she was able to show that the Broads were deep depressions cut out of peat, because they are straight-sided and flat-bottomed, a shape never found in natural lakes. This could only have come about, she thought, if they were ancient peat-cuttings. More evidence was clearly needed before her case would be convincing, so she enlisted the help of other experts, N. Jennings and C. T. Smith. A historian found documentary proof that in the early Middle Ages peat was widely used in the neighbourhood and that it ceased in the fourteenth century because the pits became flooded. An archaeologist and a civil engineer discovered firm evidence that in the thirteenth century the land was about thirteen feet higher above the sea than it is now – hence the pits were dry enough to dig. The story was nearly complete. These great pits, eight to ten feet deep, were dug at a time when they could be kept dry, but as the level of the land sank in relation to the sea, water seeped in and drainage became a problem. In 1287 there was a great flood which inundated the peat diggings, although in many places the industry was not finally extinguished by floods until the fourteenth century. The only important fact not known as a result of these studies was the date that peat digging had started. Archaeologists worked out the total amount of peat dug out of the pits – about 900 million cubic feet – and estimated that it would have lasted 350 years. This enabled them to say that the practice of using peat for fuel probably began in the tenth century. The Danes settled East Norfolk at the end of the ninth century, so perhaps they were already familiar with peat-digging in their homeland where it is plentiful, and recognized the potential in Norfolk. However, the Romans before them had dug peat to fuel their Fenland saltings, while the main extractions were made by medieval monks of St Bene't's Abbey – and Norwich alone would purchase some 200,000 blocks or 'turves' of peat in a single year.

The Broads were dug in peatland adjacent to the river and separated from it by a clay rond (causeway) which, in some instances, became eroded in the course of time, joining river and broad. Some of the peat cuttings were very shallow so that as silt was deposited the marsh vegetation soon spread over the water, once more forming a closed marsh. Sutton Broad has reached this stage in the last fifty years, and now has no open water except the navigation channel. Hoveton Great Broad is at an earlier stage, but the open water is so shallow that only a rowing boat is safe on it. Perhaps, in time, all the Broads will silt up and disappear, but the process may be indefinitely delayed in those with a dredged navigation channel. Each year thousands of holiday craft cruise along the Broadland waterways, the churning action of their propellors keeping the silt in suspension. Some of this will be deposited in quieter waters and some carried downriver. The silt, together with algal blooms (enormous numbers of single cell aquatic plants), makes the water opaque and prevents growth of bottom vegetation in the dykes and waterways. Holiday craft have been on the Broads for almost 100 years but the pastime did not 'take off' until after the last war when larger numbers of boats became available for hire. In 1890 a book on how to prepare for a sailing holiday from Wroxham advised that water supply was no problem; the rivers and Broads were so pure that one had only to drop a bucket over the side to meet all one's needs. No one would think of drinking water from the Broads today.

Clean water can still be found in Britain but it is necessary to go to the upland lakes and mountain streams where there is no industrial or agricultural pollution. Many upland lakes, for example in the Lake District and Highlands of Scotland, are situated on rocks which are not calcareous so that they tend to be rather acidic and to have what the scientist calls a low productivity. This means that nutrients in solution available for plant growth are low. Although these waters are beautifully clear they tend to have relatively little plant and animal life. Waters which are richer in nutrients and not so acid have a plant and fish life which is much more varied.

Before man began to alter the environment, most lowland rivers were probably moderately rich in nutrients, but today these waterways are very unnatural because they carry a heavy nutrient load of phosphates and nitrates from domestic, industrial and agricultural sources. Fish life is virtually non-existent in waters which have either been deoxygenated by pollution or contain poisonous chemicals. In the industrial areas of Britain many waterways are without aquatic life, as was the lower Thames until recent years, and it has been estimated that in 1980 there were 640 miles of grossly polluted rivers. Greater control of the type of effluent flowing into the river has gradually improved water quality so that fish are now being caught in parts of the Thames where they have not been seen for many years. A few hundred years ago the Thames was a well-known salmon river, and there is even a record of apprentice boys in London complaining at being given salmon too often for supper. As industrial settlement expanded along the lower Thames, salmon disappeared, and it is only very recently that one was caught again in the London area. On this occasion its appearance was headline news, and the apprentice boys of today would be only too pleased to have a share of it.

Rivers which are important for navigation are regularly dredged by the water authority. As a result they tend to lose the marginal aquatic vegetation, because the dredge deepens the bed of the watercourse. The natural marshy zone between water and land is destroyed and the wash of heavy boat traffic can prevent it re-establishing by constant erosion. If this is severe, then the banks must be strengthened by hammering in metal or wooden piles, which complete the ultimate destruction of all marginal aquatic vegetation. Small watercourses are dredged and sometimes straightened to ensure that land drainage is not impeded. The caterpillar tracks of the dragline move along the stream bank and any trees in the way must come down. There were instances in the past when the water authorities completely spoiled an attractive landscape scene by this all-or-nothing treatment. Fortunately some authorities are now prepared to leave

groups of trees, or those growing along one side of the waterway. In the case of minor waterways which are particularly interesting to the naturalist, it would be good to have the agreement of the drainage authorities to allow the stream to develop naturally.

Throughout many parts of lowland England, Ordnance Survey maps show a remarkably high scattering of tiny field ponds. Many were dug to provide water for domestic animals, others to obtain calcareous marl to put on fields where the soil was too acid. When these pits were abandoned they filled up with water and became a haven for freshwater pondlife. But when the use of the land was changed and a field was ploughed, a pond would hinder the tractor and also take up valuable space, so it was filled in. This has happened over considerable areas of our countryside. Pond water is often remarkably clean, being isolated from polluted watercourses, and those situated in meadows, although manured by cattle dung, will not suffer from toxic chemicals. This may be the reason why some

The common frog, now a threatened species in many parts of England.

The common toad. Unlike the frog, it has not declined and is a good friend to the gardener by eating pests.

animals and plants are able to survive in ponds but have disappeared from the nearby river where they formerly occurred. An example is the common frog. Forty years ago it was widespread throughout the country and bred in all manner of waterways, but today it is local and even absent from many areas. It still occurs in clean ponds, although recent surveys in parts of Suffolk show that it has even declined in grassland ponds, so pollution and habitat loss may not be the only factors in its decline. On the other hand the introduced edible frog is spreading in parts of southern England. It is much more aquatic than our common frog, spending most of its time in the water where its brighter green colour and loud voice are unmistakeable. The common toad, unlike the frog, is still very widespread. It is more terrestrial than the other British amphibia and only returns to water for breeding. As it tolerates shady ponds which are avoided by the common frog, it may have a greater range of water habitats from which to choose.

Much of this is speculation, as we do not have much data. In other animals the commonest causes of population decline are the destruction of a preferred habitat and/or a fall in the food supply. How this has affected a temporarily aquatic animal such as the frog is not clear, but we know that aquatic insects decline in number as water becomes polluted. Dragonflies are a case in point: twenty-six species were recorded along the Basingstoke canal in the 1930s, and by 1974 only four species could be found. An inadequate food supply for the aquatic larvae could be an important factor, but poor water quality may affect development in other ways. For instance, it is known that very low concentrations of pesticides may cause deformities in frog tadpoles and development cannot proceed.

In the last 200 years, Britain has lost several birds of wetland habitats. Nevertheless our *total* bird fauna is richer now than it has been for many years, thanks to effective protection laws and, even more important, a well-informed public opinion. The losses during the last 200 years include the black tern, which nested in some

A fenland scene at Wicken Fen in Cambridgeshire, where an old wind pump has been re-erected and restored by the National Trust.

numbers on several Broads in the first half of the nineteenth century but was no longer a regular breeder by about 1850. When the Broads were flooded in 1853 and 1858 it bred again, as it did in Romney Marsh, Kent, in 1885 and again during the last war when the marsh was flooded to deter invasion aircraft. The old Norfolk name for the common tern was 'dar', and in the seventeenth century Rockland Broad was known as 'Dares Meer'. As the common tern nests on sandy coasts or similar inland areas, it is more likely that Rockland Broad had a regular nesting colony of black terns, or 'blue dares' as they were called. Why it left this Broad as early as 150 years ago is unknown.

The largest natural lake in lowland Britain, Whittlesea Mere in the old Huntingdonshire part of Cambridgeshire, was drained in 1851. This event is well documented, and so is the mere itself, because many naturalists were attracted to its rare plants, birds and that glory of British entomology, the large copper butterfly. In 1697 the mere was recorded as being three miles broad and six miles long (over 11,000 acres) but it was shallow, only between three and six feet, and silt accumulated until the marginal reedswamp was able to creep out over the water surface. A hundred years later there was open water over only 1570 acres, with a circumference of eight-and-three-quarter miles. After 1800 the water table began to fall significantly, new islands began to appear and the mere nowhere was deeper than three-and-a-half feet. During the drought of 1826 it dried out completely for a short period, and was obviously near the end of its natural life in 1851 when the steam pump was invented and enterprising engineers managed to drain it, in only three weeks of pumping. This was the end of an era of wetland wildlife which we shall not see again in this country.

The quantities of fish and wildfowl obtained from Whittlesea Mere were legendary. Marsh harriers and bitterns were common only a few years before its end, but bearded tits, Savi's warblers, spotted crakes, greylag geese and black terns were recorded as nesting. In the seventeenth century spoonbills and cranes were regularly seen, and nine of the latter were recorded as being eaten at a banquet. In 1890 a visitor to the fens wrote: 'all is gone – reeds, sedges, the glittering water, the butterflies, the gypsies, the bitterns, the wildfowl, and in its place . . . a dreary flat of black arable land, with hardly a jacksnipe to give it charm'.

Whittlesea's wildlife did not completely die out. Adjacent to it was an area of deep acid peat which proved difficult to cultivate. As it dried out it was used for rough grazing, and then became a private game reserve, when many birch trees were planted. Finally, in 1954, it became the Holme Fen National Nature

Reserve. Some of the relict bog plants can still be seen there – saw-sedge, the creeping willow, heather, cross-leaved heath, bog myrtle, and there is even a recent record of the bilberry. But as the fen has been gradually drying out for many years, the species which need wet boggy conditions such as bog asphodel, sundew and grass of Parnassus have all disappeared, although sphagnum moss still lives in an old duck decoy dug in 1911.

About a mile and a half to the south is a second National Nature Reserve, Woodwalton Fen, with quite a different history. It is a fragment of marshy ground between the Mere and the clay upland; a survivor in the area which was the last to be drained and cultivated. In the middle and late-nineteenth century it was used as a turbary and several layers of peat were dug out from most of the fen surface, except in the southern tip. Much of the firm bog peat, usually regarded as the best, has therefore disappeared from the greater part of the reserve. The plants growing on the few remaining patches are similar to those at Holme Fen, with finer stands of bog myrtle, some cranberry and also the rare fen violet, which in the early years of the nineteenth century must have been quite widespread. It grows in areas which have been cleared or disturbed and there is evidence that seed may persist in the soil for a long time. An area covered by hawthorn, including some about forty-four years old, was cleared some years ago, exposing bare ground. The vegetation had been suppressed by the dense shade of the hawthorn, but in the first season after clearance the glade was carpeted with the milky white flowers of the fen violet.

Woodwalton Fen is best known for its colony of large copper butterflies. The British race of this insect had formerly been well established on the Whittlesea Mere marshes but when, in the 1820s, it was discovered that its larvae fed on the abundant great water docks, the local people gathered large numbers and sold them to collectors at fourpence per dozen, and in twenty years the population declined almost to extinction. To make matters worse, in 1841 there were severe floods which according to contemporary reports drowned the surviving larvae, and in 1848 a visiting entomologist could find only one specimen. Excessive predation by man seems to have been the main reason for its extinction, although it would almost certainly have disappeared shortly afterwards when Whittlesea Mere was drained and its marshy habitat cultivated.

For more than half a century British entomologists mourned the loss of one of our finest insects; then in 1915 a very similar race of the large copper was found in the marshes of the Dutch fens in Overijssel and

*Oak trees and other species from the ancient British wildwood have been preserved in
peat bogs like those of the Fens. Some may be over 10,000 years old and date back to
the Mesolithic era.*

Female large copper butterfly.

Friesland. It was almost indistinguishable from the British large copper, and entomologists lost no time in obtaining specimens from their Dutch friends so that in 1927 they were able to liberate twenty-five males and thirteen females on an area in the centre of Woodwalton Fen which had been specially prepared by planting many water docks. The butterflies did so well in the early years that a further introduction was made to Wicken Fen in Cambridgeshire in 1930. The Wicken population prospered for a number of years, but was already beginning to decline in the season or two before

1942 when the breeding area was drained and cleared for agriculture – a vain attempt to produce more food, in a time of scarcity, which completely failed.

The Woodwalton large coppers continued to live on the Fen although the population experienced many ups and downs when climatic conditions or predation by birds and mammals on the larvae reduced the population to very low levels. In the 1930s, the warden began to collect a number of larvae, usually about 100, and rear them in muslin cages which had been placed over one of the great water dock food plants on the Fen and then liberate the adults as they emerged. This protected them from predators and parasites at a very vulnerable period in their life cycle. This practice was continued until recently, and there is no doubt that it saved the copper from extinction on a number of occasions. One could say that the population is therefore not a natural one, and some entomologists have argued that this, plus the fact that it has been introduced, makes it of little scientific interest. The reverse is more likely to be true, because with the loss of so much wildlife habitat in the countryside we shall have to learn how to reintroduce lost species on our nature reserves in the future. A reserve population of the large copper has been maintained in captivity by the reserve warden, so that reintroduction can be made from the same genetic stock should it become extinct on the Fen. This happened in 1968, when a July flood drowned the food plants and prevented the female butterflies from laying their eggs.

In the last few years the warden has not maintained cages or liberated any butterflies from his captive stock on the Fen in order to test whether the population can survive without any help. So far it has, but in very small numbers, so the butterfly is vulnerable to a summer flood or other catastrophe. The Dutch race of this species is very localized in its own country, as much fenland has also been reclaimed there. In Britain the large copper is more at risk because it only exists in one place, and one ought to spread the risk by establishing it in other fens. There are very few from which to choose: Wicken is probably not suitable without the appropriate management, and although attempts have been made in the Norfolk Broads they were not successful. The great water dock is a very widespread plant throughout Britain but the large copper seems to be very choosy about which plant is suitable for laying its eggs. The female is on the wing in July/August when it oviposits; the eggs soon hatch and the young larvae feed for a time before migrating down to the dead leaves at the base of the food plant in early September and hibernating there until the following spring. Floods during the winter have no effect on the larvae, but when they become active in the spring to search for the first shoots of the great water dock, they may be drowned by flooding. Growth is rapid when conditions are favourable, and the large green larvae begin to pupate in early June and the first butterflies emerge in late June or early July.

In the marshes of the Norfolk Broads we have a genuine native butterfly in the swallowtail, which is larger and more striking then even the purple emperor. The larval food plant is the rather local milk parsley, a species which in contrast to the great water dock is

perhaps only really widespread in the wet fens of the Norfolk Broads. The swallowtail overwinters as a pupa but does not emerge until June in the following year, so it is on the wing a few weeks earlier than the large copper. This butterfly has been declining in numbers for some time in the Broads, partly due to natural changes on the marshes. Fifty years ago sedge and 'fen litter' (a mixture of different fen plants) were cut on a wide scale so that the marshes were kept open and the milk parsley was at its best. In the absence of this traditional cutting, bushes and alders spread over the marsh, gradually suppressing the herbaceous vegetation making the fenland habitat unsuitable for the swallowtail.

Not far from Cambridge on the edge of the Fenland Basin is Wicken Fen, probably the most famous fen nature reserve in Britain on account of the studies made on it for over 100 years. Parts of this reserve have been protected since the last years of the nineteenth century. In spite of many changes during the past 150 years, it seems to be a genuine relict of the original fens where local people were entitled to cut sedge and litter. Peat cutting was another activity that helped to preserve those plants which prefer open situations. When these common rights fell into disuse, Wicken Fen gradually became a thicket of alder buckthorn. In recent times these bushes have been cleared from large areas and plants which were last recorded many years ago have reappeared. One of the most remarkable is the fen violet, which had not been seen on Wicken Fen since 1910. As at Woodwalton Fen, the seed must have lain dormant in the peat for all those years.

Milk parsley grows quite commonly in parts of Wicken Fen and the swallowtail lived there until the last war when, in the absence of the fenmen who harvested reed and sedge, bushes invaded and made the habitat unsuitable. Attempts at reintroduction have been made from time to time, but without success. A recent detailed study has shown that because there is a lowered water table on the fen the milk parsley plants do not grow large enough to provide sufficient food for the swallowtail larvae. In addition, they grow later in the season than the plants on the Norfolk marshes, which are also generally much wetter. Without a careful study over several years it would have been difficult to be convinced that this was really the cause, as there is a good deal of milk parsley, and when it is in flower the habitat seems ideal. Almost all rare insects which have been studied by scientific methods have been shown to have complex habitat requirements, and though the food plant may be present or even common on a nature reserve, it does not necessarily mean that the insect itself is able to flourish there.

A sedge warbler singing around the margins of its territory at Wicken Fen Nature Reserve.

Mute swans nesting in fen country near Ely.

A young swan inspecting an interesting burrow.

The destruction of wetlands is not entirely a conservationist's story of gloom. In some parts of the country magnificent wetlands have been created by man and have subsequently developed into very interesting ornithological sites. It has proved relatively easy to recreate the conditions that birds need, but much more difficult to do the same for insects or plants. The mobility of birds enables them to range over a wider area, and they are quick to exploit new habitats when they appear. One well-known example is the colonization by the little ringed plover of the numerous flooded gravel pits which we now have in Britain as a result of extensive exploitation for building and road construction. Equally important are the many reservoirs, particularly in lowlands where there are few natural water sources apart from rivers. In recent years two of the largest reservoirs have been constructed in the old counties of Huntingdonshire and Rutland. Both are excellent wintering areas for waterfowl and for migrants. It is unlikely that reservoirs of this size will be built in the future, because they submerge so much valuable agricultural land.

The washlands along the rivers Nene and Ouse in the Fenland Basin were constructed in order to absorb flood water which might otherwise inundate agricultural land. The Washes still fulfil this function, but as the pumps carrying excess water to the sea are now so efficient, the flood water does not remain for as long on the marshes as it did previously. During the summer months they are valuable grazing areas, enriched with nutrients deposited by annual flooding, which stimulates a luxuriant growth of vegetation. The Nene Washes are famous for their flocks of wintering Bewick swans as well as many other wildfowl, and the Ouse

A mallard and her young.

Washes achieved fame in the 1950s when the black-tailed godwit was found breeding there. This wader was well known on migration and as a common breeding bird in the wet meadows of the Netherlands, but ceased to breed regularly in Britain in the 1820s or 1830s. There were very few attempts at breeding for over 100 years, until in 1952 the first pair bred of what proved to be a permanent colonization. Since then, aided by strict protection, the black-tailed godwit has thrived. They have many interesting species of wild-fowl as nesting companions including shovelers, gad-walls, garganeys and numerous redshanks, lapwings and snipe. The ruff is another recent colonist, and breeds on the Wash. Black-tailed godwits now breed in a number of localities throughout Britain, but nowhere as successfully as on the Ouse Washes, where it can range over an area of nearly nineteen miles by 866 yards.

There are two wetland areas on the Suffolk coast which are on every bird-watcher's list of places to visit. Yet they would probably not be nationally important bird reserves if it had not been for the last war. These are the Minsmere Nature Reserve of the Royal Society for the Protection of Birds (RSPB) and, a few miles north, the Walberswick National Nature Reserve. Both consist of shallow valleys draining directly into the sea. Before 1939 they were cattle-grazed meadows, but both were flooded during the war because it was thought this would reduce the risk of invasion aircraft landing successfully. Even in the early 1930s, drainage was a difficult problem because the sand dunes which separated the two valleys from the sea were gradually being pushed inland, blocking up the sluice which took drainage water out at low tide. After the war the expense of installing pumps capable of taking the drainage out to the sea was not considered a high

Heron, one of our largest wild birds and fortunately still fairly common although many die in hard winters.

priority, and very soon pools formed and reedbeds replaced the meadows. Marsh harriers, bitterns, bearded tits and many duck soon colonized the developing marshes, and bird-watchers were not slow in discovering them.

Minsmere was acquired as a nature reserve by the RSPB in the early 1950s, and by clever management and protection this reserve is today one of the best places for the rarer wetland birds of lowland England. The bird fauna of Walberswick is similar to that of Minsmere but the numbers of marsh harriers and bitterns are less, perhaps because there are several public footpaths which cause disturbance. Similarly, avocets breed successfully at Minsmere but attempts at Walberswick are generally not successful. Both areas are rather poor in plants and the rarer marsh invertebrates associated with East Anglian fenlands, and this may be due to their recent origin.

In north-west Lancashire, on the south side of the Lake District, the Leighton Moss reserve of the RSPB has a similar history. It lies in a small shallow valley flanked by limestone hills, and was formerly drained by

a steam pump and the land used as grazing meadows. In 1917 drainage ceased, and the water from small springs and streams collected on the clay valley bottom to form a large shallow lake. A good deal of reed and scrub has grown up in the last sixty-seven years, and although the water surface is reduced the present management preserves a balance between reed swamp and water. The most remarkable ornithological feature of this reserve is the large breeding population of bitterns, from ten to twelve pairs. It is the only place in northern England where bitterns breed regularly. Bearded tits bred for the first time in 1973 and now there is a well-established colony.

In Britain there is only one largish native mammal which spends most of its time in the water – the otter. It is almost entirely a fish eater, and until thirty to forty years ago it was well established in most of our rivers. It was hunted on foot with long-legged otter hounds, and this writer remembers these packs operating success-

Mute swan, one of our most familiar water birds.

The otter, now only really common in western Scotland and Ireland.

fully in 1936/1937 in east Leicestershire along comparatively small brooks where otters were then found quite easily. There are no otters there now, and few are left in lowland England. The decline seemed to have started in the 1950s in some parts of the country, when the otter hunts reported a sharp decrease in the number of animals found. This decrease continued until the otter had retreated to Devon and Cornwall, north Norfolk, parts of Wales, and Scotland. Happily, in Ireland it is still widespread and common. In the clean water of upland areas it is also still common, but it no longer occurs in regions of intense agriculture. Like the corncrake, which forty years ago was in all our hayfields, its only refuges are now in the north and west, where pollution and machines have not had such a profound effect on the environment.

There is no doubt that there has been a considerable loss of suitable otter habitat wherever agriculture is highly mechanized. They prefer streams and rivers where there is plenty of vegetation cover along the margins and a good number of trees so that they can hide among the roots. Modern agriculture requires full control over drainage, which too often means that streams are deepened, sides levelled and trees removed.

This would not have been responsible for the sharp decline in otter numbers, but the two factors of water pollution and habitat destruction may have combined to prevent recovery. The same fall in numbers has been reported in all the western industrialized countries. The only exception (apart from Ireland) is Greece, where in several regions the otter is still common.

Quite a few animals which never occurred here naturally have been introduced, mainly for their furs. As so often happens, some escape, and the first to establish itself in our rivers was the muskrat, a native of North America, which started to breed about 1930 and for a time occupied considerable areas in central Scotland, the upper Severn in Shropshire and in Surrey and Sussex. The damage caused by burrowing into banks was well known, but prompt and effective action by pest control officers finally exterminated the muskrat in 1937.

Our second successful but unwanted aquatic mammal which was accidentally introduced was the coypu, a native of South America and regretfully still with us. It is a large rodent weighing nearly 15 lbs and was bred, as was the muskrat, for its fur. It managed to escape during the early 1930s and found a habitat very much to its liking in the Norfolk Broads, and gradually increased in numbers until 1946, when the severe winter almost exterminated it. In the 1950s it began to increase rapidly and extended its range. For a time it seemed to be fairly harmless, apart from consuming a good deal of marsh vegetation and making a large number of well-trodden trackways. This unfortunately was short-lived; high population densities resulted in a good deal of damage to marsh vegetation on nature reserves and the coypu were said to disturb ground-nesting birds. On some of the smaller broads the aquatic vegetation was destroyed so extensively that the open water surface was substantially increased. Perhaps because it was so numerous it began to wander away from the marshes in search of other food supplies. It would eat grass, cereals, and in the winter found that potatoes and sugar beet were good to eat. Soon there were complaints about this large exotic mammal damaging agricultural crops; the Ministry of Agriculture were called in and in 1962 a campaign started to exterminate the coypu. This turned out to be very difficult because there are so many places on the marshes where it could hide although the numbers were greatly reduced.

The best coypu control is probably severe winters. Its tail and feet are susceptible to frostbite, and the 1962 winter killed so many that for a time it was thought they had gone for good; but a few survived to build up the population again in the following years. The meat,

The coypu, this large destructive aquatic-mammal still persists in the Norfolk Broads.

as one might expect with a herbivore, is said to be quite tasty to eat, but there is no market for it and the pelt has fallen in value, so that it is not worthwhile hunting the coypu commercially.

The most recent introduction of a semi-aquatic mammal in Britain is the North American mink. Its fur is very valuable and mink farms are still operating in different parts of the country. It grows to a larger size than the common ferret, and although it lives by waterways and hunts fish, it is quite able to catch small mammals, birds and even domestic poultry and game. It is a very versatile predator and most people think it is too destructive to have in our countryside. On the other hand, we rightly protect our native polecat, which is a

predator of about the same size and very rare outside Wales.

At first it was thought that the increase and spread of mink throughout the country coincided with the decline of the otter. However, it seems unlikely that the activities of these two mammals are related, because the otter disappeared from a number of areas before the mink arrived, and in the south-west mink and otter seem to be living together along the same waterways.

This account of British wetlands is a rather sad story, because so much of their wildlife heritage has been lost due to man's activities. Too many of our waterways are expected to function mainly as sewers and drains for unwanted effluents, and it is not surprising that wildlife suffers and eventually disappears. The quality of our rivers is being improved, but there is a long way to go and we cannot change their well-established use in the forseeable future. On the other hand, where unpolluted streams can be identified we should seek the co-operation of the water authorities to protect them and ensure that they are preserved in as natural a state as possible. These will then provide a baseline for assessing what a freshwater fauna and flora should be like.

We have briefly mentioned the increase in the number of water-filled gravel pits and reservoirs and the value they have for water birds, particularly migrants and winter visitors. Not so long ago no other activity except angling was permitted on reservoirs for domestic water supplies, but today there is a much more liberal approach and parts of the great reservoirs of Rutland and Grafham Waters are allocated for fishing, boating and nature reserves. Picnic sites, car parks, information boards and footpaths are facilities now provided at reservoirs for the visiting public. Water-filled sand and gravel pits are landscaped instead of leaving them as a series of spoil heaps, which was the practice not very long ago.

Artificial wetlands have also formed in mining areas following land subsidence, and several have become important ornithological sites with fine beds of reeds. Reed beds are themselves limited in Britain, and only 109 of more than five acres were recorded in a recent survey. Open water without reed beds and marshland margin is of limited interest, but these habitats can be created artificially, and this is perhaps what must be done in the future. A new approach to the environment is developing, an understanding that exploitation must be followed by restoration to leave something of value for the community, providing opportunities for wildlife conservation that should not be missed.

— 11 —

THE COAST

Although one of the smaller countries of Europe, Britain, with its elongated shape, islands and indented shores, has one of the longest coastlines. The range of latitude, from less than 50°N at the Lizard in Cornwall to about 61°N at the furthest point of the Shetlands, encompasses almost every type of coastline that can be found in the west temperate region, from the low coast of sand dunes, shingle beaches and salt marshes in the south and south-east of England to the high cliffs on the Scottish isles. Although the south generally has a low coast, apart from the famous chalk cliffs of Dover, Folkestone and the Seven Sisters, parts of Norfolk and Suffolk have soft cliffs of glacial drift and outwash material, such as boulder clay, sand and gravel, which were deposited during the Ice Age and the floods which followed. In the west and south-west the cliffs are mainly of tougher rocks – changed or 'metamorphic' rocks like slate, schist and gneiss, with some granite, volcanic basalt and the softer Old Red Sandstone – forming loftier cliffs.

The average height of most sea cliffs in Britain is somewhere between 150 and 300 feet. The highest are on the islands off the north of Scotland, including the granitic cliffs of St Kilda in the Outer Hebrides which reach to almost 1400 feet, while the Old Red Sandstone precipice of Foula in Shetland is about 1200 feet. The famous vertical offshore pillar by the island of Hoy in Orkney (known as the Old Man of Hoy) has the highest vertical rock wall in Britain, of 1080 feet, and was only climbed for the first time a few years ago. The highest cliff in mainland Scotland is the 680 foot Clo Mor of Torridonian Sandstone on the coast of Sutherland. On the English coast the highest cliff is at Boulby (650 feet) in Yorkshire.

Although there is a longer stretch of continuous sand dunes and salt marshes on the coasts of East Anglia than elsewhere, there are many fine dune systems all the way from north Devon to the north of Scotland. In Wales there are splendid dune formations on Gower, at Harlech and on the north coast. On the north-east coast of Scotland, in the former county of Moray, is the largest dune system in Britain, the Culvin Sands, and on the north coast of Caithness is the sweeping curve of dunes at Dunnet Links.

An important feature of our coastline is the numerous estuaries where rivers have brought down large quantities of silt to form tidal mud and sand flats so typical of estuaries. Many of these are internationally important feeding places for waders and wildfowl, notably in the Cheshire Dee, Morecambe Bay, the Solway, the Wash, and the Wildfowl Trust grounds in the Severn estuary.

Britain also has some fine shingle beaches which are rather rare elsewhere in Europe. The finest (some think in western Europe) is the great shingle promontory of Dungeness. Further west Chesil Beach, off the Dorset coast, extends for many miles west of Weymouth. On the Suffolk coast the National Nature Reserve of Orford Beach runs south from the extensive promontory of Orfordness. All these have been built up by the tidal currents which sometimes scour our coasts with enormous power. The tide has also fashioned sand and shingle spits such as Spurn Head at the mouth of the Humber, and Scolt Head Island and Blakeney Point off the north Norfolk coast. All the formations described have been moulded, built, eroded or changed in some way by the action of the sea. In some instances storms have built up new ridges of sand and shingle almost overnight, as at Winterton Dunes in Norfolk.

The difference between the height of mean low and high tides varies according to location. For instance, at Southampton there is about a twelve foot difference, at London Bridge it is twenty-three feet, at Liverpool thirty feet, and at Avonmouth it reaches forty-four feet. Exceptional levels are sometimes reached by the flow of the tide being pushed to an even greater height by the force of a gale blowing in the same direction. On occasions this has caused serious damage, as in 1953 when the low dunes of the Norfolk and Suffolk coasts were overtopped by the waves and a great deal of land was flooded with sea water. The power of the running tide can perhaps best be seen in the River Severn where the tidal bore, or wave, flows up the estuary sometimes with a wall of water four or five feet high.

Coastlines are ever changing, due to tidal currents and the south-westerly gales, which build up dunes

This church at Llandanwg near Harlech has been overwhelmed by drifting sand.

and shingle banks in one place and erode them in another. The force of the wind, when it blows persistently from one direction, even affects the coastal vegetation, pruning trees and shrubs into curious lopsided shapes by preventing or slowing down growth on the weather side. Even rocky shores are not immune; the waves force water into cracks so that the softer rocks are eroded away. The sea is sometimes able to excavate caves deep into the rocky cliffs and occasionally breaks through the cave roof at the inland end forming a water spout. There are some fine examples of this on Horn Head in Donegal where the sea has eroded a number of caves. The largest water spout, known locally as McSwyne's Gun, shoots an enormous jet of sea water 100 feet into the air with a thunderous roar.

The effect of the weather and the tides on the coast of Britain is also compounded by the relative height of the sea in relation to the land. The British Isles are gradually tilting so that the east coast is sinking and the west coast is rising. Proof of this is shown by the large number of raised beaches, which form inland shelves but were originally cut by wave action in the past. Some of these old beaches are now raised up as much as sixty-five feet above mean sea level. There are examples in the Isle of Man, North Wales, the Western Islands and on the west Scottish mainland. Erosion is most evident on the east coast of England: fine dune systems and shingle ridges such as Spurn Point, Yorkshire, are gradually being cut back and the material deposited elsewhere along the coast. The east coast has even lost a town which used to be one of the most important commercial centres in East Anglia in Anglo-Saxon times. Dunwich, which is now a small village with only one church, previously had more than a dozen. By the middle of the eleventh century erosion by the sea was beginning to take its toll and throughout the following centuries the town was gradually swallowed up by the

North Sea. Old photographs in Dunwich Museum show parts of the last church lying on the beach and of coffins in the churchyard about to fall down the cliff face.

But although the east coast is gradually eroding, thousands of years ago the land which is now the North Sea was part of the vast estuary formed by the River Rhine. The land link with the continent was finally flooded around 8000 BC, a few millennia after the last Ice Age. During the glacial era, water evaporating from the sea became locked on the land in the form of great glaciers and ice sheets. The sea level fell, but meanwhile the great weight of the ice depressed the land-mass, particularly the mountainous areas which carried the heaviest burden. When the ice sheets thawed the water returned rapidly to the sea, but the land level rose more slowly following the removal of the ice load. The raised beaches of the north and west mark the steps in the re-emergence. The firm land was forest-covered and evidence of this can still be traced along the coast in many places where the fossilized tree stumps project from a type of peat deposit at low tide. Submerged forests of many different ages are clear proof that the sea level has fluctuated on numerous occasions; in the cliffs of Lulworth Cove in Dorset are the remains of a petrified forest which is far older than the stumps found on the beach below. Excavations of the dock basins at Southampton and at Barry in Glamorgan have revealed remains of these old forests. Peat and tree trunks can be seen at low tide on the coast

The fragrant evening primrose is an introduced plant and found mainly on dunes in south-west England and in the Channel Islands.

near Formby in Lancashire, along the Wirral and near Harlech and at Borth in the Dovey estuary. At Pentuan in Cornwall there is a layer of sediment containing oak stumps and roots which is now sixty-five feet below the present sea level. Much of the coastline has therefore been submerged, further evidence being the steep-sided flooded inlets on the Devon and Cornish coasts, the numerous sea lochs with islands on the west coast of Scotland and the Outer Hebrides, sometimes known, as in Orkney and Shetland, by the Scandinavian name 'voe'.

The fauna and flora of the intertidal zone together form one of the richest marine ecosystems. The light and the rich oxygen supply promote a luxuriant growth of plants and a remarkable zonation of animals depending on the degree of exposure which can be tolerated at low tide, and on the type of substrate. Even where there are vast mud flats with no vegetation there is an extensive marine life of crustacea, worms and bivalve molluscs living below the surface, where they shelter until the incoming tide brings detritus and other food material on which they feed. Shallow waters offshore are also rich in fish because they are the spawning grounds of species which normally live in deep water. It is on this food supply that the cliff-nesting birds and the tern colonies depend to feed their young.

Sand dunes

Sand consists of small particles varying in size from .02 to 2.0 mm and is derived from many different sources. Some of it comes from the breakdown of rock by mechanical and chemical erosion processes, the pounding of the sea fragmenting the rock into small pieces, and from the shells of marine animals which are worn down into tiny fragments by wave action. On the beach of Connemara, Ireland, a so-called 'coral' sand occurs, consisting of pieces of coralline algae which live below the low tide mark. Sand derived almost entirely from shells is found in the machair of Scotland and in other places along the Welsh and English coasts. In areas where quartz forms a high proportion of the sand, what little calcareous material there is in it may be leached out by rainfall. Surface sand of this type is very poor in nutrients and supports only a few plants, such as lichens and mosses, forming what is usually known as dune heath. Sand is moved about both by the sea and the wind; winter storms change the profile of the beach by depositing or eroding sand and, at low tide, winds dry out the surface and blow the sand onto the dunes.

Building or 'accreting' dunes slowly grow higher as

wind-blown sand is trapped by the stiff leaves of marram grass, whose deep roots support and strengthen the dunes. If the marram cover is broken by trampling or a storm, protection against the wind is lost and a great excavation, or 'blow-out', is formed. If nothing is done to repair the breach, these blow-outs can eat through a dune system, but it is usual to build a barrier or fence across the gap to break the force of the wind and so allow sand to be deposited again. If successful, marram is planted and the hole fills up by natural processes.

A well-formed dune system has a marked zonation of plant and animal life of great interest to the ecologist. Just above the high tide line is a thin broken line of salt-resistant plants, usually prickly saltwort and sea rocket. These are the pioneers of living vegetation closest to the sea but there is another zone, known as the driftline, consisting of dead and rotting marine algae or salt marsh plants mixed up with the accumulated flotsam and jetsam to be found on most beaches. Where there are no rocks to support the larger marine algae or no nearby salt marsh, the driftline may consist almost entirely of debris with no plant life, living or dead. Slightly higher on the beach and nearer to the tall dunes one sometimes finds tiny sand hills a few inches high with a little sea couch-grass growing on them. These are known as embryo dunes because they may be the beginnings of a new big dune system or dune ridge.

Although a driftline may consist of dead material it is nevertheless part of the coastal ecosystem and the organic material is utilized by a number of different animals. Sandhoppers are everywhere, and a number of small flies breed in the wet seaweed, sometimes in such large numbers that they can be a nuisance to people on the beach. One of the best-known insects is a sandy coloured ground beetle almost entirely confined to the driftline and nearby dunes. There are sometimes enormous numbers of small money spiders which no doubt feed on the small flies, and both are sought after by small migrant birds which forage on the shore. In the north of Scotland and on Orkney and Shetland seaweed is a valuable fertilizer, collected by horse and cart and taken to the ridged arable fields or 'lazy beds', where the potatoes need the organic material to help them grow. On the island of Eynhallow in Orkney this writer has watched sheep wander far out onto the sand flats at low tide to feed on these marine algae growing on rocky outcrops.

At the head of the beach, perhaps reached only by the highest tides, is the main dune ridge. Tall accreting sand hills have much loose sand but it is protected by scattered tussocks of marram grass. This zone is called the 'yellow' or 'mobile' dune stage, names recalling the high proportion of bare sand and the fact that it is not stabilized but moves about by wind action. Marram grows best on accreting sand and when the supply ceases, growth and vigour tend to decline. As we move inland from the mobile or yellow dunes onto the landward side of the dune ridge we find that although there is still a good deal of marram it is thinner and does not form tussocks, and many other plants, particularly grasses, grow with it. The sand is not completely stabilized at this point, there being much loose material in the vegetation, but the supply of wind-blown sand is greatly reduced. It has been called the marram transition zone because this is where marram is beginning to fade out and a different type of vegetation becomes

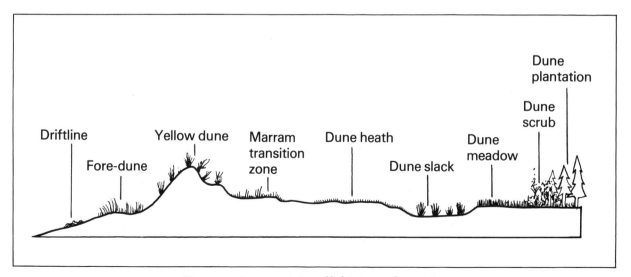

Diagrammatic representation of habitats on a dune system

established.

As we go still further inland grass and other plants become more abundant and marram virtually disappears; we are now in the dune meadow. On calcareous dunes this zone is rich in flowering plants and very colourful. Dune meadows are important grazings for domestic stock, usually sheep and cattle, and they fulfil another role in the summer by providing camping and caravanning sites for thousands of tourists. At Tentsmuir on the east coast of Scotland, where the sand is not calcareous, there is much dwarf scrub heath on the stabilized dunes instead of the dense turf found elsewhere. This large system grew over some forty years, demonstrating how rapidly the coastline can change. If the dune meadow is not grazed a scrub of sea

buckthorn may develop, or if there are wet hollows, willows, alders and birch will grow.

Conifer plantations are frequently established on dune systems, either to control wind blow or on stabilized dunes to provide timber. On the north Norfolk coast near Wells a large area of the dunes just inland of the mobile dunes was planted with Corsican pine to help as a sea defence by stabilizing the dunes. During the 1953 sea flood most of these trees were killed by sea water and when they were removed the exposed sand dunes had no vegetation to protect them for a time. However, there was a good deal of sea buckthorn nearby which was able to take over from the trees. It is a better stabilizer of loose sand than conifer plantations but it is very prickly – and an effective

The ringed plover is a common bird of sand and shingle coastlines but in the north of England and particularly in Scotland it nests in many inland areas such as shingle banks by rivers and gravel pits.

The oystercatcher is a large conspicuous bird, widespread on low coastlines and rocky shores. In the north of England and in Scotland large numbers breed along rivers and in gravel pits.

barrier against people.

Some dune formations develop depressions between the ridges which are marshy for at least part of the year or even have standing water. The water is usually fresh but may be brackish where sea water is able to seep through the dunes at high tides or where salt spray can reach them. Many slacks, as these are called, are transient and may become filled with sand again where there is an eroding coast so that wind-blown sand is brought nearer. Wet dune slacks are wonderful places for plants and animals. Until recently they were one of the favourite haunts of the natterjack toad, which has now become so scarce in Britain. This interesting amphibian, easily recognizable by the pale yellow line down the middle of the back, can still be found in several places on the east and west coasts.

Dune slacks may be fringed by rushes of different species and are often a paradise for the bryologist, who is a specialist in mosses and lichens. If the dunes are rather acid then deep banks of *Polytrichum* and *Sphagnum* mosses occur, the latter often with orchids and other flowering plants. Calcareous dune slacks have a paticularly interesting flora; at Ainsdale in Lancashire, the fourth largest British dune system, the slacks have marsh helleborines, common spotted orchids, the round-leaved wintergreen and grass of Parnassus. There is a considerable difference between the floras of calcareous and of acid dune slacks, the former having many sedge species with plants such as marsh arrow-grass, marsh lousewort and grass of Parnassus, while

the latter has mosses and cross-leaved heath. The creeping willow, which forms a low, almost prostrate shrub, is found in both sorts of dune slacks but can grow upwards, keeping pace with the accretion of wind-blown sand. As each shrub grows taller an almost vertical-sided hummock is formed. These humps have a curious bristly appearance which perhaps accounts for their local name of 'hedgehogs'. There are some good examples of these strange dunes on Newborough Warren, Anglesey, and some really big ones on the Whiteford Burrows in Gower.

Shallow water bodies, generally less than six feet deep, form coastal lagoons on some parts of our coast. The most typical have developed behind sand or shingle ridges, as at Slapton Ley in Devon and the Loch of Strathbeg in Aberdeenshire. The lagoon known as Little Sea at the Studland National Reserve in Dorset is well documented. It was flooded at normal high tide in the eighteenth century but since then has been sealed off from the sea by natural processes of accumulating marine deposits and is now mostly fresh water with reed-beds and an interesting birdlife. Another lagoon, The Fleet in Dorset, is still tidal and the coastal broads of Benacre and Covehithe in Suffolk are brackish, although formerly fresh water. Other important coastal lagoons are the machair lochs in the Outer Hebrides, shallow lakes formed on the inner areas of blown sand.

The sand terraces and dunes are greatly favoured as nest sites by many sea birds. The common tern and sandwich tern nest in low dune areas, often in dense colonies. The roseate tern is rare in Britain as a breeding species but more common on the Irish coasts, while the arctic tern is largely confined to Scotland. The black-headed gull prefers to nest on islands but it also occurs on dunes; one of the largest known colonies in Britain is on the Ravenglass dunes on the Cumbrian coast. The little tern, ringed plover and oystercatcher often nest on shingly ground at the head of the beach. This zone is also where people like to walk or picnic and the disturbance may be the reason why little terns have declined on well-used beaches. Sand dunes are even more popular as recreation areas, an activity incompatible with nesting colonies of terns. The only solution on nature reserves is to exclude the public during the breeding season and have a warden on the spot to deter trespassers.

The snowy owl, a very rare visitor to Britain, surprised everyone by nesting in Shetland in 1967 and for the following eight years. Since 1975 none have nested although occasional birds are seen each year in Shetland and Orkney.

Salt marshes

Salt marshes often form at the mouth of estuaries where the silt carried down by the rivers is deposited and a fine sticky mud or sand flats are built up. Some extensive salt marshes also occur along the open coast, particularly in north Norfolk and Bridgwater Bay in Somerset. Here the silt is brought in by the tides and deposited in still, shallow water, gradually building up until it can be colonized by plants. At Scolt Head, Norfolk, the salt marshes have formed between the island, which is a narrow line of dunes over four miles in length, and the mainland, and similarly at nearby Blakeney Point, marshes have formed along part of the mainland sheltered from the sea by the shingle and sand of Blakeney Point. In these sheltered places the sea is not disturbed by waves or tidal currents, so that its load of silt is deposited more readily than elsewhere.

One of the first plants to colonize the mud flats of a salt marsh is the glasswort, whose fleshy stems are a popular delicacy with many people who live in coastal areas. It can be eaten raw chopped up in a salad or lightly cooked, like asparagus. In sheltered areas away from the force of the waves the thin wavy leaves of eelgrass form vivid green swards in shallow water or where exposed at low tide. It is an important food for wild geese, especially the brent goose, which is more or less confined to salt marshes where eelgrass grows. In spite of the name, these plants are not grasses, but rather unusual herbs with long filamentous leaves. For some years our mud flats have been threatened by a recent plant invader first recorded in Southampton Water in 1870. This is the hybrid cordgrass, which has the capacity to grow over bare saltings with great speed and may completely dominate the salt marshes. It traps suspended silt, building up the level of the marsh until other plants are able to colonize. In some places it has destroyed the beds of eelgrass and, as it is unpalatable, the wild geese have been forced to go elsewhere. The wading birds who found their food on the open mud flats before the cordgrass arrived have also had to go to other marshes.

At the highest level in the intertidal zone seameadow grass creates a rather straggly turf. It is submerged on the highest tides but at other times its nutritious leaves are sought after by the sheep, cattle and horses which are often grazed on the salt marshes and the nearby dune meadow. At this level on older marshes there is an abundance of sea aster, sea lavender, sea blight, sea plantain and the sea arrowgrass.

Salt marshes are criss-crossed by channels cut by the flow of the ebb tide and forming fantastic patterns, best shown on aerial photographs. The edges of the chan-

nels, even when dry, can be picked out by the growth of
the woody plant sea purslane. It traps sediment
brought in by the tide and gradually builds up the sides
of the channels so that they stand up above the rest of
the salt marsh. It is rather tough and twiggy, growing
to about the same height as heather but fading out
when the ebb and flow of the tide has ceased due to
accretion of silt.

Although there are numerous marine animals on
the salt marsh at high tide, particularly crustacea,
molluscs and worms, there are also many insects
which are really terrestrial that exploit the various
plants growing on the marsh. Sea aster and sea
lavender are the homes of a number of interesting
beetles and small moths. Sea wormwood and sea
plantain are the food plants of the ground lackey moth,
confined to Essex and north Kent, the Essex emerald,
and the scarce pug. Salt marshes are surprisingly very
interesting places for unusual spiders. These are not
truly marine because they do not live in the water, but
on the other hand most can withstand submergence at
high tide for at least twelve hours. For instance, if one
cuts out a piece of seameadow grass turf when it is
submerged at high tide, there will be several spiders in
it. The most typical salt marsh species is a wolf spider
called *Pardosa purbeckensis*, but where vegetation litter
has accumulated, many different species may be found.
One of these is a small money spider, *Erigone arctica*,
which also occurs in beach driftline material and is
found occasionally inland by salt mines. The larger
wolf spider *Arctosa fulvolineata*, rather rare on south-
east coasts, has a bright spear-shaped orange mark on
the abdomen, making it quite unmistakable. It seems to
prefer estuarine marshes but has been taken in one or
two saltings along the mainland coast of south-east
England. Living on the bare mud underneath sea
purslane, and also confined to the south-east coasts of
England, is a curious money spider called *Praestigia
duffeyi*. It is small and black with red legs and has a
curious projection on its head, which can only be seen
under a microscope and looks a little bit like a
policeman's helmet.

For obvious reasons, salt marshes do not have
nesting birds, although black-headed gulls will occasionally try to nest in tall sea purslane, only to have
their eggs floated away on the first high tide. But as a
feeding area the salt marsh is very valuable indeed. In
the winter and migration periods large numbers of
waders and geese congregate to feed on the abundant

*Salt marsh vegetation at Salthouse in Norfolk. Note the dune
barrier between the marshes and the sea.*

animal life or to graze the seameadow grass, eelgrass and other palatable species. Fine filamentous algae are common on many salt marshes and are taken as an alternative food by brent geese in the absence of eelgrass.

Man has known for a long time, and certainly since the Romans occupied Britain, that salt marsh mud can be made into fertile agricultural soil. For two thousand years saltings have been enclosed by building out banks from the shore to keep out the sea. Gradually the salt is washed out by rain and the land is ready for cultivation. The most remarkable example of this on a large scale is the Dutch polders. Enormous areas have been reclaimed, adding a great deal of valuable agricultural land to the country. The best examples in Britain are in the region of the Wash – the site of some of our oldest enclosures. Some engineers think that virtually the whole of this area could be reclaimed by embanking, partly for new agricultural land and partly for the construction of a freshwater reservoir. The cost would be astronomical and a wildfowl feeding area of international importance would be destroyed.

Shingle beaches

Britain is unique in Europe in having some of the finest shingle formations. Banks, beaches and spits are fairly frequent around our coasts but large formations almost entirely of pebbles are rather rare. They are built up by strong tidal currents and by wave action, although Europe's finest, Dungeness in Kent, was probably formed by a series of storm beaches. Its great size has attracted a number of developments, including the construction of a nuclear power station, which caused some concern among biologists but has the advantage of being well away from large centres of population. Dungeness has several coastal lagoons, both natural and artificial and varying from freshwater to saline, where the introduced marsh frog thrives. Many years ago this writer remembers watching a singing marsh warbler in a willow bush by one of the lagoons, the first time I had seen this bird in Britain. The ornithological interest of Dungeness is considerable and the Royal Society for the Protection of Birds has its own nature reserve there. In the winter the wide open spaces of shingle attract hen harriers, short-eared owls, merlins and small finches including the snow bunting. It is a famous landfall for migrating birds in spring and especially in autumn, when black terns, whitethroats, lesser whitethroats and firecrests are seen. Migrating butterflies and moths also pass through. Dungeness is well known for its rare and local lepidoptera, particu-

larly moths, and there are also several rare spiders including one species which is not known from any other locality in Britain.

Other large shingle beaches, Chesil Beach in Dorset and Orford Beach in Suffolk, have been formed by tidal currents depositing shingle in a long ridge parallel to the coast and forming a spit. Chesil Beach is a beautiful example; it is completely straight and over eighteen miles in length. It encloses the interesting tidal lagoon known as The Fleet, where the three British species of eelgrass occur together in an extensive population. Large numbers of duck congregate there in winter, attracted by this source of food. Growing amongst the pebbles on the shingle ridge are large populations of some local species of plants, the tall sea kale, the beautiful yellow horned poppy, the sea pea, a very characteristic plant of shingle, and the rough trefoil. The shrubby sea blight, which is confined to the southern and south-eastern coasts of Britain, is regarded as a shingle plant but prefers the stones to be well consolidated with debris or salt-marsh mud. The most extraordinary invertebrate animal recorded from Chesil Beach is the scaley cricket. It has no wings, is quite dark in colour, and has been taken nowhere else in the British Isles. It is really a characteristic species of Mediterranean regions. Both the Dungeness shingle and Chesil Beach have large breeding populations of little terns and together account for a substantial proportion of the total British population of this species.

The third outstanding shingle formation is on the Suffolk coast by the village of Orford, from which it gets its name. The beach extends for about ten miles along the coast from the town of Aldeburgh and is separated from the mainland by the River Alde. This river probably entered the sea close by the town of Aldeburgh in the distant past but has been deflected ten miles south by the movement of shingle along the coast. A long ridge has been formed which is broadest at a point known as Orfordness, close to the village of Orford. South of Orfordness is the National Nature Reserve of Orford Beach, a superb shingle ridge about seven miles long. From north to south one passes through a series of vegetation types, from long-established to new, until one finally reaches the bare, mobile shingle of the southern tip where there is no vegetation. The constant movement of the waves and the ebb and flow of the tides makes the shingle very unstable and it is still extending southward.

The spectacular beach of Orford Ness in Suffolk seen from the air. Note how Orford Ness has diverted the rivers as they approach the sea.

Much of the older part of Orford Beach is grass-covered and the pioneer plants of horned poppy and sea pea have gone. A few shrubs try to maintain a foothold, including a small oak tree which may be of considerable age but is only bush size, its growth being retarded by the cold winds off the North Sea. The sea beet, the sea pea, and the yellow horned poppy are all very common on the more recent, loose shingle and there are also a number of invertebrate animals of great interest. In particular there are two rare jumping spiders which frequently lay their eggs in the empty shells of the common whelk. The adult spiders are very difficult to catch because they disappear with great speed into the crevices between the stones. There is an extensive shingle bank on the mainland opposite the south end of Orford Beach near the small village of Shingle Street. This deposit is thought to be originally part of the spit but it was thrown onto the mainland shore during a violent storm in the past. Common and little terns nest at the southern end of Orford Beach, but not so abundantly as at Chesil Beach and Dungeness.

Elsewhere on the British coasts there are substantial deposits of shingle but the pebbles are usually mixed with some other material. At Scolt Head, the National Nature Reserve on the north Norfolk coast, shingle occurs widely with sand, or it lies on the salt marsh and is mixed with mud. It is only the west point, where the island is still growing, that it may consist of clean, loose pebbles. A glance at the map of Scolt Head shows that there is a series of shingle bars at right angles to the main line of the dunes for almost the whole of the four miles length. These shingle bars once formed the growth point of the embryo Scolt Head, the tide and wave action building up a spit which was curved round until it was at right angles to the dune ridge. By the time it had reached this state the growing point of the island had continued further west, sheltering the newly formed shingle spit from the effects of the sea. As each successive ridge was built up salt marshes formed between them with the most mature vegetation on the oldest, grading to eelgrass and glasswort on the newest. Today the shingle ridges lie only a little above the salt marshes but because they are partly submerged by high tides, muddy material has filled the gaps between the stones.

Consolidated shingle is soon colonized by plants. On the east and south-east coasts the shrubby sea blight is one of the most typical. It is a low bush with rather hard stems and fleshy leaves. Its main area of distribution is along the Mediterranean and in this country it is confined to the more southern coasts. During migration times the banks of sea blight are favourite places for small birds – finches and warblers – which shelter during periods of bad weather. The high tides deposit a great many seeds in the drift material that collects around the sea blight stems on which the migrant and winter-visiting finches are glad to feed. The sea blight has tiny inconspicuous flowers but on a summer's day the shingle ridges are covered with banks of the white flowers of the sea bladder campion and the pinky flowers of thrift, both often growing in great quantity. With them may be carpets of stonecrop with lichens. Where the high tide reaches the mud-packed shingle a small sea lavender with delicate stems and spreading inflorescences grows from a rosette of leaves, the little blue flowers hardly noticeable against the shingle substrate. It is another rarity confined to a few places in the south-east of England.

Cliffs

Of the different types of British coastline, nothing is so majestic and awe-inspiring as a rocky cliff. It does not have to be particularly high, even 150 feet is enough to experience the full might of the ocean which for thousands of years has battered our cliffs. The chalk cliffs of the south-east are protected to some extent by a beach which breaks some of the force of the waves, but the soft material of the south coast is vulnerable in other ways. In Dorset a strange cliff structure not seen anywhere else in Britain – the Axmouth-Lyme Regis Undercliff – was a modest chalk and greensand cliff with no special features but on Christmas Day 1839, when William Pritchard and his wife were returning home at 1 am, they found that the ground had sunk a foot since they passed by a few hours earlier. Earth movements continued and at 3 am the Pritchards and their neighbours hurriedly had to evacuate their houses. Contemporary accounts describe how rocks were rent asunder and trees uprooted, as a chasm half a mile long opened up, ranging in width from 200 to 400 feet and from 100 to 200 feet deep. A large piece of land of about thirteen acres that had been part of two fields with the hedge between had moved outwards towards the sea. This dramatic event attracted many people who sketched, wrote about, and later photographed it, so that it is unusually well documented. The next year, turnips and wheat were harvested on the detached portion of land on 25 August, but in the following years this island and the floor of the chasm developed its own vegetation. Today, after 144 years, a natural ash forest covers the old scars.

In the south-west the Cornish coasts are granitic and although not very high, form a picturesque coastline. Although the birdlife of the Cornish cliffs is not of

*A late summer view of plants in grassland on a cliff top at Muchalls near Aberdeen.
Harebells, bracken, thrift and several other plants can be seen.*

A rich growth of lichens, sheep's sorrel and a stonecrop growing on the walls of an abandoned dwelling in Snowdonia.

special note, there was formerly a population of choughs which local people claimed were different in some slight respect from choughs elsewhere. It last bred in Cornwall in 1952. This handsome black bird, with its conspicuous red legs and beak, is still common in western Ireland and in parts of Wales, the Isle of Man and south-west Scotland. In Pembrokeshire the chough can still be seen feeding on cliff tops and it also breeds on the islands of Skokholm and Skomer.

The coastline along the Lizard peninsula attracts many tourists, some of the most popular places being Kynance Cove and Cliff and Vellan Head. To the biologist it is renowned for its unusual flora on the

The gnarled cliffs of schist a few miles south of Aberdeen.

An adult black-headed gull.

An immature black-headed gull which is gradually acquiring adult plumage.

*A young herring gull which has just left the nest. Note how the mottled plumage
provides excellent camouflage in the beach shingle.*

serpentine rocks which outcrop on the peninsula. Serpentine is a rock-forming mineral containing magnesium and attractively coloured with shades of green, white and sometimes streaked with red. It is soft and is used locally for making ornaments. Many rare plants grow on the cliffs and adjacent heathland, some found nowhere else in Britain, particularly species of clovers. There are vast areas of the Cornish heath, which although very common here scarcely occurs anywhere else in Britain. Abroad it is found in western France and is abundant on similar heathlands in the northern regions of Spain.

Cliff flora is specialized because the habitat is very exposed and the plants must be tolerant of salt spray. Rock ledges are often rich in plants, particularly thrift and sea bladder campion, with golden samphire and the rock sea lavender in sheltered crevices. Some plants, for example lovage, that tall umbellifer with yellowish flowers, are more common in the north,

although found in many coastal areas further south. Roseroot, an ally of the stonecrop, is widespread on the western cliffs of Scotland.

The chief glory of Britain's cliffs are without doubt the nesting colonies of sea birds. Anyone who has not seen the teeming masses of guillemots, puffins, razorbills, kittiwakes and fulmars on the northern cliffs has missed a thrilling experience. Seabird colonies occur on almost all cliffs where there are ledges but the finest are on the St Kilda group of islands, several of which tower over a thousand feet above the sea. The black guillemot is probably the most local of our sea birds and is confined to the north and west of Britain, but the other auks, and the kittiwake, gannet and fulmar, nest as far south as the north-west coast of France. The common guillemot, perhaps our most abundant auk, seems to like to crowd densely on the nesting ledges while the razorbill prefers more space and is seldom so numerous. The puffin, as everyone knows, is a hole-nester and

Wildlife of the rocky shorelines.

Common limpets (conical shell), mussels (the cluster of bivalves) and large numbers of common barnacles scattered over the rock face. All these species have evolved a strong attachment to the rock so that they can withstand the force of the waves.

An Enteromorpha alga growing on cliffs where water drips down over the rocks at Port Quin, Cornwall. The Enteromorpha species are filamentous algae frequently very common on salt marshes or in rock pools and form nutritious food for waterfowl, particularly some geese.

The fascinating wildlife of an Irish rockpool. The white coating on the rocks is a living plant, a calcareous alga Lithothamnion; *the centre of the picture is occupied by a common seaweed (*Chondrus crispus*) and the reddish sea anenome, often common in rock pools, is* Actinia equina. *There are two species of limpet in the picture, the common (grooved shell) but also a much more local one,* Mondonta lineata, *occurring only in the south-west of Britain and Ireland. A specimen of this species is just below the seaweed. In the top right-hand of the picture are some barnacles. The rock pool is often so rich in species that it is a good place for the young student to begin if he wants to know something about marine biology.*

shares this habit with the Manx shearwater, storm petrel and Leach's petrel, which choose burrows or similar crevices on rocky slopes for their nests. The last three are nocturnal, keeping away from the nesting localities while it is light, but the puffin hunts in inshore waters during the day.

The black guillemot frequently nests on very low cliffs, provided there are suitable crevices in which to hide the nest. It does not need ledges and so frequents rocky coasts where other auks are not seen. The strange fulmar nests on exposed cliff ledges but on islands it will nest on the ground. In Orkney this writer has seen nests at the base of stone walls and also inside a ruined chapel. The spread of the fulmar along our coasts has been well documented. For many years it was confined to St Kilda and did not spread to other parts of the Scottish coast until the end of the nineteenth century. However, experts believe that the fulmars which colonized mainland Britain, from Shetland to the Isle of Wight, originated from Iceland and not from St Kilda. The stupendous cliffs of Foula in the Shetlands were the second breeding locality, the first birds being recorded there in 1878. It has now been estimated that all available cliff sites around the British coasts are occupied and the fulmars' range has virtually stopped expanding.

Birds of prey and crows often nest on cliffs but are not necessarily dependent on the sea. The buzzard and kestrel occasionally nest but the raptor most bird-watchers want to see is the peregrine. This beautiful falcon was greatly affected by agricultural pesticides, which infected it through its prey, causing a sharp drop in breeding success, but in recent years a recovery has been made and pairs have reappeared in many of their old nesting haunts. The golden eagle has been known to nest on sea cliffs, and the true sea eagle, extinct since the last century, has recently been restored to Scotland by a series of introductions. The island of Rhum was chosen for this experiment, which was carefully planned and carried out over several years. If the introduction is successful one hopes that this largest of European eagles will spread to the Welsh and English coasts as well as to the rest of Scotland. Finally, the harsh-voiced raven, which although in the past has been accused of misdeeds by sheep-farmers, is in many ways the spirit of the wilderness on our coastal cliffs.

The British coast is one of our finest environmental assets. Although much has been overdeveloped with unsightly buildings, particularly in the south, stricter control has been exercised by the planning authorities since the last war. Several agencies have contributed to the protection of unspoilt coastlines. County Conservation Trusts have created nature reserves and the National Trust has been presented with land for safe keeping. The National Trust followed up the early initiatives by obtaining further coastal property at every opportunity and now has over 400 miles under its protection. The designation of Areas of Outstanding Natural Beauty (ANOBs) has helped to prevent development along our most attractive coasts and this

The common seal, which breeds on the coasts of Scotland, Ireland and eastern England, with the greatest numbers in the Wash. It is the smaller and less numerous of our two breeding seals.

has been reinforced by the establishment of long-distance coastal footpaths, as in the south-west and in Wales. The Nature Conservancy Council, the Wildfowl Trust and the Royal Society for the Protection of Birds have all made significant contributions to the protection of estuary saltings and other areas where there are important coastal feeding areas for wildfowl and waders.

On our east coasts, as far as Orkney and Shetland, a new activity has arrived in recent years – offshore oil and the terminals built on the coast. No one doubts the value of this oil to our economy but with it we have oil spills and seabird deaths. Industry is doing its best to correct these faults and it is to be hoped that a means will be found of harvesting our oil riches without harming our coastal environment.

Conservation Issues

The countrysides of Britain are the products of many millennia of evolution. It was probably during the Mesolithic period that man in Britain ceased to be a part of the natural ecosystems and began deliberately to modify the environment in attempts to increase its productivity. Local transformations of the landscape, involving the felling and burning of patches of the wildwood in order to produce deer pastures and open hunting ranges, may have begun about 10,000 years ago. With the introduction of farming, around 5000 BC, the transformations became more purposeful and extensive, so that by the end of the Bronze Age, around 700 BC, England had become a place of open agricultural landscapes, and there could have been no more woodland than today. Throughout the millennia which followed, change was continuous, until the landscapes of Britain reached their glorious maturity in Victorian times.

Although the countrysides were periodically reshaped, change was never absolute, so that fragments of old countryside and landscape features inherited from former times could survive the transformations. Many lowland countrysides would display hedgerows dating from the recent Parliamentary Enclosures, others which were of a medieval vintage, and others still which were first established in Dark Age or even Roman times. In this way the countrysides were like palimpsets – documents which still carry the traces of earlier inscriptions. Animals, birds and plants usually survived or even flourished during the processes of change, for example, although the Parliamentary Enclosures virtually eradicated the surviving open strip fields, the new Enclosure hedgerows were havens for a galaxy of wildlife.

Today, however, the nature of change is different. Now we have not only the power to eliminate the plants, fungi and animals which threaten the harvest, but also the ability to obliterate every form of wildlife and to convert the countryside into a featureless agricultural factory. Few farmers might wish to do this and some care very deeply for their land and setting. Even so, the bare facts which describe the dismantling of the countryside are chilling. In 1983 a Nature Conservancy Council report estimated that since 1947 Britain has lost 95 per cent of herb- and flower-rich meadows; 80 per cent of sheep grazed calcareous (lime-rich) pasture; 50 to 60 per cent of heathland; 30 to 50 per cent of deciduous woodland; 45 per cent of limestone pavement, and 30 per cent of our upland grassland, heaths and mires. Careful studies have shown that twelve British plant species have become extinct due to man's modifications to the countryside, the populations of rare species have declined, and many more species which were common or widespread until recently are now found only in a few places. This process is not confined to Britain – almost every country in western Europe can tell the same tale and in some, for example, the Netherlands, the human impact on wildlife has been even greater. When practised with the degree of efficiency expected nowadays, agriculture and forestry are great levellers of the natural environment; that is, they reduce the countryside to a monotonous uniformity in which habitats for wildlife are lost and aesthetic appeal is minimal.

On rich soils such as the Fenlands of East Anglia, drained from a vast marsh in the eighteenth and nineteenth centuries, little natural vegetation can survive outside the few nature reserves. Elsewhere, however, where change has been gradual, it is possible to preserve a variety of habitats from trees to hedgerows and ponds. There are several examples of farmers who have successfully maintained habitat variety, and evidence is accumulating which proves that this form of management need make no difference to profits. The Farming and Wildlife Advisory Group, an alliance of farmers and conservationists, are doing good work in demonstrating how these two interests can be reconciled, but can they influence a large enough proportion of farmers to have a real effect on the countryside?

From both the aesthetic and the conservation viewpoints one of the greatest problems concerns the grubbing-out of hedgerows. In 1970 it was estimated that the period 1946–1970 witnessed the removal of some 50,000 miles of hedgerow, with 2000 miles disappearing from one lowland area of only 6 million acres. More recently it has been realized that this estimate understated the problem; the Council for the Protection of Rural England now estimates that during the 1960s the removal of hedgerows reached a peak rate of between 8 and 10 thousand miles lost annually. Since this time the rate of hedgerow removal has slowed because there are fewer hedges left to be removed. The farmers who accomplished this destruction were not always aware of the implications of their actions, being encouraged to grub-out their hedges by the agricultural authorities and only later realizing that they had brought the prairies of Dakota to the English heartlands. One of the writers was recently talking to a farmer who deeply regretted the changes which he had wrought in his corner of Essex, and who took great delight in a shelter belt which he had just planted.

Conservationists who have criticized the dismantling of old countryside have often been accused of attempting to stand in the way of progress. The experiments conducted in recent years at the reconstructed Iron Age farm at Butser Hill, near Petersfield in Hampshire, present some salutary facts. Here the workers have grown 'primitive' cereals, such as emmer wheat, using entirely Iron Age methods – yet have achieved yields of grain which compare favourably with those obtained by British farmers in the 1950s. There is also concern in some quarters that the 'progressive' agricultural techniques of today may be causing lasting damage to the environment. Bad conservation is not a new phenomenon, and archaeologists believe that they can detect the disastrous consequences of the over-working and neglect of the land at a number of periods in the past – the late-Neolithic, the late-Bronze Age, the late-Roman period and also the environmental crises of the fourteenth century, which resulted in the desertion of a multitude of villages which were situated on marginal agricultural land. It seems that at the end of the Roman period in Yorkshire there was 'the great silt-up', which resulted in a number of rivers being choked by silt washed down from the ploughlands. It has been argued that the silt-up was caused by an over-concentration on the cultivation of winter wheat, which exposed vast areas of bare soil to erosion by winter rain. A recent landscape history conference at York learned that very similar circumstances prevail today in parts of the Yorkshire Wolds, where only massive applications of fertilizer allow crops to be grown in what is now the chalky sub-soil.

In the past some popular countryside books tended to paint a false picture of the countryside – one based on the countrysides of the Victorian era rather than those of modern times. It was sometimes argued that readers did not want to read 'upsetting' facts. In this way such books did a considerable disservice to the cause of conservation and fostered complacent outlooks. But readers are entitled to expect an honest account of the transformations of the environment, one which is in tune with reality rather than based on false, romantic stereotypes.

During the 1939–1945 war the devastating effects of submarine warfare against our essential imports of foodstuffs resulted in a campaign to extend the arable area; some wetlands were drained and extensive areas of permanent pasture and meadow land were brought under the plough. The decline in ancient pasture such as the chalk downs and valley meadows was one of the main causes of wildlife loss. Anyone who can remember the countryside before the last war will know that a ploughed field on the Downs was a rarity, but today it is the reverse. One of us can remember a boyhood in the hunting country of the east Leicestershire Wolds in 1937–1938 – rolling green hills with wonderful hedges – but today most of it is ploughed. Traditional valley meadows which depend for their fertility on regular winter floods and still retain a rich distinctive flora are now so rare that they are teetering on the brink of extinction. The Water Authorities are doing all they can to prevent flooding so that these meadows can be 'improved' or else ploughed up for cereal growing. A farmer friend has said that even if river valley ploughland is covered by floods after sowing so that the resulting crop is poor, one really good harvest in seven years is enough to make ploughing financially worthwhile. There is no doubt that the extension of the arable acreage and the ploughing and reseeding of old, flower- and herb-rich pastures can be largely explained by the agricultural subsidies made available by government and EEC grants.

In 1982 the Conservative MP and farmer Richard Body estimated that taxpayers' support represented 188 per cent of farmers' income. Two thirds of the EEC budget go to the 8 million people in the community who are associated with agriculture, while in 1983, 201,000 British farmers received £1688 million – an average sum of £8440 per farmer paid by national and EEC sources. *The Sunday Times* has calculated that in addition, disguised subsidies, such as freedom from rates, add a further £20,000 to the income of the average farmer. The enormous financial benefits available in the form of such subsidies helps to explain the rocketing increases in the value of agricultural land, which has risen sevenfold since 1970. As a result, it has become very difficult for aspiring small farmers to obtain holdings, while the high costs of lands, rents and equipment can result in pressures for the repayment of capital loans which encourage the farmer to seek the maximum yield from every patch of ground. Very frequently this results in the removal of hedgerows and woodlands, the ploughing-up of heathland and moors and the draining of wetlands. The destruction of habitats results in turn in the disappearance of plants and wildlife. While certain plants and animals must always have been rare in Britain, we are now witnessing the gradual disappearance of species which were extremely common during the childhood of many readers – the primrose, the ragged robin, some nine species of bumble bee and even the 'common' frog.

The decline of the common frog is a mystery never properly explained and the same can be said for the otter. Both are very local or absent in lowland England, although common almost everywhere forty years ago. They are still well established in the cleaner waters of the north and the west. Water quality has almost certainly had some influence, particularly in the case of the frog, because research has shown that tadpoles may develop deformities in the presence of certain pesticides. Industry pollutes the rivers with a wide range of chemicals while fertilizers and pesticides drain off from agricultural land. The effluent from sewage works, although hygienically safe, loads the waterways with nitrates and phosphates which promote algal growths, often making the water opaque. Nevertheless, great efforts have been made to improve the state of some rivers and the Thames is probably cleaner now than it has been for two hundred years. Another important factor for the decline in otters and frogs is loss of habitat. The former need tall waterside vegetation and the overhanging roots of trees to provide places in which to hide and breed, but river management often results in this cover being destroyed. Similarly the common frog found ideal conditions in the field ponds which were formerly abundant in many counties. Modern agriculture demands that they should be filled and converted to usable land and so the frog and many other water creatures disappear.

While our long-established deciduous woods are disappearing at an alarming rate, this century has witnessed the introduction of extensive conifer plantations. In biological and visual terms such plantations of alien conifers are often unwelcome. They tend to support a much narrower range of plants and wildlife than flourished in the broad-leaf woods, heaths and upland pastures which the plantations have replaced, and the conifers are frequently economically and ecologically poorly-adapted to the British environments. The great drive to establish a domestic supply of softwood timber can be traced to the submarine threats

to timber imports during the 1914–18 war. In addition, it is now believed that the conifers increase the problems of acid rain pollution by intercepting acid-bearing mists and clouds. The continuing establishment of conifer plantations is partly explained by a range of very attractive if intricate tax concessions which are available to wealthy investors in this form of land-use.

Other conservation problems derive from the lack of concern and awareness for our threatened rural assets which are current amongst a small minority of the public. When one of the authors attempted to obtain a photograph of a small colony of rare fritillaries in a meadow near Huntingdon to illustrate this book he discovered that all sixty blooms had been picked by vandals on the previous day. Another problem concerns the over-use of certain reserves and fragments of the countryside by ramblers and strollers. This threat is greatly exacerbated by the rapid removal of established rights of way, which has the effect of concentrating visitors on those pathways where the rights of access are still intact. The creation of prairie fields has been accompanied by the removal or diversion of the old footpaths which followed the now-vanished hedgerows. In 1983 the Ramblers' Association and the Open Spaces Society estimated that between 1978 and 1982 orders were made for the creation of only 242 public paths but the diversion of 5410 footpaths and the extinguishment of 1162 rights of way.

In addition to the threats to wildlife and the visual landscape the vogue for ploughing areas of permanent pasture is resulting in the destruction of a remarkable heritage of archaeological sites – settlements, fortifications, tombs and earthworks of many different ages. Only in some of the most notable cases is the finance available to allow a rescue excavation to explore the evidence before destruction commences. There are many competitors for public finance, and country-lovers may feel that, given the widespread enthusiasm for natural history and landscape history, the rural heritage is under-supported. Currently all the ten National Parks together receive direct government support of £6.5 million, and this has been compared to the grant of £10 million paid to support just one theatre – Covent Garden.

This curious imbalance between support given to the arts and that given to the more tangible work of saving the countryside which we all enjoy is partly historical (the arts were the first to receive government help) and partly because an education in the former is regarded as being cultured, while the protection of the environment is taken less seriously by the decision-makers or even thought to be a little cranky. Nevertheless, we do not have to look far to find that there is an enormous groundswell of public opinion deeply committed to protecting our rural heritage. This interest reaches all social classes and manifests itself in scores of voluntary organizations from the National Trust with over one million members, the Scottish National Trust, the County Conservation Trusts with a membership of about 120,000, the Royal Society for the Protection of Birds, with 350,000, and the rapidly growing Woodland Trust, with 38,000. These are all land-owning bodies and have protected many areas as nature reserves and for amenity. Others such as the Friends of the Earth, Greenpeace, British Association of Nature Conservationists, Council for the Preservation of Rural England, and the Ramblers Association, represent different interests in the countryside and are doing a fine job in collecting facts, educating the public and supporting the cause of conservation at public enquiries. All these organizations are financed by private subscriptions, a demonstration of the interest felt by the British public in the protection of our environment. No one who owns large areas of country-side or who is responsible for waterways and forests can say that what he does with them is not the concern of others. The aesthetic appeal of land and water, the treatment they receive, the future of the plants and animals, *are* the business of all who love the country-side.

One is reluctant to end any book on a pessimistic note, and yet, when one considers the statistics which describe the rates of removal of hedgerows, woodlands, heathland, wetlands and so on it is difficult to avoid a feeling of helplessness and despair. People who were born in the 1940s saw the British landscape in its glory during their childhoods, but if they live to see the opening decades of the twenty-first century they may find that all the beauty and biological richness of the British scene has been extinguished *in the course of a lifetime*. All our best literature, music and painting have been inspired by our landscape. The love of the British for their countryside is renowned throughout the world, and so it is surprising that this wonderful legacy is being so easily surrendered.

Appendices

Planning for Leisure

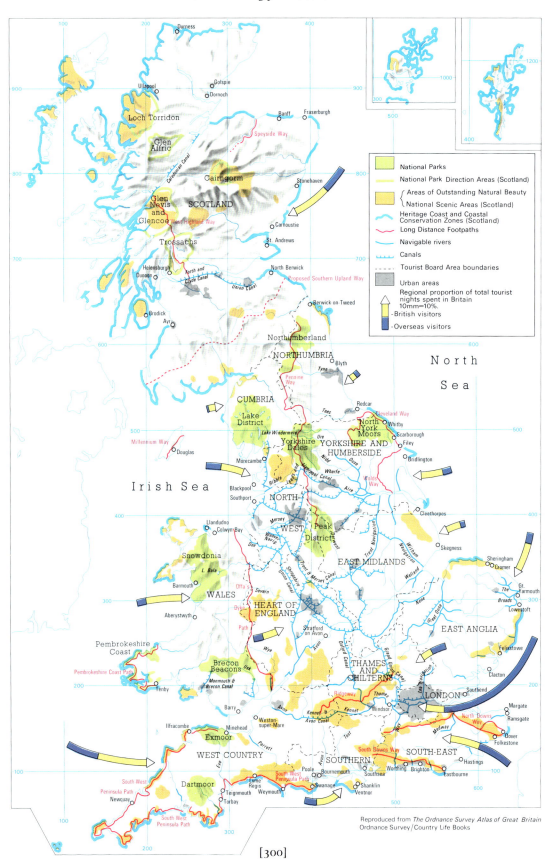

Reproduced from *The Ordnance Survey Atlas of Great Britain*
Ordnance Survey/Country Life Books

National Nature Reserves

RSPB Reserves

North Hill, Papa Westray
Noup Cliffs
Marwick Head
Dale of Cottasgarth
The Loons
Copinsay
Hobbister
Lumbister
Fetlar
Loch of Spiggie
Handa
Balranald
Culbin Sands
Loch of Strathbeg
Loch Garten
Insh marshes
Killiecrankie
Fowlsheugh
Loch of Kinnordy
Vare Farm
Lochwinnoch
Rathlin Island Cliffs
Lough Foyle
Ken/Dee Marshes
Shanes Castle
Geltsdale
Castlecaldwell
Mull of Galloway
St Bees Hd
Leighton Moss & Morecambe Bay
Bempton Cliffs
Hornsea Mere
Fairburn Ings
Blacktoft Sands
Eastwood
Tetney Marshes
South Stack Cliffs
Point of Air
Coombes Valley & Rough Knipe
Titchwell
Gayton Sands
Snettisham
Coed Garth Gell
Nene Washes
Strumpshaw Fen
Lake Vyrnwy
Ouse Washes
Minsmere
Ynys-hir
The Lodge
Fowlmere
North Warren
Wolves Wood
Havergate
Gwenffrwd & Dinas
Rye House Marsh
Stour
Grassholm
Nagshead
Church Wood
Northward Hill
Elmley Marshes
Chapel Wood
West Sedgemoor
Barfold Copse
Blean
Aylesbeare Common
Langstone Harbour
Dungeness
Fore Wood
Radipole Lake
Arne

0   80 km

0   50 miles

The Rare Breeds Survival Trust Ltd.
Approved centres open to the public

COTSWOLD FARM PARK,
Guiting Power,
Cheltenham,
Glos.

APPLEBY CASTLE,
Appleby-in-Westmorland,
Cumbria,

PARKE RARE BREEDS FARM,
Bovey Tracey,
Devon

CRAWLEY NATURE RESERVE,
Parks Department,
Town Hall,
Crawley,
West Sussex

PARADISE PARK,
Hayle,
Cornwall

WIMPOLE HOME FARM,
Arrington,
Royston,
Herts.

A selection of open-air museums

ACTON SCOTT WORKING FARM MUSEUM,
Acton Scott,
Nr Church Stretton,
Shropshire

NORTH OF ENGLAND OPEN AIR MUSEUM,
Nr Chester-le-Street,
Beamish,
Co. Durham

CHALK PITS MUSEUM,
Houghton Bridge,
Amberley,
Nr Arundel,
West Sussex

WEALD AND DOWNLAND OPEN AIR MUSEUM,
Singleton,
Nr Chichester,
West Sussex

THE AVONCROFT MUSEUM OF BUILDINGS,
Stoke Heath,
Bromsgrove,
Hereford and Worcester

ELVASTON CASTLE MUSEUM,
The Working Estate,
Elvaston Castle County Park,
Borrowash Road,
Elvaston,
Derby

MUSEUM OF EAST ANGLIAN LIFE,
Stowmarket,
Suffolk

MANOR FARM MUSEUM,
Cogges,
Nr Witney,
Oxfordshire

List of metric equivalents

1 foot = 0.3048 metres
1 yard = 0.9144 metres
100 feet = 30.48 metres
200 feet = 60.96 metres
300 feet = 91.44 metres
400 feet = 121.92 metres
500 feet = 152.4 metres
600 feet = 182.88 metres
700 feet = 213.36 metres
800 feet = 243.84 metres
900 feet = 274.32 metres
1000 feet = 304.8 metres
2000 feet = 609.6 metres
3000 feet = 914.4 metres
4000 feet = 1219.2 metres
1 mile = 1.6093 kilometres
1 acre = 4046.9 metres^2

Bibliography

General

F.H.A.AALEN *Man and the Landscape in Ireland* Academic Press, 1978

M.W.BERESFORD AND J.K.ST JOSEPH *Medieval England, An Aerial Survey* CUP, 1979

W.G.HOSKINS *The Making of the English Landscape* Hodder and Stoughton, 1955

R.N.MILLMAN *The Making of the Scottish Landscape* Batsford, 1975

R.MILLWARD AND ADRIAN ROBINSON *Upland Britain* David and Charles, 1980

R.MUIR *The Shell Guide to Reading the Landscape* Michael Joseph, 1981

Villages

M.W.BERESFORD *The Lost Villages of England* Lutterworth, 1954

G.DARLEY *Villages of Vision* Paladin, 1978

R.MUIR *The Lost Villages of Britain* Michael Joseph, 1982

B.K.ROBERTS *Rural Settlement in Britain* Hutchinson, 1979

T.ROWLEY *Villages in the British Landscape* Dent, 1981

C.C.TAYLOR *Village and Farmstead* George Philip, 1983

Fields and Farms

G.DARLEY *The National Trust Book of the Farm* Weidenfeld and Nicolson, 1981

P.J.FOWLER *The Farming of Prehistoric Britain* CUP, 1983

M.SHOARD *The Theft of the Countryside* Temple Smith, 1980

Dwellings and Churches

R.W.BRUNSKILL *Traditional Buildings of Britain* Gollancz, 1981

A.CLIFTON-TAYLOR AND A.S.IRESON *English Stone Building* Gollancz, 1983

J.G.DUNBAR *The Historic Architecture of Scotland* Batsford, 1966

E.FERNIE *The Architecture of the Anglo-Saxons* Batsford, 1983

E.MERCER *English Vernacular Houses* RCHM, 1975

J. AND J.PENOYRE *Houses in the Landscape* Faber, 1978

R.REID *The Shell Book of Cottages* Michael Joseph, 1978

W.RODWELL *The Archaeology of the English Church* Batsford, 1981

M.WOOD *The English Medieval House* Ferndale, 1975

Roads

F.GODWIN AND S.TOULSON *The Drove Roads of Wales* Wildwood House, 1977

A.R.B.HALDANE *The Drove Roads of Scotland* Nelson, 1952

C.C.TAYLOR *Roads and Trackways of Britain* Dent, 1979

Woods

J.G.EVANS *The Environment of Early Man in the British Isles* Elek, 1975

O.RACKHAM *Trees and Woodland in the British Landscape* Dent, 1976.

G.WILKINSON *A History of Britain's Trees* Hutchinson, 1981

Natural History

H.ANGEL et al *The Natural History of Britain and Ireland* Michael Joseph, 1981

G.B.CORBET AND H.N.SOUTHERN *The Handbook of British Mammals* (second ed) Blackwells, 1977

E.DUFFEY et al *Grassland Ecology and Wildlife Management* Chapman & Hall, 1974

A.MITCHELL *A Field Guide to the Trees of Britain and Northern Europe* Collins, 1974

G.PETERKEN *Woodland Conservation and Management* Chapman & Hall, 1981

D.S.RANWELL *Ecology of Salt Marshes and Sand Dunes* Chapman & Hall, 1972

F.ROSE *The Wild Flower Key* Warne, 1981

D.A.SCOTT (ed) *Managing Wetlands and Their Birds* International Waterfowl Research Bureau, Slimbridge, Glos, 1982

C.TAYLOR *Fields in the English Landscape* Dent, 1975

A.WARREN AND F.B.GOLDSMITH (ed) *Conservation in Perspective* John Wiley, 1983

Acknowledgements

Newnes Books for permission to reproduce the following maps:
Great Britain: Geology
Great Britain: Physical Relief
Great Britain: Climate
Planning for Leisure

Merton College, Oxford, for permission to reproduce the map of Gamlingay, 1601

The Royal Society for the Protection of Birds and The Nature Conservancy Council for supplying the relevant maps

Royal Commission on Historical Monuments for permission to reproduce line drawings from their publication *English Vernacular Houses: Study of Traditional Farmhouses and Cottages*

Bedfordshire County Council for permission to reproduce the drawing of Stevington Post Mill, Bedfordshire.

Eric and David Hosking for the photograph of the female large copper butterfly (Chapter 10).

The photographs reproduced in the Introduction are of Borrowdale, Cumbria (p 7), Land's End, Cornwall (p 9), Wasdale Head, Cumbria (p 12) and Fountains Abbey, Yorkshire (p 13).

Index

Aalen F 220
Abbots Salford 85
A Collection of Roses from Nature 205
Adare 156
Agricultural Revolution 235
Ainsdale 279
Aislabie, John 192
Aldeburgh, 285
alder 53, 63, 238
alder buckthorn 265
Aldwincle 110
Alfred the Great 158
algae
    Enteromorpha 292
    Lithothamnion 292
    marine 277
alkanet
    green 98
Altarnun 109
Alvingham 110
Amberley Wild Brooks 36, 255
Anglesey Abbey 186–187, 199, 226
animal road casualties 101
ant 73
Antioch Farm 213
Appleton-le-Moors 162
Areas of Outstanding Natural
    Beauty 294
Arun, river 255
ash 45, 47, 48, 52, 53, 63
    forest 286
    mountain 46, 246
Ashwell 113, 117
assarts (*see also* woodlands) 20, 21
auk 291
autumn crocus (*Colchicum*) 39, 40
Avebury 90, 91, 225
Aviemore-Glen Feshie track 87
axe 80
    factories 13
Axmouth-Lyme Regis Undercliff 286
Aysgarth 99

bacteria 65
badger 69, 101
Bakewell 105
Banbury Lane 85
Barden Tower 182–183
Barfreston 112, 115
barnacles 293
barns (*see also* farming and
    livestock) 222ff, 227

tithe 224
Barrington 155
Barry 276
Barton 29
Barton-on-Humber 109, 113, 146
Bassingbourn 224
bat
    greater horseshoe 132
    mouse-eared 132
Batcombe 122
Bayfield 114
Bayham Abbey 192
Beachamwell 110
beaches (*see also* coast)
    raised 274, 275
    shingle 274, 275, 281, 285ff
bearberry 44
bee 131
beech 45, 54, 55, 56, 63, 192
beetle 45, 48, 101, 199, 282
    ground 131, 247, 277
    longhorn (*Cerambyx cerdo*) 200
    stag 200
    water 209
Belchamp St Paul 223
Beltane 23
Belton 128
Benacre 281
Benedictine Abbey 105
Beresford, M W 164
Big Glyder 244
Big Moor 17
bilberry 41, 65, 242, 262
bindweed
    hedge 47
birch 51, 53, 238
birds (*see individually named*)
bird breeding (*see also* dovecotes and
    game) 246
Birstwith 35, 174, 176
Bishop Aelnoth 104
Bishop Eadnoth 104
Bishops Castle 86
bistort 39
    alpine 41
bittern 267
bittersweet 43
blackberry 47, 48
blackbird 48, 61, 72, 208
blackcap 72
Black Death 93, 113, 164, 165, 181
black medick 42

black poplar 52
black-tailed godwit 267
black-throated diver 247
blackthorn 43, 45, 47, 72
Blaise Hamlet 156
Blakeney Point 274, 281
Blenheim 188
Blickling 189
bluebells 45, 47, 64, 65
blue tit 206
Blythburgh-Southwold line 102
Blyth estuary 102
boar 179
Body MP, Richard 296
bog asphodel 41, 262
bog myrtle 262
bog plants (*see individually named*)
Boothby Pagnell 217
Borrowdale 7
Borth, Dovey estuary 276
Botanical Society of the British
    Isles 132
Boulby 274
Bourn 232
Bouthwaite 172, 173
Bradford-on-Avon 112, 224
Bradwell 87
bramble 45, 47, 208
Braunton Great Field 25
Breamore 137
    church 144
Breckland 48, 61, 100, 182
Brecon Beacons National Park 244
brickworkings 144–146, 232
bridges (*see also* roads and tracks)
    clapper 89
    Cotswolds 89
    Lakeland 89
    pack-horse 88, 89, 93
    Pennines 89
    West Country 89
    Yorkshire Dales 89
Bridgwater 146
    Bay 281
Brime 160
Brimham Rocks 246
British Fishery Society 175
British Lichen Society 132
Brixworth 112
Bronze Age 17, 50, 105
    fields 17
    holy wells 109

settlement 158
standing stone 108
Brown, Lancelot 'Capability' 88, 190, 192, 193
Browne family 217
Bruton 225
Buckingham Palace 210
buckthorn
common 69
buddleia
common 208
bunting
snow 247, 283
Bure, river 255
burial sites, *see* religious sites
burnet
great 41
Burnham Beeches 198
Burren 41, 44, 73, 239
buttercup 35, 96
meadow 41
Butterflies
black hairstreak 72
brimstone 69
chalkhill 101
comma 69, 129
forest 69
gatekeeper 69, 130
green hairstreak 69
green-veined white 69
hedge brown 69, 130
holly blue 131
large copper 262, 264–265
little blue 129
meadow brown 129, 208
orange-tip 131
peacock 69, 131
pearl-bordered fritillary 44
purple emperor 72
purple hairstreak 69
red admiral 129, 130
ringlet 69, 208
small copper 129, 264
small heath 129
small and large skippers 69
speckled wood 69, 208
swallowtail 265
tortoiseshell 69, 129
white admiral 47, 72
woodwhite 44
Buttermere 250
buzzard 244, 294
Byland Abbey 173

Cader Idris 244
Cairngorms Nature Reserve 247, 248
Cambridge 82, 91
Cambridge University 63
Cambridgeshire Naturalists' Trust 64
campanula 99
Canford Magna 156
Cannock Chase 179, 180

Canterbury 85
Carlisle 87
carnation grass 41
Carn Euny 158
carts and wagons (*see also* roads and tracks) 93ff
barge wagons 94
boat wagons 94
bow wagons 94
box wagons 94
carriers' wagons 94
farm wagons 94
four-wheeled wagons 93
harvest carts 94
mail coaches 93
muck carts 93
regionalism 94
Scotch carts 94
spring carts 94
tumbrils 94
two-wheeled carts 93
wheelwrights 94
Castle Acre 162
Castle Ashby 193
Castle Camps 110
Castle Donington 110
Castle Howard 188
Castlerigg stone circle 105
Castle Rising 162
Castleton 25
caterpillar (*see also* butterflies and moths) 69, 129, 208
Cawston 117
Caxton 110
cedar 192
chaffinch 72
Chaldon 117
Challacombe 23
Charnwood Forest 181, 198
Chater, A 129
Chatsworth 188, 192
Chelsea Physic Garden 210
Cheshire Dee 274
Chesil Beach 274, 285, 286
chestnut 193,194
horse 188, 192
sweet 63
Cheviots 238
chiff-chaff 72
Chile pine 192
chimneys 147, 152, 220
chough 288
churches (*see also* religions and burial sites) 104ff
Catholic 163
carving 121
chapels 120, 127, 173
Cornish 122
craftsmen 112, 117
crosses 105
Dark Ages 104, 105
Decorated 104, 109, 110, 113, 117, 118
Early English 104

Eighteenth-century 118
Fenland 105, 110
field 105, 159
Flamboyant tracery 124
Gothic Revival 104, 119, 122
images 117
Jacobean 118
medieval 106, 114, 128, 168
Minster 104
neo-Classical 104
Norman 104, 109, 110, 113, 114
paintings 117
Perpendicular 104, 113, 119, 122, 124, 168
pews 118
pre-Reformation 117
Presbyterian 163
pulpits 118
regional styles 104ff
rood screens 117
Saxon 104, 105, 108, 109, 110, 112, 113, 114, 124
stone 121, 124
timber 124
tombs 118, 124, 127
upland 122
village 104
Welsh 120, 122
wool 119, 122
churchyard flora and fauna 127ff
Chysauster 158, 178
cinquefoil
alpine 41
spring 100
Cirencester 117
Clare, John 33, 36
Clare 136
Cleveland Way 91
cliffs (*see also* coast) 286ff
chalk 286
sea stack 287
climate (*see also* Ice Age) 13, 17, 40, 41, 59
Clint 220–221
Clonmacnois 105
clover 208
coast (*see also* beaches, cliffs, dunes and lagoons) 273ff
caves 275
coral sand 276
erosion 275, 279
estuaries 274
shingle formations 283ff
tide variation 274
Cokerington 110
collembola 200
Colt Park Wood 238
Combe Martin 25
Comberton 225
Commonwealth (*see also* Reformation) 117, 119
conifer (*see also* plantations and *named varieties*) 45, 192, 278
Connemara 276

conservation (see also named bodies) 58, 73, 100, 102, 132, 295ff
Coombe Bissett 23
cordgrass 281
cornflower, wild 35
corn marigold 35
Corsican pine 53, 278
cotoneaster 208
cottage (see also timber-framing and settlements and dwellings) 134ff
    brick 144–145
    clunch 139, 144
    cob 138, 144
    Flemish bond 145
    gardens 178, 202ff
    grazing rights 134
    industries 134, 136, 138, 148, 227
    Irish 136
    medieval 136
    mud 138, 144
    stone 134, 138, 139, 140, 142, 146, 160
    thatch 134, 142–143, 146
    tile hanging 145, 146, 147
    vernacular 137ff
    wattle-and-daub 138
    weatherboarding 144, 145
    Welsh 136
cottar 134
Cottesbrooke 118
Council for the Protection of Rural England 296, 298
County Conservation Trusts 58, 73, 102, 238, 294, 298
Countryside Commission 248
    Scottish 248
Covehithe 120, 281
cowberry 40, 41, 242, 244
cow parsley 98, 208
cowslip 36, 45, 69, 129, 208
coypu 270–271
crabapple 45, 48, 208
cranberry 262
Cranborne Chase 179, 180
crane 179, 262
cranesbill
    bloody 41
    meadow 98
    wood 41
Crathes Castle 225
crepis 38
crested hairgrass 41
Cronckley Fells 41
Croscombe 118
Cross Fell 238
cross-leaved heath 281
crow 72
crowberry 41
Cublington 93
Culloden, battle 25, 163, 175, 218
Culvin Sands 274

Culworth 160
curlew 243
    common 41
current 48
cypress 188, 192
    spurge 42

Dacre 174
Dacre Banks 174
daisy 35, 208
    ox-eye 35, 41, 96
Dalham 127
dandelion 101, 208
Dark Ages (see also Saxon) 18, 25, 58
    church 104, 105, 113
    farming 18, 25
    missionary sites 124
    religious relics 110
    settlements 158
Darley 174, 176, 218
Dartmoor forests 178
deadly nightshade 43
de Caux family 182
deer (see also forests)
    fallow 69, 179, 197
    hunting 61
    red 61, 67, 179
    roe 61, 179
    sika 198
Deerhurst 110
deer sedge 41
Delabole 146
de Mowbray family 172
Denver 233
Dere Street 82, 84
Derwent, river 255
Derwent Water 34, 51
Devil's Dyke 161
Devil's Elbow road 90
Devizes 182
Diapensia 248
Din Lligwy 158, 159
Dissolution 112, 173, 217
dock 208
Doddington 105
Dodgshon, R A 23
dog's mercury 47, 64
dog's violet
    common 41
dogwood 47, 192
Domesday 110, 159, 168, 170, 172
Donington Park 201
dotterel 243, 247
Douglas fir 61, 192
Dounby 228
dovecotes 225
Dover cliffs 274
dropwort 40
duck 285
    mallard 132
dunes (see also coast) 276ff
    accreting 276
    driftline 277

dune heath 276
embryo 277
hummock 281
meadow 278
slacks 279
stabilization 278
yellow or mobile 277
Dungeness 283
    promontory 274
Dunmore 156
Duxford 110
dyers greenweed 40

Earls Barton 113
earthnut 41
earthworks 24, 109, 168, 180, 182, 193, 194, 222
Eastnor 156
Easton 156
Easton-on-the-Hill 127
East Tanfield 168, 169
Ebernoe Common 198
Edward I 182
EEC 296
Eel Crag 241
eelgrass 281, 283, 285, 286
Egham-Staines road, 86
Egmere 165
elder 45, 46, 48, 192, 208
Ellis, Ted 208
elm 45, 52, 53, 63, 65, 69, 188, 192, 193, 238
    Dutch Elm Disease 45, 65, 199
Eltisley 213
Elton, Charles 200
Ely Cathedral 131
Enclosure Acts (see also Parliamentary Enclosure) 45
Epping Forest 202
Ermine street 82
Eskdale 109
Evelyn, John 53
Ewhurst 127
excavations 16, 124, 137
Exmoor forests 178
Exmoor National Park 198
eyebright 39, 41
Eynhallow, 277

Fairford 117
fairs (see also livestock and markets) 87, 161, 169
farming (see also appropriate historical period, field systems, grasslands, meadows and Parliamentary Enclosure) 13, 16, 18ff, 33, 179
    ancient 16
    commons 18, 22, 26, 238
    courtyard 222
    dairies 225
    furlongs 18, 21
    garden 21, 178ff
    garths (tofts) 21

grainfields 35
grazing 18, 23, 238
infield 21, 22, 23
inland 22
open field 18, 20, 25, 26, 47, 159
outfield 21, 23
paddocks 17, 32, 159
pastures 18, 21
pollution 36, 266, 270, 271, 272, 297
ploughlands 18
runrig 22
stockpens 17
strip 18, 20, 26
tools 16
transhumance 23
Farming and Wildlife Advisory Group 295
Fearby 153, 169
Fens (see also named sites, Nature Reserves and Wetlands) 48, 85, 100, 160, 232, 255, 256, 263, 265, 266, 268
ferns 40, 45, 129
adder's tongue 40
Hart's tongue 66
ferret 271
fieldfare 246
field mallow 208
field maple 45
field names see place names
field systems (see also farming, hedgerows, Parliamentary Enclosure and stone walling)
Bronze Age 17
Celtic 16
enclosures 20, 25
medieval 23, 24
Norman Forest Law 31
pen-field 45
ridge and furrow 24, 40
Roman 17
Saxon 18, 30
strip lynchets 23, 24
field wormwood 100
Fiennes, Celia 218
Finmere 84
firecrest 283
fish 209, 258
salmon 258
sea 276
trout 252
fishponds 182, 225–226
Fleet, The 281, 285
Fleming, Andrew and Ralph, Nicholas 30
flies 101, 277
blowflies 131
dragonflies 250
sawflies 247
flycatcher
pied 72
Folkestone cliffs 274
footpaths, see roads and tracks

Forest of Dean 63, 178
Forests (see also deer, plantations, woodland and individual named sites) 8, 41, 53, 178ff
amenities 58
boar 179
flora and fauna 58ff
hunting chase 172
hunting lodges 182
Law 178, 179, 180
management 52
pine 61
royal hunting 52, 178ff
submerged 276
Forestry Commission 58, 61
Formby 276
Forrabury 25
Foster, W Gilbert 87
Foula 274
Fountains Abbey 13, 173, 174, 176, 192, 195, 214, 226
Fowlmere 251
fox 48, 61, 63, 69, 102, 179
foxearth 213, 215
foxgloves 98, 204
Freefolk 156
Friends of the Earth 298
Friston 232
fritillary 36, 38
frog 101, 209, 259, 301
Frome St Quintin 182
fulmars 291, 293
fungi 65, 74, 76, 200
Coriolus versicolor 74
fly agaric 75
gill 76
honey 75
mushroom 65, 76
Phlebia radiata 74
Pleurotus sapidus 75
shaggy pholiota 74
Fyfield Down 90

Gait Barrows 238
game (see also deer and rabbit) 64, 245
grouse 40, 41
pheasant breeding 63, 179
silver pheasant 199
Gamlingay 18ff, 26, 27
gannet 291
gardens and parks (see also appropriate historical periods, deer, forests and woodland) 178ff
cottage 202ff
Elizabethan 188
emparking 165
flora and fauna 96ff, 205
formal 188ff
hybrids 204–205
lost 194
Gardenstown 175
garganey 267

geese
wild, 281
greylag 262
geology 8, 41, 44, 80, 121, 129, 140, 218, 238–239, 241, 246, 258, 274, 279, 286, 288
glabrous rupturewort 100
Glandford 114
Glasshouses 176
glasswort 281, 286
Glastonbury 85
Glengariff Forest 73
globe flower 41
Gloucester, Earl of 179
glow-worms 129
Godiva 104
Godshill 109
Godwick 165
Gog Magog 100
goldcrests 61
golden eagle 244, 246, 294
golden plover 41, 243
golden samphire 291
goldfinch 45, 207, 208
Goodwick 194
gooseberry 48
Gordon, Duke of 163
Gosforth 105
Gough, Richard 118
Grantchester 225
grass of Parnassus 262, 279
Grassington 17, 87
grasslands (see also climate, geology, farming, soils and meadows) 23, 34, 36ff
artificial watercourses 37
chalk 17, 18, 36, 42, 100–101
Downs 36
fertilizers 36
flora and fauna 36ff, 101
management 40
marshes 38
moorland 40, 41
pastures 34, 36
upland 20, 40ff
Great Coxwell 224
Great Gable 15
Great Rebuilding 137, 141, 217, 222
Great West Road 90
Great Yeldham 225, 276
greenfinch 101, 207, 208
Greenhow Hill 88
Greenpeace 298
Green Park 210
Greensted-juxta-Ongar 113
Greenwood, John 176
Grimspound, Dartmoor 158
Grisedale Forest 58
guelder rose 43
guillemots 291
black 293
gulls
black-headed 281, 282, 290

herring 291

Hadstock 110
Hall Barn, Beaconsfield 188
Hampton Court 188
Hangleton house 137
Hard Knott pass 80
hare 65, 101
harebell 41
Harford, J S 156
Harlaxton 156
Harlech, Gower 274
Harrington 193, 226
Haverah Park 182
hawthorn 43, 45, 47, 48, 58, 208, 262
Hayley Wood 56, 64, 65, 69, 102
hazel 45, 47, 48, 52, 53, 63, 238
heartsease (*Viola tricolor*) 39, 205
heather 40, 44, 244, 262
  bell 41
heathrush 40
hedgerows (*see also* field systems, Parliamentary Enclosure and stone walling) 16, 25, 28, 29, 31ff, 36, 46
  dating 45
  flora 38, 43, 45ff
  medieval 192
  open-field boundaries 47
  relic wood-edge 47
  removal 47, 297
hedgehog 48, 101, 209
Helvellyn 241
hen harrier 244, 246, 283
Henry II 178, 182
Henry III 179
herbs 281
  angelica 41
  lovage 291
  wild thyme 41
herb paris 64
herbicides and pesticides (*see also* pollution) 36, 96, 102, 205, 208
heron 179, 268
High Street 82
Hinderskelfe 188
Hindle, B P 86
History of Nidderdale 173
hogweed 41
Holderness 179
Holkham Hall 191
holly 45, 63, 192, 208
Holme Fen National Nature Reserve 262
Holne Moor, Dartmoor 30
Holywell 109
honesty 204
honeysuckle 47, 72, 208
Honister pass 80
Hooper, M 45
hornbeam 56, 63
Horn Head, Donegal 275

Horningsea church 104
Hosking, E and D 264
Hoskins, W G 45
Houghton 126, 229
houseleek
  common 208
houses, *see* settlements and dwellings
Howgrave 169
Hurst, John 164
Hyde Park 210
hymenoptera 101

Ice Age (*see also* climate) 41, 51, 274, 276
Icknield Way 80, 96, 100
Ickworth 166, 192
Ilkley 105
Industrial Revolution 163, 174, 226
Ingleborough Fell 239
Ingleton 88
Inglewood forests 178
Inkpen Old Rectory, Berkshire 188
insects (*see also* invertebrate fauna *and named species*) 44–45, 47, 48, 49, 61, 65, 69, 72, 101, 129, 130, 131, 199–200, 282
Institute of Terrestrial Ecology 102
International Wetlands Convention 255
Invertebrate fauna (*see also* insects) 59, 101, 129, 131, 200, 202, 210, 243, 247, 248, 282, 285, 292
Ipplepen 118
Iron Age 17, 50
  farm 178, 212
  hillfort 225
  holy wells 109
  village 158
ivy 44, 45, 64, 129, 208

jackdaw 48
jay 65
Jefferies, Richard 48
Jeffrey's Map 169
Jennings, N 258
Jodrell, Sir Alfred 114
juniper 44
Jurassic Way 80

Keighley 176
Kensington Gardens 210
Kent, William 188
Kentmere Hall 217
kestrel 48, 179, 294
Kilpeck 112
Kings Forest 61
Kingston Wood 20, 21, 25
Kirby Hall 188
Kirkby Malzeard 172, 173
kittiwake 291
knapweed 208
Knaresborough 82
Knightwood Oak 54

Knocknarea 239
knot grass 101
Knowlton 109
Knox, John 138

Lacey Green 232
Lacock 223
ladies smock 208
lady's mantle 41
lagoons (*see also* coast) 281
  coastal broads 281
  machair lochs 281
Lake District National Park 239ff, 248
Lambert, Joyce 256
Lancashire cotton workers 204
Lancaster, Earl of 179, 180
Landbeach 226
Land's End 9
lapwing 267
larch 53, 61, 188, 192
Lavenham 115, 122
Lawrence, May 205
Laxton 45, 182
lead industry 164
Ledbury 93
Legs Cross 84
Leighton Moss reserve 268
Leofric of Mercia 104
lichen 127, 129, 132, 197, 200, 201–202, 245
Lichfield, Bishop of 179, 180
lime 56, 63, 188
limpet 293
  Mondonta lineata 293
Lindsey 91
Ling Gill 238
linnet 208
Linton 23
Little Langdale 150
Little Ouseburn 110
Little Sea 281
livelong 66
livestock (*see also* fairs, markets)
  Ayrshire 236
  black cattle 23
  British Saddleback 236
  cattle 40, 44, 48, 86, 129, 179, 218, 225, 235, 238, 242, 267, 278
  Chianina cattle 236
  Charolais cattle 236
  Cotswold sheep 236
  goats 238
  Highland cattle 86
  horses 52, 93, 179, 222, 224
  Jacob 236
  jagger ponies 97
  Kerry cattle 235
  Large Black pig 236
  long horn 193, 235
  Manx sheep 235
  Montgomery cattle
  Orkney sheep 235

oxen 225
pack ponies 87–88
pigs 52, 64, 179, 235
Soay sheep 235
sheep 40, 41, 44, 48, 86, 129,
    165, 175, 179, 227, 235, 238,
    244, 278
  Shirehorse 236
  Simmental cattle 236
  white calf 236
  white park cattle 196
Lizard 274, 288
Llandanwg, Harlech 275
Ll'anddewi Brefi, Lampeter 25, 114,
    193
Llandovery valley forests 72
Llandygan 156
Llanegryn church 117
Llangelynin church 113
Llanhowel church 113
Llyn Idwal 244
Loch Aber 244
Loch Awe 244
Loch Garten 246
Loch of Strathbeg 276
lodgepole pine 53
Lofthouse 172, 173
London 82
London, George 188
London Lead Company 164
London Natural History Society 210
Long Coombe 117
Longleat 188
Long Melford 119, 212
lords and ladies 66
Loughborough Great Meadow 37
Lower Slaughter 160, 170–171
lowland/upland zones, distinction
    between 8ff
  landscape 18
Ludborough 226
Lulworth Cove 276

Macadam, John Loudon, 96
Madeley Great Park 181
magpie 65
Malham Cove 237, 239
Malham Tarn 88
mallard 267
Malton 214
Manx shear water 291
maple 47
March 110
Marden 109
marine ecosystems 276ff
market (see also fairs, livestock and
    village greens) 160, 169, 173,
    245
  cattle droves 169
  medieval 169, 232
  pack-horse traders 169
Markings Farm, Whittlesford 214,
    216, 217
Marmion family 168

marram grass 277–278
  transition zone 277
marsh arrow grass 279
marsh harrier 268
marsh lousewort 279
martin
  house 132
Marton 105
Masham 109, 169
Mastiles Lane 88
mat grass 40, 41
Maxey 109
may 45
mayweed 97
meadow pipit 41
meadowsweet 41
meadow saffron (autumn crocus) 39
meadows (see also grasslands and
    named sites) 18, 21, 22, 27, 35,
    37
  dune 278
  flood 35, 37
  grazing 267, 268
  hay 18, 21, 22, 34, 38, 39
  water 35, 40
  watercress meadows 251
medieval period (see also
    Norman) 48, 58, 110, 137,
    174
  archers 127
  brothels 93
  chantry chapels 93
  church architecture 106, 114,
    128, 168
  cottage 136
  cross 232
  deer parks 178ff
  dovecotes 225
  dwellings 136, 137, 146
  farmsteads 155, 156, 212, 213,
    223
  fishponds 182, 225–226
  gardens 185, 204, 205
  guildhall 232
  hedgerows 192
  hermitages 93
  hunting forests 179
  kings 179
  longhouses 148
  markets 169, 232
  New Town 162
  peat 258
  roads 85–86, 88, 92, 93
  settlements 110
  swine pastures 52
  village planning 162
  villages 160
  wayside inns 93
Melbourne 113
Melbourne Hall 188
Men of Trees 73
merlin 244, 283
Merton College, Oxford 18
Mesolithic period 13, 80

hunters 238, 263
Mevagissey 175, 176
Mickleham church 129
Middlesmoor 158, 172, 173
Middleton 83
milk parsley 265
Millium effusum 64
mills 228ff
  click 228
  drainage 232
  post 230, 231, 232
  smock 232
  tower 232
  water 229
  wind 231–232, 250
Ministry of the Environment 100
mink 271
Minsmere marshes 255
Minsmere Nature Reserve 267, 268
Monasterbois 105
Monewden Meadow 40
Monks Wood Experimental
    Station 47
Monks Wood National Nature
    Reserve 69
Montgomery 86
Moore Head Lane 88
moorlands see grasslands
Morecambe Bay 274
moss 129, 200, 201, 247, 281
  lesser clubmoss 41
  Polytrichum 279
  Sphagnum 41, 262, 279
  Rhacomitrium 243, 244
moss campion 244
moth 282, 283
  ground lackey 282
  hummingbird hawk 208
  mottle umber 65
  mullein 208
  oak roller 65
  winter 65
Mottisfont Abbey 190, 192
Moulton 88, 89
mountain avens 41, 244
mountain everlasting 41
mouse 65
  wood 209
Muchalls 287, 289
Muchelney 127
mudflats, see salt marshes
mullein
  great 38
museums and farm parks 95, 178
  Avoncroft Museum of
    Buildings 223
  Bunratty folk museum 222
  Butser Hill 178
  Dunwich Museum 276
  East Anglian Life 214, 223, 228,
    231
  Easton Park 225
  Lanhydrock 225
  Singleton 137

Weald and Dowland 148, 225, 231
mushroom, *see* fungi
muskrat 270
Myddle 118
myxomatosis (*see also* rabbit) 36

Najas marina 256
National Parks *see* named sites
National Trust 202, 217, 223, 232, 241, 294, 298
  of Scotland 248, 298
Nature Conservancy Council 100, 102, 132, 196, 197, 248, 294, 295
Nature Conservation Review 196
Nature Reserves (*see also named sites*) 36, 40, 58, 100, 161, 238, 247, 248, 249, 255, 281
  coast 274, 281, 285
  woodland 64ff, 198ff, 267
  wetland 238ff
Nene, river 255, 256, 266
Nene valley 37
Nenthead 163
Neolithic period 13, 50, 80, 105, 168, 274
  hut cluster 158
nettles 48, 69, 129, 208
Nevern, Fishguard 106, 110, 127
Newborough Warren 281
New Bradwell 232
New Buckenham 162
New Forest 58, 59, 63, 178, 180, 198, 201
  ponies 60, 201, 202
New House Farm, Bishopdale 220–221
Newton 139
Newton on Rawcliffe 135
New Winchelsea 162
Nicholas, Ralph, see Fleming, Andrew
Nidderdale 169, 170, 173, 218
nightingale 72
Norfolk Broads 254, 256ff
  Hickling Broad 256
  Hoveton Great Broad 258
  peat cuttings 258
  Rockland Broad 262
  Sutton Broad 258
  Water Authority 256
Norman period (*see also* Medieval period)
  architecture 104, 109, 110, 113, 114
  Conquest 105, 159, 160, 170, 172, 178
  church 104, 109, 110, 113
  Forest Law 217
  Harrying of the North 172
  hunting forests 179
  kings 180
  occupation 110, 170

priest's house 124
  stone carvings 112, 115
  stone manor houses 217
North Carlton 84
North Downs Way 91
North Petherton 113
North Sea 276
nuclear power stations 283
Nun Monkton 85, 154, 251

oak 45, 47, 48, 49, 52, 53, 58, 63, 65, 69, 192, 193, 208, 238, 263
  bog 200
  dermast or sessile 63, 201
  pedunculate 63, 201
Offa's Dyke Path 91
Okeford Fitzpaine 160, 162
Old Bath Road 90, 91
Old Man of Hoy 274
old man's beard 47
Old Warden 156
Ongar 182
open-air museums 303
Open Spaces Society 91
orchids
  common spotted 41, 208, 279
  dark red helleborine 41
  early purple 40, 41
  fragrant 41
  frog 41
  green-winged 40
  marsh helleborine 279
  twayblade 41
Ordnance Survey 259
Orford Beach National Nature Reserve 274, 285
Orford Ness 147, 284–285, 286
Orkney Islands 34, 281
orpine, *see* livelong
osprey 244, 246
Otley-Knaresborough road 88
Otley Hall 213
otter 101, 270
Oundle-Thrapston line 102
Ouse, river 255, 256, 266
Outer Hebrides 276, 281
owl 48, 129
  barn 72, 132
  little 72
  long-eared 72
  short-eared 283
  snowy 280
  tawny 61, 72, 73
  white 132
oxlip 64, 69, 204
oystercatcher 279, 281

Painsworth 127
Paisley weavers 204
Palmer, John 90
pargetting 136
Parliamentary Acts 26
Parliamentary Enclosure 25, 26, 28,

31, 82, 91, 212, 213
Parrett, river 255
parsley
  hedge 48
partridge 101
Pateley Bridge 88, 173
Patrington 112, 113, 118
pasque flower 36
peacock 193, 199
Peak, The 238
peatbog 258, 262, 265
Peddars Way 82
Pembroke, Earl of 178
Penmon Priory 225
Pennine Way 91
Pen y Gadair 244
peregrine falcon 179, 243, 244, 293
Pestilence, see Black Death
Peterborough Abbey 110
Peterken, George 197
Petre Ifan tomb 98
petrel
  Leach's 293
  storm 293
Picturesque 204
Piercebridge 84
pigeons 48
  wood 61, 72
Pike of Blisco 243
Pike O'Stickle 213
pine (*see also named specimens* and plantations) 51, 61
place names 23, 58, 93, 134, 180
  'borth' 93
  'cot' 134
  field names 20
  'grange' 173, 214
  'lidgate' 93
  Old Norse 172, 176, 213
  'saltways' 85
  Saxon 178
  Welsh 110
Plantations 40, 53, 55, 61, 69, 73, 219, 278
plover
  ringed 273, 281
polecats 101
pollen 238
pollution 129, 201, 210, 256, 258, 259, 267
  acid rain 129, 258, 259
  agricultural 136, 266, 270, 271, 272, 297
  sea 294
Polperro 174, 176
polyanthus 205
pond life 208–209, 249–250
Pope, Alexander 188
poppy 35
  yellow horned 285, 286
Port Errol 163
Portmeirion 156
Port Quin 175
Port Way 86

prehistoric
  climate 13
  farming 16
  settlement 50
  vegetation 13
prickly saltwort 277
primrose 64, 65, 66, 69, 205
  bird's eye 41
  primrose/cowslip hybrid 69, 205
Primrose Hill 210
Prior 110
Prior's Manor House 214
privet 47
Protection of Wild Creatures
    Legislation 132
pseudoscorpion (Dendrochernes
    cyrneus) 201
Pudding Norton 165
puffins 291, 293
Pultneytown 175
purging flax 41
purple moor grass 40

Quakers 164
quaking grass 41
quickthorn, see hawthorn

rabbits 43, 48, 65, 179, 182
Rackham, Oliver 50, 179, 197
Radwinter 156
ragwort 129
  common 39
  great fen 100
railway, embankment wildlife 101,
    102
  disused lines 101–102
Ramblers' Association 91, 298
Ramsgill 172
Rare Breeds Survival Trust 236, 303
raven 244, 294
Raven Crag 240
Ravenglass dunes 281
razorbill 291
Reach 85, 160
reaves, see field systems
Red Data Books of Endangered
    Species 255
red kite 244
redshank 267
redstart 44, 72
  black 132
red-throated diver 247
redwing 246
redwood 192
Reformation (see also churches and
    Commonwealth) 117, 119
Regents Park 210
religious and burial sites (see also
    churches; named abbeys,
    cathedrals, churches, standing
    stones and stone circles)
  burial barrows 109
  Celtic cross 109
  Cistercian Abbey 173

cross 110
cross slab 110
Dark Age 110
early Christian 113
flora 129
holy wells 109, 113
monastic (see also named
    sites) 105, 173
open air 105
shrine 85, 109
tombstone 126
Welsh 113
Repton, Humphrey 190, 192
Rhum Island 298
Richmond, Earl of 179
Riders Rings, Dartmoor 158
ring ouzel 246
Ripley 156, 181
Ripley Castle 181
Ripon 88
Rivenhall 109, 110, 124, 212
rivers, see wetlands and individually
    named rivers
river transport system 85
roads and tracks (see also carts and
    wagons and named sites) 52, 77,
    80ff
  abandoned 81
  ancient 80, 82, 90, 91, 96
  bridleway 91
  causeway 85
  coach 90
  country 80ff
  droveways 23, 86–87, 93, 169
  flora and fauna 96ff
  harepaths 92
  holloway 82, 87, 93
  leyline 92
  maintenance 89
  market 169
  medieval 85, 86, 88, 92, 169
  military 90
  pack-horse 87, 88, 93, 169
  Parliamentary Enclosure 82, 91
  paved 88
  public footpaths 91, 297
  Roman 82ff, 104, 182
  saltways 85
  Saxon 84–85
  stiles 93
  timber trackways 50
  toll houses 90
  turnpike 26, 27, 90
  Turnpike Trusts 90
Roberts, Brian K 134
robin 72, 207
Rockingham 50
rock sea lavender 291
Rodwell, Warwick 109, 212
Roman period 17, 63
  brick-making 145
  fields 17
  fort 105
  gardens 178

land drainage 250
milestones 83
occupation 110
rituals 117
roads 82ff, 104, 182
settlement 50, 104, 109
use of peat 258
villa 124, 178, 212
waterway 160
Romanticism 192, 204
Ronas Hill 40
rose 45, 47, 205
  wild 42, 48
rosebay 99
Rose, Francis 197, 201–202
roseroot 242, 291
Rossington 118
Rosthwaite 34, 80
rough hawkbit 42
Rough Tor 17, 158
round-leaved wintergreen 279
Rousham 188
rowan 46, 246
Rowley, Trevor 178
Royal Society for the Protection of
    Birds 208, 246, 267, 283, 294,
    298
Rudston 108
ruff 267

St Ives 17
St James Park 210
St Kilda islands 291, 293, 294
St Mary's church, Whitby 118
St Non's chapel 113
St Tudy 122, 123
Salcott 85
Salford Priors 85
Sall 118
sallow 45
Saltaire 163, 164
Salterford 85
Salterforth 85
Salthouse 85
salt marshes 281ff
Sandbach 105
sand hoppers 277
Savi's warbler 262
saw-sedge 262
saw wort 40
saxifrage
  mossy 244
  opposite-leaved golden 242
  pepper 40
  purple 244
  yellow mountain 242
Saxon 48, 84, 168
  architecture 104, 105, 114
  cemetery 109
  charter 45
  churches 104, 105, 108, 109,
    110, 112, 113, 114, 124, 159
  county map 169
  cross 173

deer parks 180ff
  farmsteads 212
  fields 18, 30
  hunting forests 52, 178ff
  mills 231
  place names 178
  roads 84–85
  settlements 48, 173, 176
  village 160
Saxtead Green 231
Scafell Pike 241, 242
scaley cricket 285
Scar Close 239
Scolt Head Island 274, 281
Scolt Head National Nature
    Reserve 286
Scots pine 48, 53, 69, 192
sea arrow grass 281
sea aster 281, 282
sea beet 285
sea bladder campion 286, 291
sea blight 281, 286
sea buckthorn 278
sea campion 242
sea couch-grass 277
sea eagle 294
sea kale 285
sea lavender 281, 282, 286
sea meadow grass 283
sea pea 285, 286
sea plantain 281, 282
sea purslane 281, 282
sea rocket 277
seaweed 277
  Chondrus crispus 293
  fertilizers 277
sea wormwood 281
seal
  common 295
Sennen Cove 31
Sesleria 41
settlements and dwellings (see also
    cottage, farming and appropriate
    historical period)
  baffle entry house 151, 152
  Blackhouses 148, 220
  bothies 23
  Bronze Age settlements 158
  clachans 23
  coits 150
  cross passage houses 151
  Dark Age village 158
  deserted villages 108, 110, 137,
    164, 165, 166, 168, 169, 188,
    222
  double-depth house 153
  double-pile house 151, 152
  Edwardian 154
  emparking 165
  farmsteads 153, 155, 156, 176,
    212ff
  fermtouns 23, 218
  fishing village 174, 175, 176
  Georgian 218, 222

granges 173
  kirktouns 124
  laithe-houses 150, 151, 214
  longhouses 148, 149ff
  medieval 110
  moated manor sites 213
  Neolithic hut cluster 158
  Norse 172, 174
  polyfocal village 176
  priest houses 124, 127
  Romano-British settlement 159
  shielings 23
  shrunken village 104, 110, 193
  single fronted cottage plan 154
  spinning galleries 227
  summer settlements 23
  unplanned village 173
  vernacular dwellings 137ff
  Victorian 154, 218, 222
  village layout 204
  Wealdon house 155, 156, 216
  Y-shaped settlement 170
Severn estuary 274
Seven Sisters cliffs 274
Severn, river 270, 274
sheep's fescue 41
Sherwood Forest 180, 182, 201,
    202
Shingle Street 286
Shoard, Marion 31
shovelers 267
Shrewsbury 86
sickle-leaved hare's ear 100
Sinclair, Sir J 23
Singing Way 96
Sites of Special Scientific Interest
    248
Sitka spruce 53
Skara Brae 158, 274
Skelton 113
Skiddaw 241
Skipton 252
Skokholm Island 288
Skomer Island 288
Skythorns 88
slate (see also cottage, geology and
    stone for building)
  quarries 146
  Swithland 146
Sleningford 169
sloe 43, 45, 48, 72
Smelthouses 176
Smith, C T 258
snake 210
snakeshead 36
snapdragon 129
Snape 234
snipe 267
Snowdonia National Park 244, 248
Soar valley 37
soils (see also geology and
    invertebrate fauna)
  acid 40, 42, 238–239, 241,
    244, 268, 269, 279

calcareous 208, 279
clay 69, 164, 208, 274
coastal 279ff
grassland 40, 41
sandy 59, 274
woodland 63
Solway 274
Somerleyton 156
Somerset level 50
sorrel 41, 208
  mountain 242, 244
Southampton 276
Spanish catchfly 100
sparrow 132
sparrowhawk 61, 72
spiders 45, 48, 73, 101, 131, 200,
    210, 248, 282, 285
  Amaurobius ferox 73
  Arctosa fulvolineata 282
  Dipoena 73
  Erigone arctica 282
  Lepthyphantes carri 201
  jumping 210, 286
  Micrommata virescens 73
  money 243, 277, 282
  Pardosa purbeckensis 282
  Praestigia duffeyi 282
  Tetrilus 201
  Textrix 45
  Thyreosthenius parasiticus 199
  Tuberta 221
  Uloborus 73
  wolf 282
  zebra 210
spindle tree 45, 47, 192
spoonbill 262
spotted crake 262
spotted flycatcher 45, 129, 208
spring gentian 44
spruce 61, 192
spurge laurel 64
Spurn Point 274, 275
squirrel 65, 72
  grey 67
starling
  common 44
standing stones (see also stone
    circles) 108
Stevington 109
Stevington Post Mill 230
Stewkley 113
stitchwort
  greater 98
stoat 48, 101
stocks 174
stone for building (see also slate and
    stone walling) 44, 45, 80, 121,
    129, 138, 139, 140–141, 142,
    146
stone circles (see also standing stones
    and named sites) 77, 105
stone walling 15, 17, 22, 28, 30,
    32, 40ff, 131
  Cotswolds type 32, 44

drystone 30
flora and fauna 44ff, 210
granite 32, 44
Millstone Grit 30, 32
moorstone 32
reaves 17, 30
Welsh 32
Stow 104, 105, 113
Stowe Park 84
Strixton 193, 194
Studland National Nature
    Reserve 281
sulphur clover 40
Summerbridge 176
Sunday Times 296
sundew 41, 262
Swaffham Prior 112
Swaledale 173
swallow 132
swans 179, 266
    Bewick 266
    mute 266, 269
Swavesey 160
sweet briar 42
swift 132
Swinside stone circle 77
sycamore 45
Sylva 53

Tame, John 117
Taplow 109
Taylor, Christopher 50, 160
teazel
    common 38
Teesdale 41
Telford, Thomas 96, 175
tern
    arctic 285
    black 260, 262, 283
    common 262, 281, 286
    little 281, 286
    roseate 281
Test, river 252–253
thatching, *see* cottages
Thetford 182
Thetford Chase 59, 63
thistle 208
    carline 42
    melancholy 41
Thornborough circles 168
Threlkeld 22
thrift 291
thrush 48, 61
    song 72, 208
Thurne, Norfolk Broads 254
Thwaite Lane 88
Tidenham 109
tile-hanging, *see* cottage
timber-framing 137, 141ff, 160,
    212, 220, 223, 224
    box-framing 141, 142, 155
    cruck-framing 141, 142, 144,
        223
    medieval farmsteads 156, 214

Tiptree Heaths 52
Titchmarsh 113, 160
tits 129
    bearded 262, 268
    blue 72, 207
    coal 61
    crested 61
    great 72
toad 250
    natterjack 279
toadflax
    ivy-leaved 210
toadstool, *see* fungi
Tomintoul 163
tools 16
Townend, Troutbeck 217, 218, 227
tree creepers 129
trefoil
    birdsfoot 42, 100
    greater birdsfoot 42, 100
    rough 285
Tresco Abbey gardens 192
Trifolium 208
Trotten church 229
Tudor sheep clearances 175
Tyrells pass 156

Ullapool 175
Up Cerne 184–185
upland/lowland zones, distinction
        between 8ff
Upsland 169
Upwood Meadows National Nature
        Reserve 40
Ure, river 257

valerian 41
Vanburgh 188
Verbascum 210
Veronica 100
vetch 41
    horseshoe 36, 41
    kidney 36, 41
Via Devana 82, 100
Victoria, Queen 163
village greens (*see also* fairs and
        markets) 159, 160, 161, 176,
        232
violets 64
    Fen 262

Wade, George 90
Wadenhoe 29, 225
    church 182
wagons, *see* carts and wagons
wagtail
    pied 44
Walberswick National Nature
        Reserve 255, 267, 268
wallflowers 129
Walsingham 85
Wandlebury 56, 70, 225
warbler
    common 61

garden 72
grasshopper 61
marsh 283
sedge 266
willow 61, 72
wood 72
Warner Comb Valley Woods 198
Warwick Castle 188
Wasdale Head 12, 15, 22, 89
Wash, the 274, 283
wasp 48
    queen 131
Wast Water 15, 241
water avens 41
watercress meadows 251
Water Stratford 84
Watling Street 82, 84
Waveney, river 255
wavy hairgrass 41
waxwing 208
weazels 48
Wells 278
Wells Cathedral 109, 113
Welsh lily 244
Wessex chalk downlands 16, 33, 80
Wessex Ridgeway 80
Westbury White Horse 28
Westminster Abbey 132
West Tanfield 168, 169
wetlands 250ff (*see also* meadows)
    artificial 272
    land drainage 251–252
    marshland 252, 255, 256, 262
    mere 262
    pollution 258, 259
    reedswamp 262
    rivers 255ff
Wharfedale 24
Wharram le Street 165
Wharram Percy 137, 165
wheatear 41, 44
wheelwrights, *see* carts and wagons
whelk
    common 286
whimbrel 246
whinchat 101
white byrony 43, 48
white campion 45
whitethroat 61, 283
    lesser 283
Whitford Burrows, Gower 281
Whittlesea Mere 262
Whittlesford 117, 124–125, 214
Whitwick Park 181
Whymper, Edward 247
Wick 175
Wicken Fen Nature Reserve 161,
    232, 249, 251, 264
Wickham St Paul 109
Widdy Bank 41
wild clematis 47
Wildfowl Trust 274, 294
wildfowl (*see also* named species) 37,
    252, 266, 283, 292

Williams-Ellis, Clough 156
Williamson, Tom 212
Willington 225
willow 63, 69
    creeping 262, 281
    dwarf 247
    goat 72
Wilmington 127
Wimborne Minster 104
Wimborne St Giles 182
Winchester, Bishop of 179, 180
Windsor Castle 188
Windsor forest 202
Winterbourne Steepleton 24
Winterton Dunes 274
Wirral 276
Wise, Henry 188
wolf 179, 244
Wolves Wood 52, 53
wood anemone 47
wood bastwick 177
wood melick 47
woodland (*see also* forests, nature

reserves, named woodlands and
    nature reserves) 20, 50, 52ff,
    196ff
    amenities 58
    ancient 56, 198ff
    clearance 52
    coppiced timber 52, 56, 57, 63,
        64
    crafts 52, 56
    deciduous 51, 61, 63, 238, 297
    fencing 63
    flora and fauna 58ff
    game preservation 63
    landscaped 189
    pastures 73, 198ff
    pollarding 198
    private 63
    protected 201
Woodland Trust 73
woodlark 61
woodpecker 129
    greater spotted 72
    green 72

lesser spotted 72
wood sandpiper 246
Woodstock 180
Woodwalten Fen National Nature
    Reserve 262, 264, 265
woody nightshade 43
Wordsworth, William 241
Worth Matravers 23
woundwort
    hedge 41
whortleberry 40
wren 72
Wychwood National Nature Reserve
    202
Wymondham 112

Yare, river 255
yellow rattle 38
yew 53, 127, 129
York 173
Yorkshire Dales National Park 239